T0139880

Flexible Systems Management

Series editor

Sushil
Department of Management Studies
Indian Institute of Technology Delhi
New Delhi
India

Editorial Board

Gerhard Chroust, Institute for Telekooperation, Johannes Kepler University Linz, Austria
Julia Connell, Curtin Business School, Curtin University, Perth, Western Australia
Stuart Evans, Integrated Innovation Institute, Carnegie Mellon University, USA
Takao Fujiwara, Toyohashi University of Technology, Toyohashi, Aichi, Japan
Mike C. Jackson OBE, University of Hull, UK
Rashmi Jain, Montclair State University, Montclair, New Jersey, USA
Ramaraj Palanisamy, St. Francis Xavier University, Antigonish, NS, Canada
Edward A. Stohr, Stevens Institute of Technology, New Jersey, USA

The main objective of this series on Flexible Systems Management is to provide a rich collection of research as well as practice based contributions, from different contexts, that can serve as reference material in this upcoming area. Some of these books will be published in association with 'Global Institute of Flexible Systems Management'.

It will help in cross-fertilizing ideas from different perspectives of flexibility so as to consolidate and enrich the paradigm of flexible systems management. The audience for the volumes under this series includes researchers, management students/teachers, and practitioners interested in exploring various facets of flexibility research and practice.

The series features five types of books:

- *Post conference volumes* containing peer reviewed high quality research papers around a theme and clustered in sub-themes that can act as good reference material.
- *Contributed thematic volumes* based on invited papers from leading professionals, from academia as well practicing world, containing state of the art on an emerging theme.
- *Research monographs* based on research work making a comprehensive contribution to the body of knowledge.
- *Books based on novel frameworks and methodologies* covering new developments that are well tested and ready for wider application in research as well as practice.
- *Business practices and case-based* books documenting flexibility practices, strategies and systems in real life organizations.

More information about this series at http://www.springer.com/series/10780

Natalia Kryvinska · Michal Gregus
Editors

Agile Information Business

Exploring Managerial Implications

 Springer

Editors
Natalia Kryvinska
Department of e-Business,
   School of Business, Economics
   and Statistics
University of Vienna
Vienna
Austria

and

Department of Information Systems,
   Faculty of Management
Comenius University in Bratislava
Bratislava
Slovakia

Michal Gregus
Department of Information Systems
Comenius University in Bratislava
Bratislava
Slovakia

ISSN 2199-8493
Flexible Systems Management
ISBN 978-981-10-9853-6
DOI 10.1007/978-981-10-3358-2

ISSN 2199-8507   (electronic)

ISBN 978-981-10-3358-2   (eBook)

Printed on acid-free paper

This Springer imprint is published by Springer Nature
The registered company is Springer Nature Singapore Pte Ltd.
The registered company address is: 152 Beach Road, #21-01/04 Gateway East, Singapore 189721, Singapore

Preface

With this book, we start to explore challenges and opportunities of Agile Information Business and its managerial implications. We attempt to include different aspects of this research area and explore their insights in this book.

In 1961, G.J. Stigler wrote the following: *"One should hardly have to tell academicians that information is a valuable resource: knowledge is power"* (Stigler 1961). Similarly, Stiglitz (2000) specifies: *"In the field of economics, perhaps the most important break with the past - one that leaves open huge areas for future work - lies in the economics of information"*. Stiglitz (2000) goes further and explores crucial challenges: *"It is now recognized that information is imperfect, obtaining information can be costly, there are important asymmetries of information, and the extent of information asymmetries is affected by actions of firms and individuals"* (Stiglitz 2000). In the (Foley 2013), the author discusses *"popular idea that "economic growth" can continue indefinitely in postindustrial capitalist economies through the shift of labor to "service" sectors, particularly finance and information-based activities,…"*. Other scholars (Shapiro 1999) claim that *"We use the term information very broadly. Essentially, anything that can be digitized - encoded as a stream of bits - is information"*. They also state that *"We focus on the value of information to different consumers. Some information has entertainment value, and some has business value, but regardless of the particular source of value, people are willing to pay for information"*. And, we conclude with a statement from (Evans and Wurster 1997)—*"Every Business is an Information Business"*.

Accordingly, this book involves works considering research outputs on varied perspectives of 'Information Business' Management. In particular, the work entitled "Capturing and Analyzing Information on Fiscal Policy of EU Countries: Viewpoint—Government Expenditure on Education Since 2008" (Chap. 1), by Holubjaková and Bohdalová, determines and analyses the relation between amount of government expenditure on education and development of the basic macroeconomic indicators of GDP, as well as public debt using EU countries data relating to time of economic and debt crisis.

Further, the chapter authored by Okasa and Bohdalová "Math Analysis of Informational Factors Affecting State Fiscal Policy in Short-term Development Prediction" (Chap. 2), focuses on the usage of mathematical tools, to deal with information processing, within a broader macroeconomic application. The prime objective of the case study is to predict a short-term development of the most important macroeconomic variable, GDP, and to analyse its influence on the state's fiscal policy.

In the paper "Business Information Consideration for Labour Market Study of the Slovak Republic" (Chap. 3), Kurdyová and Bohdalová observe the main economic indicators of the labour market, such as gross domestic product (GDP), minimal wage, inflation rate and unemployment rate in the selected Central European counties: Czech Republic, Hungary and Slovak Republic. Based on this observation, they analyse the influence of GDP on the number of advertised vacant positions on the Slovak labour market, as well as the relationship between vacancies and unemployment rate. Then, the authors evaluate the results of job offer investigation based on data collected between 2010 and 2013.

Thanh van Do et al., in "Social Financial Benefit Assessment of the Mobile Birth Registration" (Chap. 4), study the usability and the usefulness of mobile technologies, which are, as the authors claim, far beyond personal communication. And, according to authors' finding, it has been demonstrated by the Mobile Birth Registration (MBR) concept. They go further and realize that in order to remove the hindrances like long distances, time-consuming travels, high costs—MBR makes use of 'gatekeepers', i.e. trusted, reliable and community based individuals that carry out birth registration using mobile phones. It is also shown that MBR brings lots of advantages and conveniences to all parties from the children, parents, government, gatekeepers and NGOs. The authors perform a simple social benefit assessment that re-affirms the social value of MBR.

The chapter, "Mobile Banking Services—Business Information Management with Mobile Payments" (Chap. 5), authored by Markoska, Ivanochko and one of the editors, Gregus, covers three aspects of contemporary society: the importance of the tertiary sector of the economy—services in the developed countries, the development of new (mobile) technologies, and the high penetration rate and acceptance of "the device" of the contemporary history—the smart phone. The authors attempt to translate these three aspects into the banking service sector in Austria with a focus on the payments.

In the "Organizational Service Management as an Umbrella for Information Business" (Chap. 6), Hanudelova and Prochazkova explores different aspects of service management and business, and its core part—information business—in relation to the service science. The growth of service sector and its relevance for businesses, as we now live in a service-based economy, results in the need for many organizations to adjust everyday operations that enable them to respond quickly to changing market conditions, and to be more efficient and effective in the application of services. Thus, the main aim of this work is to perform recherché, examination, and systematization on the different aspects of service management and business.

Writing this work, the authors combine the study of mostly scientific literature, with their own analytical, proposal, and recommendation capabilities.

Žilinčan, in the "Improving Information Accuracy with SEO for Online Marketing Services" (Chap. 7), deals with a trend in the online marketing named search engine optimization, often shortened to SEO. Quality SEO thus ensures information accuracy for first positions without any financial investments. Some optimization techniques do not change over time, and still form the basis of SEO. However, as the Internet and web design evolve dynamically, new optimization techniques arise and some even die. Accordingly, the author provides a summary of the most important factors and techniques that can help to improve position in search results.

And finally, in the chapter "Sharing Knowledge and Information Through Corporate e-Learning" (Chap. 8), Vančová and Kovačičová claim that implementation of e-learning has an increasing tendency in many companies and countries. And e-learning applications therefore can be used almost anywhere and anytime, in turn being a rich source for sharing knowledge and improving the education level of people in companies. Thus, the authors dedicate this chapter to the three points of view—the view of a company producing LMS, the view of a company using e-learning as a form of education for its employees and last but not least, the view of people, who are using e-learning for education in a company where they work.

Vienna, Austria   Natalia Kryvinska
Bratislava, Slovakia   Michal Gregus

References

Stigler GJ (1961) The economics of information. J Polit Econ 69(3):213–225

Stiglitz JE (2000) The contributions of the economics of information to twentieth century economics. Q J Econ 115(4):1441–1478

Foley DK (2013) Rethinking financial capitalism and the 'information' economy. Rev Radical Polit Econ 45(3):257–268

Shapiro C, Varian HR (1999) Information rules: a strategic guide to the network economy. Harvard Business School Press, Boston

Evans P, Wurster TS (1997) Strategy and the new economics of information. Harvard Bus Rev 75(5):70–82

Contents

1 Capturing and Analyzing Information on Fiscal Policy of EU Countries.. 1
Dominika Holubjaková and Mária Bohdalová

2 Math Analysis of Informational Factors Affecting State Fiscal Policy in Short-Term Development Prediction............ 43
Gabriel Okasa and Mária Bohdalová

3 Business Information Consideration for Labour Market Study of the Slovak Republic............................ 93
Eva Kurdyová and Mária Bohdalová

4 Social Financial Benefit Assessment of the Mobile Birth Registration.. 113
Thanh van Do, Clark Swafford, Loc H. Khuong and Van Thuan Do

5 Mobile Banking Services—Business Information Management with Mobile Payments...................... 125
Katerina Markoska, Iryna Ivanochko and Michal Gregus ml.

6 Organizational Service Management as an Umbrella for Information Business................................. 177
Jana Hanudelova and Lenka Prochazkova

7 Improving Information Accuracy with SEO for Online Marketing Services...................................... 217
Jakub Žilinčan

8 Sharing Knowledge and Information Through Corporate e-Learning... 255
Martina Halás Vančová and Zuzana Kovačičová

Editors and Contributors

About the Editors

Assoc. Prof. Natalia Kryvinska is University Lecturer at the University of Vienna's School of Business, Economics and Statistics. She received her Ph.D. in Electrical and IT Engineering from the Vienna University of Technology in Austria, and a Habilitation in Management Information Systems from Comenius University in Bratislava, Slovakia.

Prof. Michal Gregus is currently Professor at the Comenius University in Bratislava. He is Head of the Department of Information Systems, and Vice-Dean for International Relations at the Faculty of Management. His main interests are in the field of ICT. Professor Gregus obtained his Ph.D. degree is in the field of mathematical analysis. He was working for few years at the Joint Institute for Nuclear Research in Dubna, Russia, mainly on computers mathematical modelling.

Contributors

Mária Bohdalová Department of Information Systems, Faculty of Management, Comenius University in Bratislava, Bratislava 25, Slovakia

Van Thuan Do Wolffia AS, Oslo, Norway

Thanh van Do Telenor Research, Fornebu, Norway; Oslo & Akershus University College, Oslo, Norway

Michal Gregus ml. Department of Information Systems, Faculty of Management, Comenius University in Bratislava, Bratislava, Slovakia

Jana Hanudelova Faculty of Management, Comenius University in Bratislava, Bratislava, Slovakia

Dominika Holubjaková Department of Information Systems, Faculty of Management, Comenius University in Bratislava, Bratislava 25, Slovakia

Iryna Ivanochko Faculty of Management, Comenius University in Bratislava, Bratislava, Slovakia

Loc H. Khuong Keller Graduate School of Management, DeVry University, Irving, TX, USA

Zuzana Kovačičová Faculty of Management, Comenius University, Bratislava, Slovakia

Eva Kurdyová Faculty of Management, Comenius University in Bratislava, Bratislava, Slovakia

Katerina Markoska School of Business, Economics and Statistics, University of Vienna, Vienna, Austria

Gabriel Okasa Department of Information Systems, Faculty of Management, Comenius University in Bratislava, Bratislava 25, Slovakia

Lenka Prochazkova Faculty of Management, Comenius University in Bratislava, Bratislava, Slovakia

Clark Swafford Keller Graduate School of Management, DeVry University, Irving, TX, USA

Martina Halás Vančová Faculty of Management, Comenius University, Bratislava, Slovakia

Jakub Žilinčan Faculty of Management, Comenius University, Bratislava, Slovakia

Chapter 1
Capturing and Analyzing Information on Fiscal Policy of EU Countries

Viewpoint—Government Expenditure on Education Since 2008

Dominika Holubjaková and Mária Bohdalová

Abstract The aim of this chapter is to determine the relation between the amount of government expenditure on education and development of the basic macroeconomic indicators of GDP and public debt using EU countries data relating to times of economic and debt crisis. This paper is a combination of theoretical knowledge with practical examples. Theoretical area includes mainly the definition of fiscal policy, its application in the European Union as well as the economic background characteristic of the factors examined during times of crisis. The analysis of examined variables is based on both comparative and correlation method, and the results are further processed using cluster analysis and linear regression to predict the future values of the amount of government expenditure on education. The results of work will help the reader better understand the relation between the amount of government expenditure on education and development of the economy in times of crisis. People interested in the subject will be enriched by an explanation of how to effectively predict future changes in the amount of government expenditure on education.

Keywords Fiscal policy · The European Union · Economic and debt crisis · Government expenditure on education · Gross domestic product · Public debt

D. Holubjaková · M. Bohdalová (✉)
Department of Information Systems, Faculty of Management, Comenius University in Bratislava, Odbojárov 10, P.O. BOX 95, 82005 Bratislava 25, Slovakia
e-mail: maria.bohdalova@fm.uniba.sk

D. Holubjaková
e-mail: d.holubjakova@gmail.com

© Springer Science+Business Media Singapore 2018
N. Kryvinska and M. Gregus (eds.), *Agile Information Business*,
Flexible Systems Management, DOI 10.1007/978-981-10-3358-2_1

1 Introduction

Fiscal policy in the European Union is an important issue not only within EU member countries, but also for the whole organization. The main aim of fiscal policy is to ensure efficiency and sustainability of public finance that can promote economic development and improve the quality of life in the Member countries. However, when the game enters an unexpected factor in the form of a crisis or other negative interventions in the economy, nations are forced to react quickly, to abandon their initial plans and adopt appropriate measures to reduce the severity of the fall in economic activity (Auer et al. 2011). Subsequently, the government must adjust its budget in order to put the measures into effect. Consequently, government expenditure in certain sectors are considerably reduced, however, often improperly. If nations wish to break the long-term crisis, there is a need to support sectors such as education or research, because highly skilled people can contribute to economic recovery by their knowledge and new ideas (Engelhardt-Nowitzki et al. 2011; Urikova et al. 2012a). The aim of the section is to determine the relation between the amount of government expenditure on education and development of the basic macroeconomic indicators of GDP and public debt from different perspectives during the economic and debt crisis since 2008. In the case of confirmed connection between these variables, we can forecast the changes in the amount of government expenditure on education in the future or estimate the amount of government expenditure on education retrospectively in the case it was not published by EU member countries.

The first section of the chapter is devoted to issues of fiscal policy and the economic and debt crisis of the EU—describing economic background of the subsequent analysis of government expenditure on education. The section starts with a brief general overview of fiscal policy, i.e., definition of terms of fiscal policy and of the principles on which it works, then explains the different kinds of fiscal policies, and describes the limits by that fiscal policy is restricted. The purpose of this overview is to better understand the nature of fiscal policy and the development of the basic macroeconomic indicator of GDP, on which both, comparative and cluster analysis will be carried out. The next section describes the state budget as a fundamental instrument of fiscal policy with a focus on European Union Member countries. At the same time briefly explains the principle of budgeting in EU, from which education allowances in the form of different programs are allocated to Member countries.

An important part of this section is a description of budgetary classification, which allows international comparison of income and expenditure data of individual Member countries. Based on this classification it is possible to collect the necessary data for our analysis of government expenditure on education. This chapter continues with the section devoted to background description in which we will conduct an analysis—the period of economic and debt crisis of the European Union since 2008. The practical part of this chapter focuses on a comparative analysis of public debt and budget deficit of the individual EU member countries.

The section also involves a list of mechanisms for the coordination of fiscal policies that have been adopted to reduce the level of public debt of Member countries as an additional variable necessary for the analysis. The last section of the chapter is devoted to the issue of missing central fiscal policy in EU as a possible solution to the growing public debt of the EU. But on this issue there are several opinions—sovereignty versus shared responsibility of States for fiscal policy. The second section focuses on government expenditure on education as part of fiscal policy. The section describes how to collect any information necessary for the analysis of government expenditure on education and the issues connected with it (Kryvinska et al. 2009). The next section focuses on the comparative analysis of government expenditure on education and GDP figures between EU member countries from different perspectives. Subsequently, section continues with correlation detection between data (GDP, public debt and government expenditure on education) in the statistical program IBM SPSS Statistics. Finally, this chapter reveals the use of correlated variables in practice when estimating the amount of government expenditure on education based on cluster analysis, or on the basis of the linear regression model. The main findings are presented at the end of the section.

2 Fiscal Policy in EU Countries

Fiscal policy is an essential instrument of the policy of the central government. Its main objective is to balance economic development with the state budget and thus to influence the overall level of GDP, employment, price and income of population.

2.1 Fiscal Policy in Times of Economic Crisis

The economic crisis that affected the EU financial markets in the autumn of 2007 is according to some experts, the worst one since the global economic crisis after the Second World War. The impulse for the outbreak of the crisis was a crisis in the US real estate market. It was caused by providing mortgage loans to citizens with lower living standard for a low interest rate. Based on the fact that solvency of the borrowers was assessed based on the opinion of rating companies that were often bribed, financial markets began to collapse due to borrowers' insolvency to repay mortgages and related interest. Several banks appeared on the verge of collapse due to a lack of liquidity, which significantly affected the other banks in EU member countries. The first effects of the crisis influenced the European Union in the first quarter of 2008. The consequences resulted in high inflation in the form of substantial price increases mainly in oil and food prices. After the US investment bank "Lehman Brothers" declared bankruptcy due to no other funding help from the US government, ECB was forced to provide banks with 30 billion euro of loans to their rescue. The year 2009 became most critical. EU economic growth has stopped and the strong economies of Germany and England were significantly affected by the recession. Gross domestic product of EU member countries dropped significantly (by 2.5% quarter on quarter) in the first quarter, moreover, a decrease of more than 1.22 million jobs was observed and most countries had their government budget deficit over the reference value of 3% of GDP. In 2010, the economic situation started to stabilize and thanks to the austerity measures the economy started to grow slowly. Later, however, EU member countries had to face a debt crisis caused by false economic statistic data provided by the Greek (EurActiv 2012). Greece provided the statistic office Eurostat with adjusted fiscal data for many years. Thus, it was not revealed Greek debt reached 120% of GDP in 2010, which exceeded twice the limit set by the Stability and Growth Pact and moreover the government deficit exceeded 12% of GDP, thus exceeding the limit four times. Greece was forced to adopt a number of reforms regarding budget adjustment (pension reform, healthcare, etc.). After revealing of this information, investors were skeptical about lending money to Greek government, and the same situation followed in other countries with higher public debt—Italy, Portugal, and Ireland (Uhliarik 2013) deficit is a result of higher expenditure compared to budget revenue. From 2008 to the present, several countries have exceeded desired limit of public debt in the amount of 3% of GDP. It was observed mainly Ireland, Greece, or Spain. The smallest amount of public debt was spotted in small countries such as Luxembourg or Estonia, but also in Sweden, Finland, and Germany. Public debt occurs as a result of budget deficit accumulations in given period the highest public debt was in countries such as Greece, Italy, Portugal, Ireland, and Belgium. However, the limit of 60% of GDP was exceeded in several countries. The best results were reported in Estonia, Luxembourg, and Romania. Figure 1 provides an overview of public debt development of EU member countries with the limit of reference value (60% of GDP) in given period.

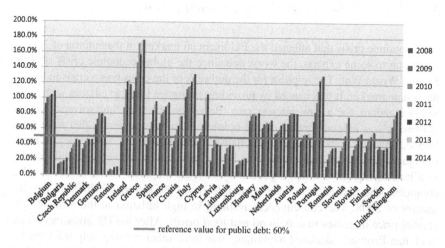

Fig. 1 Public debt development since 2008. *Source* Processing was based on data from Eurostat. *Note* Data for 2014 represent data for the period Q1–Q3 2014 (Color figure online)

2.2 Mechanisms for Fiscal Policy Coordination

The first mechanism to coordinate fiscal policy has become the Stability and Growth Pact. It consists of two parts—"preventive arm" (Art. #121 of the TFEU) and "corrective arm" (Art. #126 of the TFEU). The aim of the preventive part is a coordination of fiscal policies of EU member countries in order to meet EU goals. The principle of the corrective part (known also as excessive deficit procedure—EDP) is to define corrective measures for those EU countries which exceeded permitted limit of budget deficit or public debt set out in Protocol No. 12 of the TFEU. Protocol No. 12 on the excessive deficit procedure defines limit of 3% of GDP for budget deficit and 60% of GDP for public debt (The European Commission 2014a, b).

Based on the fact that EU member countries constantly violated set limits, despite the penalties that have never been applied in practice, EU launched a new support solution for fiscal policy: "Six-pack"—a package of five legislative regulations and one directive proposed by the European Commission, approved by European Parliament and EU member countries, which entered into force in 2011. Despite the efforts to strengthen fiscal policy through a package of six legislative regulations, it is necessary to highlight the fact that punitive measures have not been applied also in this case. However, as the crisis in EU still continued, the issue of fiscal policy began to require more and more attention (Lajčiak 2013).

The European Commission has decided to tighten up budgetary discipline by the Treaty on Stability, Coordination, and Governance in the Economic and Monetary Union, also known as the Fiscal Compact. The other measure taken with regard to fiscal policy was the package of two legislative acts called "Two-pack"—a system of two regulations, which were designed to supervise the preparation of budgetary policies of euro zone member countries and the activities of EU member countries being in financial difficulty or recipients of external financial aid. A package of two legislative acts came into force on May 30, 2013 in all euro zone member countries (The Ministry of Finance of the Slovak Republic 2014; Stoshikj et al. 2014).

It should be noted that even a package of two legislative measures have had no success so far in combating the problem of fiscal policy.

2.3 The Central Fiscal Policy Versus National Responsibility for Its Own Finances

A member of European Parliament (MEP), Slovak politician, Richard Sulik criticized the financial measures adopted by the EU, mainly Six-pack and Two-pack, from the start of their validity. He argued that if countries have not complied with the basic rules of the Stability and Growth Pact, there is no reason to respect the rules of their extended version. An example might be France, which plans to bring the deficit below the threshold of 3% of GDP until 2017, so it will comply with the rules of six legislative acts (Six-pack) after 6 years since its introduction. In 2015, the European Commission intends more in-depth analysis of economic situation of the most troubled countries, i.e., France, Belgium, and Italy. However, based on the fact that individual EU member countries have the final say in adopting the state budget, and taking into account the fact that the penalties resulting from violations of the above-mentioned measures have not been applied to any country yet, countries are not forced to improve their economic situation. Richard Sulik proposes as the only way how to stop increasing level of public debt that each country should be responsible for its own finances. In his opinion, the adoption of further measures, which are not really respected, do not solve the issues of macroeconomic instability (Sulík 2014).

On the other hand, Roman Lajčiak, an employee of MINISTRY of Foreign and European Affairs of the Slovak Republic, claims that part of the performance of fiscal policy should be shifted to the European level (Lajčiak 2013). The same opinion is also German chancellor Angela Merkel. She states that fiscal union is necessary to prevent another financial crisis in the future. A core of fiscal union should be focused on central budget and tax policies, not only in euro zone, but in all EU member countries (SITA 2011).

In the next section we will take a closer look whether EU member countries considered educated people to be an effective tool in the fight against the crisis, and so their amount of government expenditure on education was appropriate.

3 Government Expenditure on Education as a Part of Fiscal Policy

The budget surplus is not the government's money; it's the people's money.

(George Bush)

Measure everything, because everything that is measured and watched improves.

(Bob Parsons—GoDaddy)

In this section we take a closer look at how the GDP and government expenditure on education of the individual EU member countries have developed since the crisis in 2008 to the present. Then we detect whether there is a correlation between development of GDP and government expenditure on education, or the amount of government expenditure on education varied irrespective of the amount of GDP. As we evaluate the development of government expenditure on education especially in times of crisis, we will also analyze the impact of public debt of individual EU member countries to government expenditure on education. In the case of revealed connection between the development of government expenditure on education and public debt development as well as changes in the amount of GDP, we will use the relationship of correlating variables to forecast future values of the amount of government expenditure on education or to estimate the historical values of the amount of government expenditure on education that have been not published yet (Fauska et al. 2014; Gregus and Kryvinska 2015).

Government expenditure on education is primarily used to fund activities of public educational institutions, as well as private educational institutions and administration connected with their operation (OECD 2012). The biggest part of government expenditure on education represents the wages of education employees. The amount of wages increases with higher education level. However, the biggest part of government expenditure on wages is allocated to secondary education as a result of the higher number of students in high schools in comparison to the number of students at universities. Expenditures on education help contribute to the economic development of the country, support personal development of its inhabitants and eliminate disparities between countries (Kaczor et al. 2013; Kryvinska et al. 2013). The European Union allows its members to set their own level of the amount of government expenditure on education including resources from the EU budget. Investments in education are one of the key fields of the Europe 2020 strategy, under which investments in education and trainings or support of lifelong learning have become effective tools to combat youth unemployment. In respect of education, the Europe 2020 strategy should achieve the following objectives (The European Commission 2015):

- at least 95% of children (from 4 to compulsory school age) should participate in early childhood education;
- fewer than 15% of 15-year-olds should be underskilled in reading, mathematics and science;
- the rate of early leavers from education and training aged 18–24 should be below 10%;
- at least 40% of people aged 30–34 should have completed some form of higher education;
- at least 15% of adults should participate in lifelong learning;
- at least 20% of higher education graduates and 6% of 18–34-year-olds with an initial vocational qualification should have spent some time studying or training abroad;
- the share of employed graduates (aged 20–34 with at least upper secondary education attainment and having left education 1–3 years ago) should be at least 82%.

However, the economic crisis that affected the EU in 2008, and the subsequent debt crisis caused by the negative economy development in Greece meant that EU member countries had to significantly adjust their budgets to match the requirements of the Stability and Growth Pact. This adjustment also significantly affected the amount of government expenditure on education. Some countries initially increased their government expenditure on education, but then there was observed their decline, and vice versa. Therefore, we will try to find a link between public spending on education and national economic development, or to find out if there is any other important factor affecting the amount of government expenditure on education.

3.1 Analysis of Government Expenditure on Education Since 2008

Data on government expenditure on education are collected by Eurostat within the functional classification of budget expenditures COFOG (Classification of the Functions of Government—the part *709 Education*—(see Appendix 1, 2, 3 (IMF 2014)) based on the ESA 2010 standards.

International comparison of data focused only on the funding of education is provided by Eurostat in cooperation with UNESCO and the OECD based on the UOE methodology (UNESCO/OECD/Eurostat). Based on the fact that data on government expenditure on education, collected under both methodologies, in the case of EU countries are significantly correlated, in the analysis we will use the data collected under both methodologies (The Ministry of Education, Science, Research and Sport of the Slovak Republic 2013). The biggest problem when comparing individual EU member countries is to obtain current information on government expenditure on education. The information is always available with a certain delay, for example, currently latest published data on expenditures on education provided by the OECD are from the year 2011 (for EU-16), data provided by Eurostat based on the functional classification from the year 2012. The lack of current information makes it impossible to analyze and evaluate the current changes in investments in education, and to respond in time for a possible unfavorable situation that may occur in the economy (The European Commission 2014a, b).

Based on the above-mentioned problem we will carry out deeper analysis of data on the overall government expenditure on education only from 2008 to 2012, in the case of government expenditure on education per pupil/student only from 2008 to 2011.

3.2 Comparative Analysis of Government Expenditure on Education from 2008 to 2012

Based on the basic statistical indicators of the development of government expenditure on education we will carry out the comparative analysis of quantitative file "Government expenditure on education EU 2008–2012" from data available at Eurostat and in the OECD database from different perspectives.

3.2.1 The Total Government Expenditure on Education as a Percentage of GDP

Government expenditure on education EU-27 since 2008 remained above the threshold of 5% of total EU GDP (an average of 693 bil. euro). The highest average government expenditure on education were observed in 2009 (5.8% GDP), however, since then they were gradually reduced to the value of 5.4% of GDP in 2012 (Table 1). The highest average education investments compared with the amount of GDP of individual EU member countries for monitored period were spotted in Denmark (7.7% of GDP), then in Cyprus (7.1% of GDP) and in Sweden (6.9% of GDP), on the other hand, the lowest average investments in education were in Romania (3.8%), then in Bulgaria (3.9% of GDP) and in Slovakia (4% of GDP) (Fig. 2).

The mode value of government expenditure on education data in 2008–2012 amounted to 6.8% of GDP of the EU member countries (Cyprus in 2008; Sweden in 2008, 2011, 2012; Portugal in 2009; England in 2010; Lithuania and Latvia in 2009). The mean value of expenditures on education in the years 2008–2012 was around 5.7% of GDP (Table 1).

When analyzing on-year changes in the amount of government expenditure on education, there were noted no significant deviations. The level of government expenditure on education interannually changed only at around 1%. In 2012 there was observed a YoY increase in or at least the same amount of government expenditure on education in up to 14 countries (Croatia, Luxembourg, Malta, Denmark, Estonia, Sweden, Belgium, France, the Netherlands, Austria, Poland, Ireland, Italy, and Greece).

Table 1 Government expenditure on education, EU-27

Government expenditure on education (% of GDP, EU-27)						
	2008	2009	2010	2011	2012	2008–2012
Average value	5.4	5.8	5.7	5.6	5.4	5.6
Mode value	–	–	–	–	–	6.8
Mean value	5.5	5.7	5.7	5.7	5.6	5.7
Maximum value	6.9	8.0	8.1	7.8	7.9	8.1
Minimum value	3.5	4.1	3.3	3.6	3.0	3.0

Source Processing was based on data from Eurostat

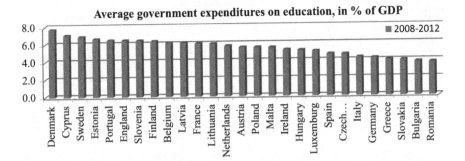

Fig. 2 Government expenditure on education, in % of GDP. *Source* Processing was based on data from Eurostat (Color figure online)

3.2.2   Government Expenditure on Education Compared to Total Government Expenditure

There is also another view, of which government expenditure on education can be analyzed, i.e., share of expenditures on education in total government expenditure. Each country has different amount of total government expenditure, and this may be subsequently reflected in the significant differences between the amounts of government expenditure on education in EU member countries.

Based on the results of the comparative analysis, EU member countries invest in education around 12% of their total government expenditure, the largest part of government expenditure went to education in 2008 (12.3%), the lowest part in 2010 (11.9%). When analyzing the total government expenditure of the Member countries, we found out that the largest part of their public expenditure in the form of investment in education was paid out in Estonia (16.5%), then in Cyprus (15.6%) and in Latvia (15.3%), on the other hand, the smallest proportion of expenditures on education was paid out in Greece (7.8%), Italy (8.7%), and Germany (9.4%) (Fig. 3). The analysis of YoY development of expenditure on education share in total government expenditure revealed no extraordinary deviation (±1%). The significant changes in the amount of government expenditure on education occurred only in Ireland (in 2010, a decline of almost 3%). The reason of the decline was the growing amount of public debt [significantly above the permitted level (Fig. 1)] that required the adoption of measures under the Stability and Growth Pact. Subsequently, the adoption caused reduction in the amount of the government expenditure in several areas, one of which was education.

3.2.3   Government Expenditure Per Pupil/Student Expressed in PPPs

Based on the fact that the countries have different number of pupils/students, there is also a need of a different amount of resources for them, what results in a different

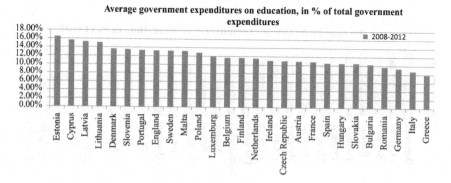

Fig. 3 Government expenditure on education, in % of total government expenditure. *Source* Processing was based on data from Eurostat (Color figure online)

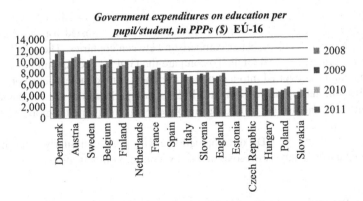

Fig. 4 Government expenditure on education per pupil/student in PPPs ($). *Source* Processing was based on data from OECD database (Color figure online)

amount of government expenditure on education (Urikova et al. 2012b). In order to determine the amount of government expenditure per pupil/student we will use available indicator—Public expenditure on educational institutions per student. Data for this indicator collects OECD. Currently are available data on government expenditure on education to 2011, but out of all EU member countries there is only 21 countries, that are also the OECD Member countries. However, only 16 countries have released the data on government expenditure per pupil/student. Data of government expenditure per pupil/student are expressed in PPPs ($).[1]

The largest average amount of government expenditure on education per pupil/student for the period 2008–2011 was invested in Denmark ($ 11,462), then in Austria ($ 10,802) and in Sweden ($ 10,459). Conversely, the lowest amount invested in education was observed in Slovakia ($ 4304), Poland ($ 4647), and Hungary ($ 4820). The government expenditure on education grew steadily year on-year in 10 countries. The largest increase was spotted in Denmark ($ 10,621 per pupil/student; FY 2008/2009). The level of government expenditure on education declined in six countries, mainly at the turn of the FY 2009/2010, with the largest decrease in Italy ($ 409 per pupil/student) (Fig. 4).

3.3   Comparative Analysis of the GDP Development of EU Member Countries Since 2008

Gross domestic product (GDP) is a key indicator of economic status of a country. GDP is the value of all final goods and services produced in the territory of the

---

[1]*Note* PPP index (Purchasing Power Parity index)—represents the rates of currency conversion that eliminate the differences in price levels between countries.

country for a given period in current prices of the year, it is called nominal GDP (Stoshikj et al. 2016). However, this indicator is then adjusted for the impact of inflation in order to ensure better comparison between countries. The result is GDP at constant prices, i.e., real GDP. To compare the GDP of each country is the GDP of each country converted into a common currency, for example to euro or dollars, or to PPS. Purchasing power standard (PPS) in comparison with the exchange rates takes into account also the differences in price levels in different regions of the EU member countries.

When analyzing the GDP development we will proceed similarly as in the case of a comparative analysis of government expenditure on education.

3.3.1 GDP at Current Market Prices

The largest volume of production of final goods and services in EU countries in the period 2008–2013 was observed in the countries of Germany, France, and England. The average GDP amount for the period was EUR 2,559,483 million in Germany, EUR 1,974,870 million in France and EUR 1,791,784 million in England.

On the other hand, the lowest volume of production of final goods and services (Kryvinska et al. 2014a, b, 2015) in the given period was observed in the countries such as Cyprus, Estonia, and Malta. The average annual GDP amount in Estonia reached the level of EUR 17,605 million, EUR 15,817 million in Cyprus and EUR 6541 million in Malta. The development of the GDP amount of EU member countries since 2008 captures (Fig. 5). However, it should be noted that macroeconomic indicator of the GDP at current market prices does not reflect the size of economy expressed by the size of population or the difference in price levels.

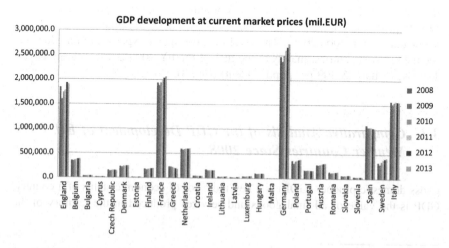

Fig. 5 GDP development in 2008–2013. *Source* Processing was based on data from Eurostat (Color figure online)

The result is that countries with larger size of population will achieve higher GDP growth in comparison with countries with smaller size of population. It is therefore recommended to use it only when comparing the rate of GDP of current year.

3.3.2 GDP Per Capita at Constant Prices

Based on the fact that the GDP indicator at current market prices does not effectively assess the living standards of population or the difference in price levels, it is better to take into account the indicator of real GDP per capita at constant prices at EUR and PPS base.

Taking into account the indicator at EUR base, the countries with the highest average GDP amount in the period 2008–2013 were Luxembourg, Denmark, and Sweden. The average GDP amount per capita in Luxembourg was around EUR 77,133, EUR 43,733 in Denmark and EUR 39,383 in Sweden. However, data on the high GDP amount in Luxembourg are partially distorted. Although Luxembourg is one of the economically richest countries, the highest level of GDP per capita is achieved, thanks to workers from neighboring countries such as France, Belgium, or Germany. Subsequently, the increased number of workers significantly increases the value of GDP, which is then calculated only by using the number of people who live there.

The average value of real GDP per capita in all EU member countries amounted to EUR 25,500 euro. This average GDP threshold managed to overcome in addition to the above-mentioned countries even countries such as the Netherlands, Ireland, Austria, Finland, Belgium, Germany, France, England, and Italy. The average value of GDP per capita of EU members was in the Euro area (18 Member countries) by EUR 3150 lower. The lowest average value of GDP per capita in the given period was observed in the countries of Latvia (EUR 9417/capita.), Romania (EUR 6467/capita.), and Bulgaria (EUR 5033/capita.). The development of the values of real GDP per capita of all EU member countries since 2008 captures (Fig. 6).

Taking into account the differences in price levels in individual regions of the EU member countries show a slight change in the order of EU member countries. Usage of data expressed in PPS compared with data expressed in EUR has the balancing effect—regions with very high amount of GDP per capita—mainly capital cities, industrial centers, etc.—are characterized in comparison with rural areas by relatively high price levels. Luxembourg remains the country with the highest GDP per capita, but then it is followed by the Netherlands and Ireland. Denmark and Sweden that, in the case of neglecting regional differences, occupied second and third places, in the case of taking them into account shifted to the fourth and fifth places. The order of the last three countries with the lowest GDP per capita in the case of taking into account regional differences remained unchanged (see Fig. 7).

Annual change in the value of real GDP since 2008 had different development. As a result of financial and economic crisis that hit EU member countries, there was

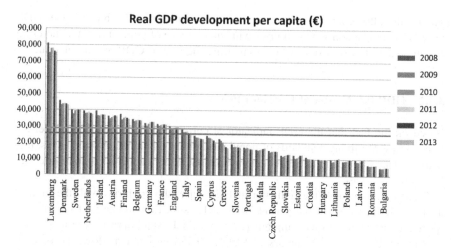

Fig. 6 Real GDP development per capita in 2008–2013. *Source* Processing was based on data from Eurostat (Color figure online)

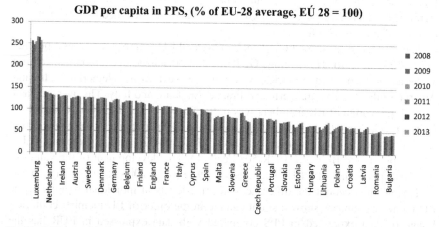

Fig. 7 GDP per capita in PPS. *Source* Processing was based on data from Eurostat. *Note* Data for 2014 are only estimated (Color figure online)

observed a significant decline in GDP growth in 2009 (a decline of approximately 5%). In 2010, the economic situation started to stabilize and thanks to the austerity measures the economy started to grow slowly. 2009/2010 annual growth of GDP amounted to 1.8% and continued until 2011 (1.5%). However, in 2011, first consequences of the debt crisis, caused by providing false data on Greek economy to EU, resulted in a decline of GDP. Real GDP in 2012 fell by around 0.7%, in 2013

Fig. 8 Real GDP growth per capita in 2008–2014. *Source* Processing was based on data from Eurostat (Color figure online)

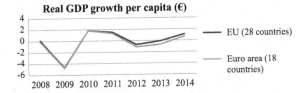

Real GDP growth per capita (€)

EU (28 countries)

Euro area (18 countries)

by only 0.1% and in 2014 there was spotted a significant economy recovery—estimated increase of 1.1% as a consequence of measures taken by the European Commission—Six-pack (2011), Fiscal Treaty (2013), and Two-pack (2013).

In the euro zone, GDP growth developed in a similar way. However, the major changes occurred in 2012—a larger drop by 4%. The changes are caused by debt crisis that hit the countries such as Greece, Italy, Portugal and Ireland and dampened so the GDP growth in the euro zone (due to necessity of financial contribution to EFSF and ESM). In 2013 there was observed a decline of 0.6% and in 2014 there is expected the GDP growth of 0.4% lower than in all EU countries. The development of values of real GDP per capita in EU member countries and in the euro zone since 2008 captures (Fig. 8).

When analyzing real GDP growth in individual EU member countries there can be observed a completely different development. While in 2008 grew real GDP per capita mainly in Romania, Bulgaria and Slovakia, along with other 14 countries, in 2009, after outbreak of the crisis, was positive GDP growth observed only in Poland. The sharp decline in real GDP was spotted in 2009; especially in less economically developed countries such as Latvia, Lithuania, and Estonia (more than 10% decline in GDP). In 2010, after economic recovery, the GDP grew in up to 21 countries, with the highest GDP growth in Sweden (5.1%). The sharpest fall in GDP in 2010 was observed in Greece (5.2%). The positive GDP growth continued in 2011 in 24 countries.

However, in 2012 the debt crisis weakened economies of several countries, especially members of the euro zone. Positive GDP growth was observed only in 11 countries with the highest growth in real GDP per capita in the economically weakest countries from the year 2009—Latvia, Lithuania, and Estonia. In 2013, the situation has not changed significantly, but in 2014 there is expected a significant increase in the number of countries with positive growth in real GDP (23 countries) as a result of successful implementation of anti-crisis measures put in effect in 2013. The detailed development of real GDP per capita in individual EU member countries is listed in Table 2.

Table 2 The EU countries with the highest real GDP growth per capita in the period 2008–2013

The EU countries with the highest real GDP growth per capita in the period 2008–2013 in %

2008		2009		2010		2011		2012		2013	
Romania	10.3	Poland	2.5	Sweden	5.1	Estonia	8.6	Latvia	6.1	Latvia	5.3
Bulgaria	6.3	Portugal	−3.1	Slovakia	4.6	Lithuania	8.5	Lithuania	5.2	Lithuania	4.3
Slovakia	5.3	Malta	−3.2	Germany	4.2	Latvia	7.0	Estonia	5.0	Romania	3.8
Poland	3.9	Belgium	−3.4	Lithuania	3.8	Poland	4.7	Malta	1.7	Estonia	2.0
Lithuania	3.7	France	−3.4	Luxemburg	3.2	Bulgaria	4.6	Poland	1.7	Malta	2.0
Slovenia	3.1	Netherlands	−3.8	Malta	3.0	Germany	3.6	Slovakia	1.4	Hungary	1.8
Malta	2.7	Austria	−4.0	Estonia	2.7	Slovakia	3.3	Bulgaria	1.1	Poland	1.8
Croatia	2.1	Greece	−4.4	Poland	2.7	Romania	2.7	Romania	1.1	Bulgaria	1.6
Czech Rep.	1.7	Spain	−4.4	Finland	2.5	Austria	2.4	Austria	0.4	Slovakia	1.3
Netherlands	1.7	Bulgaria	−4.5	Czech Rep.	2.0	Czech Rep.	2.2	Germany	0.2	England	1.0
Germany	1.2	Cyprus	−4.6	Portugal	1.9	Hungary	2.1	England	0.0	Sweden	0.4
Austria	1.2	England	−5.0	Belgium	1.6	Finland	2.1	France	−0.1	Germany	−0.1
Cyprus	1.1	Czech Rep.	−5.4	Austria	1.6	Sweden	1.9	Belgium	−0.6	Ireland	−0.1
Hungary	1.1	Germany	−5.4	France	1.5	Malta	1.8	Ireland	−0.6	Belgium	−0.2
Finland	0.3	Slovakia	−5.5	Bulgaria	1.3	France	1.6	Czech Rep.	−0.9	France	−0.2
Belgium	0.2	Denmark	−5.6	Italy	1.3	Ireland	1.6	Denmark	−1.0	Austria	−0.4
Portugal	0.1	Italy	−6.0	Denmark	1.2	Netherlands	1.2	Hungary	−1.0	Luxemburg	−0.6
France	−0.4	Sweden	−6.0	England	1.1	Belgium	0.8	Sweden	−1.0	Czech Rep.	−0.7
Spain	−0.5	Romania	−6.3	Hungary	1.0	England	0.8	Croatia	−1.9	Croatia	−0.7
Greece	−0.7	Hungary	−6.4	Slovenia	0.9	Denmark	0.7	Netherlands	−1.9	Portugal	−0.8
England	−1.1	Luxemburg	−7.0	Netherlands	0.5	Slovenia	0.4	Finland	−1.9	Denmark	−0.9
Denmark	−1.3	Ireland	−7.3	Romania	−0.2	Spain	0.3	Spain	−2.2	Spain	−0.9
Luxemburg	−1.3	Croatia	−7.3	Spain	−0.4	Italy	0.2	Luxemburg	−2.4	Netherlands	−1.0

(continued)

Table 2 (continued)

The EU countries with the highest real GDP growth per capita in the period 2008–2013 in %

2008		2009		2010		2011		2012		2013	
Sweden	−1.3	Slovenia	−8.7	Ireland	−0.7	Croatia	0.0	Slovenia	−2.8	Slovenia	−1.1
Italy	−1.8	Finland	−8.7	Latvia	−0.8	Spain	−1.0	Portugal	−2.9	Finland	−1.8
Latvia	−2.1	Latvia	−12.8	Cyprus	−1.2	Portugal	−1.7	Italy	−3.2	Italy	−2.2
Ireland	−4.7	Lithuania	−13.9	Croatia	−1.4	Cyprus	−2.3	Cyprus	−3.9	Greece	−3.3
Estonia	−5.0	Estonia	−14.6	Greece	−5.2	Greece	−8.6	Greece	−6.3	Cyprus	−5.1

Source Processing was based on data from Eurostat

3.4   Comparative Analysis of Public Debt Development Since 2008

Carried out within Sect. 2.1.

3.5   Correlation Between the Government Expenditure on Education, GDP and Public Debt Development Since 2008

In this section we take a closer look at the different relationships between the analyzed indicators of government expenditure on education and GDP and public debt development. The analysis is performed by using Pearson correlation coefficient in the IBM SPSS Statistics software. Pearson correlation coefficient (ρ) measures the strength of the linear relationship between two quantitative variables. It ranges from -1 (values are developed inversely proportional) to $+1$ (values are developed in proportion). If the value equals to 0 there is no linear relationship between the variables, but in this case, the coefficient does not deny the possibility of a nonlinear relationship. Moreover, using of the Pearson correlation population correlation coefficient ρ ("rho") enable to decide whether there is a statistical evidence of a linear relationship of two variables, or variables are dependent only randomly. The analysis of a linear relationship between the variables is performed by SPSS Statistics command—Analyze/Correlate/Bivariate Correlations. Then, the analyzed variables, the kind of correlation coefficient (Pearson correlation coefficient) and the kind of confidence interval (two-tailed test of significance—because there are no assumptions whether the possible relationship between the variables are positively or negatively correlated) are chosen.

3.5.1   Government Expenditure Per Pupil/Student Versus GDP Per Capita in PPPs

In this step, we will examine the relationship between variables of government expenditure on education per pupil/student and GDP per capita. We expect that, in the case of confirmed correlation, the countries with higher GDP per capita will invest much more in education in comparison with countries with a lower GDP. The analyzed variables represent data of the EU-16 for the period 2008–2011, as they are the latest available information on the amount of government expenditure on education per pupil/student in PPP provided by the OECD. Since we have chosen the two-tailed confidence interval, we will test the following hypotheses at the significance level $\alpha = 0.05$ (95% confidence that possible correlation between the variables is not random):

*H*0: The amount of government expenditure on education per pupil/student developed independently of GDP per capita development

*H*1: The amount of government expenditure on education per pupil/student developed dependent on the development of GDP per capita

The results of correlation analysis are shown in Table 3. Due to the fact that the observed *p*-value = 0.000 is lower than the significance level $\alpha = 0.05$, the hypothesis *H*0 is rejected. The value of the Pearson correlation coefficient $(r) = 0.905$ corresponds to a significant positive correlation between the analyzed variables (Fig. 9; Table 3). The amount of government expenditure on education per pupil/student and GDP per capita are strongly correlated, the coefficient of determination is equal to 81.8%. Thus, we can state that countries with higher amount of GDP per capita invested in education per pupil/student more.

3.5.2 The Growth in Government Expenditure on Education Per Pupil/Student Versus the Growth in GDP Per Capita in %

In this case we will try to find out whether there is a correlation between YoY growth in government expenditure per pupil/student and the growth in GDP per capita. We assume that if countries expected increased production in the following year, subsequently they also increased the amount of the planned expenditure on education. In order to find out the correlation we will analyze the same set of data as in Sect. 3.5.1.

Table 3 Correlation test #1

Correlations		GDP per capita in PPPs	Expenditure per student in PPPs
GDP per capita in PPPs	Pearson correlation	1	0.905*
	Sig. (2-tailed)		0.000
	N	64	64
Expenditure per student in PPPs	Pearson correlation	0.905*	
	Sig. (2-tailed)	0.000	1
	N	64	64

*Correlation is significant at the 0.01 level (2-tailed)
Source Processing was carried out in IBM SPSS statistics

Fig. 9 Government
expenditure per pupil/student
versus GDP per capita in
PPPs. *Source* Processing was
carried out in IBM SPSS
statistics

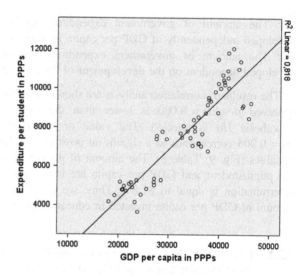

At a significance level of $\alpha = 0.05$, we will test the following hypotheses:

$H0$: Annual growth in government expenditure on education per pupil/student
developed independently of GDP growth per capita
$H1$: Annual growth in government expenditure on education per pupil/student
developed dependent on GDP growth per capita

The results of the analysis (Table 4):

p-value = 0.926; $\alpha = 0.05$, p-value > α, hypothesis H_0 will be not rejected.

Annual growth in government expenditure on education per pupil/student
developed independently of the growth in GDP per capita, that is confirmed by the
low correlation coefficient $(\rho) = 0.014$, and the coefficient of determination equaled

Table 4 Correlation test #2

Correlations				
		Education expenditure growth, per student (%)	Real GDP growth, per capita (%)
Education expenditure growth, per student (%)	Pearson correlation	1	0.014
	Sig. (2-tailed)		0.926
	N	48	48
Real GDP growth, per capita (%)	Pearson correlation	0.014	1
	Sig. (2-tailed)	0.926	
	N	48	48

Source Processing was carried out in IBM SPSS statistics

to 1.96%. EU-16 countries invested in education regardless of the fact whether their GDP per capita grew or declined.

3.5.3 Government Expenditure on Education as % of GDP Versus % of Total Government Expenditure

Due to the fact that in some EU countries there are only available data for total government expenditure on education, not calculated for pupil/student, we will also examine data on government expenditure from this perspective. We will try to find out if there is any correlation between data on government expenditure as a percentage of GDP and total government expenditure. We will analyze a set of data of the EU-27 in 2008–2012.

$H0$: There is no correlation between data on government expenditure as a percentage of GDP and total government expenditure
$H1$: There is a correlation between data on government expenditure as a percentage of GDP and total government expenditure

By the analysis at the significance level $\alpha = 0.05$ we found that there is relatively high correlation between the examined variables in the form of a positive correlation $(\rho) = 0.760$, the coefficient of determination equals to 57.76%, p-value $= 0.000$, p-value $< \alpha$, hypothesis $H0$ is rejected. Thus, we can state that if expenditure on education represented higher % of GDP, they automatically represented higher % share of total government expenditure (Table 5).

Table 5 Correlation test #3

Correlations			
		Education expenditure, % of GDP	Education expenditure, % of total expenditures
Education expenditure, % of GDP	Pearson correlation	1	0.760*
	Sig. (2-tailed)		0.000
	N	135	135
Education expenditure, % of total expenditures	Pearson correlation	0.760*	1
	Sig. (2-tailed)	0.000	
	N	135	135

*Correlation is significant at the 0.01 level (2-tailed)
Source Processing was carried out in IBM SPSS statistics

3.5.4 Total Government Expenditure on Education Versus Public Debt as % of GDP

This paper is devoted to the development of fiscal policy, especially in times of crisis, so it is necessary to examine the relationship between government expenditure on education and economic and debt crisis, by using government debt indicators. We expect that if the amount of public debt is high, EU member countries will cut investments in any sector, including education.

We will again analyze the data set of EU-27 government expenditure on education in 2008–2012 at the significance level of $\alpha = 0.05$.

$H0$: Total government expenditure on education have developed independently from the amount of public debt
$H1$: Total government expenditure on education developed dependent on the amount of public debt

Although the results of the analysis (Table 6) in the form of a negative correlation coefficient $(\rho) = -0.132$ partly confirmed our assumption of reduced expenditure on education in the context of high public debt, however, in most countries, the amount of government expenditure on education developed irrespective of the amount of public debt:

p-value $= 0.127$, $\alpha = 0.05$, p-value $> \alpha$ confirmed the hypothesis $H0$ of the independence of the investigated variables.

Table 6 Correlation test #4

Correlations		General government gross debt in % GDP	Education expenditures in % GDP
General government gross debt in % GDP	Pearson correlation	1	−0.132
	Sig. (2-tailed)		0.127
	N	135	135
Education expenditures in % GDP	Pearson correlation	−0.132	1
	Sig. (2-tailed)	0.127	
	N	135	135

Source Processing was carried out in IBM SPSS statistics

3.5.5   Government Expenditure on Education Growth Versus Public Debt Growth

Due to the low correlation between the variables in the previous section, we try to look at the relationship of government expenditure on education and public debt from another perspective. In this step, we look more closely at the fact whether countries had responded to growing amount of public debt and adjusted the amount of government expenditure on education. In times of crisis, countries should increase their investment in education, because especially educated people can contribute their ideas to help them get out of the negative situation. Therefore, we expect that if public debt grows, in the optimistic case countries invest more in education, in order to actively join the fight against the crisis using the ideas and opinions of educated people.

We will again analyze the data set of EU-27 government expenditure on education in 2008–2012 at a significance level of $\alpha = 0.05$.

$H0$: The growth of public debt did not affect the amount of public expenditure on education
$H1$: The growth of public debt affected the amount of public expenditure on education

The results of the analysis (Table 7) in the form of a negative correlation coefficient $\rho = -0.181$, however, did not confirm our assumption. With the increasing level of public debt, some countries invested in education even less money, in most countries, the amount of government expenditure on education developed independently from public debt development:

$p = 0.061, \alpha = 0.05, p > \alpha$ confirmed the hypothesis $H0$ of independence examined variables.

Further analysis of the year on-year increase in public debt in the range of 0–20% confirmed that the countries invested in education within the range of 2–10%

Table 7   Correlation test #5

Correlations		Education expenditure change	General gross debt change
Education expenditure change	Pearson correlation	1	−0.181
	Sig. (2-tailed)		0.061
	N	108	108
General gross debt change	Pearson correlation	−0.181	1
	Sig. (2-tailed)	0.061	
	N	108	108

Source Processing was carried out in IBM SPSS statistics

Fig. 10 Government
expenditure on education
growth versus public debt
growth. *Source* Processing
was carried out in IBM SPSS
statistics

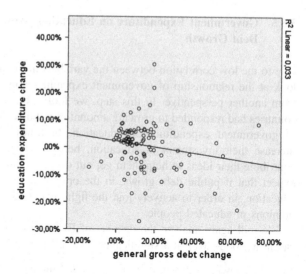

more. Moreover, some extremes can be also observed (labeled "specific values"—Fig. 10). The extreme increase in government expenditure on education during increasing public debt by almost 20% was recorded in Romania in 2011 (31%), Slovakia in 2009 (22%) and Poland in 2010 (16%). Worth mentioning is also the growth in government expenditure on education by 9% in Estonia in 2012 parallel with a huge increase in public debt by 74%. On the other hand, an extreme drop in government expenditure on education was recorded during the growth of public debt by 13% in Romania in 2012 (−27%), by 63% again in Romania in 2009 (−23%), and by 15% in Poland in 2009 (−17%).

3.6 Application of the Confirmed Correlation Between the Examined Variables

Confirmed correlation between the examined variables can help us in many ways:

- to identify the probable amount of government expenditure on education per pupil/student in EU member countries that publish this information in long lapse of time or not at all—Sect. 3.6.1
- to predict total government expenditure on education and expenditure per pupil/student in the future on the basis of the GDP amount and % share of government expenditure on education in the total government expenditure—Sects. 3.6.2 and 3.6.3.

3.6.1 Cluster Analysis of EU Member Countries (Cluster Analysis)

Based on the fact there is a problem to collect data on government expenditure on education per pupil/student, we may split EU member countries into groups with common characteristics. In the case of not publishing data on government expenditure on education, the groups can be helpful to estimate the amount of expenditure on education based on published data of the countries belonging to the same group.

To split EU member countries to groups, we use the indicator of real GDP per capita due to the highest confirmed correlation between the amount of government expenditure on education per pupil/student and GDP per capita, and based on the fact that the GDP per capita indicator best describes the living standard of countries. The cluster analysis allows us to split the EU countries into certain characteristic groups using a similar amount of real GDP per capita during the period 2008–2013. Analysis is carried out using a two-step cluster analysis "TwoStep Cluster" in the IBM SPSS Statistics 23.0 software using data on real per capita GDP from 2008 to 2013 of EU-28 published in the Eurostat database. To carry out the analysis, you need to enter following input data (Fig. 11):

- **continuous variables**: columns of data on GDP per capita for the period 2008–2013 in numerical terms
- distance between objects suitable for continuous variables: Euclidean distance
- **fixed number of clusters**: optimum 7 clusters. The number of clusters depends on the number of countries that have published data on government expenditure on education per pupil/student. In the case of active involvement of EU member countries in publishing of data on government expenditure on education there can be created a larger number of clusters. It helps us identify the amount of

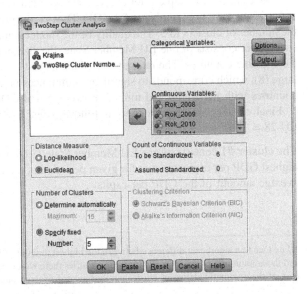

Fig. 11 Input data of cluster analysis. *Source* Processing was carried out in IBM SPSS statistics

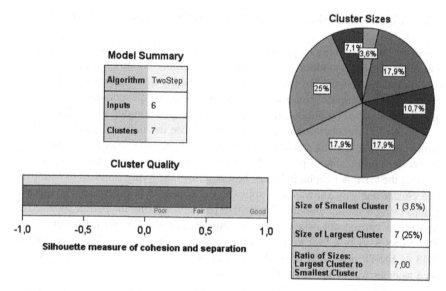

Fig. 12 Cluster sizes. *Source* Processing was carried out in IBM SPSS statistics

government expenditure on education of those countries, that have not provided data yet, as accurate as possible. Due to the fact that the data on government expenditure on education per pupil/student are usually published by OECD, there is necessary to check whether at least one country in a created cluster is a member of the OECD, and moreover whether it published its data on government expenditure on education per pupil/student or not.[2]

The result of two-step cluster analysis is seven clusters, but one cluster includes countries that are not members of the OECD. As a result, we were forced to reduce the number of clusters to 5. The quality of the model is marked as "good". Smallest size cluster consists of one EU Member State; the size of the largest cluster is eight EU member countries. The ratio of size of the largest cluster to the smallest is quite large (8), which corresponds to significant differences in the number of EU member countries with maximum and minimum average real GDP per capita (Fig. 12).

Final clusters are characterized as follows (Fig. 13—GDP per capita, in PPS, EU-28 = 100):

The cluster #1 consists of one EU Member State (3.6%)—Luxembourg, due to the highest GDP per capita amount for given period, that refers to 2.57 times the EU-28 average amount of the GDP per capita.

---

[2]*Note* Due to a significant difference between the highest amount of GDP reported in Luxembourg and the amount of GDP in other EU member countries there would be created only 2 clusters in the case of the automatic choice of cluster number instead of fixed number of clusters.

Size										
		3,6% (1)		28,6% (8)		17,9% (5)		21,4% (6)		28,6% (8)
Inputs	2008 256,00		2008 124,50		2008 106,60		2008 82,50		2008 58,00	
	2009 247,00		2009 123,12		2009 106,20		2009 83,00		2009 56,25	
	2010 254,00		2010 124,50		2010 104,00		2010 81,83		2010 56,88	
	2011 265,00		2011 125,62		2011 101,60		2011 79,67		2011 59,25	
	2012 264,00		2012 125,00		2012 100,40		2012 78,67		2012 61,25	
	2013 257,00		2013 124,25		2013 99,60		2013 79,50		2013 63,00	

Fig. 13 Cluster characteristics. *Source* Processing was carried out in IBM SPSS statistics

The cluster #2 includes eight EU member countries (28.6%): the Netherlands, Ireland, Austria, Sweden, Denmark, Germany, Belgium, and Finland with a high average amount of GDP per capita, i.e., 1.24 times the EU-28 average amount of the GDP per capita.

The cluster #3 represents 5 EU member countries (17.9%)—England, France, Italy, Cyprus, and Spain. The average amount of GDP per capita of the cluster represents 1.03 times the average amount of the EU-28.

The cluster #4 consists of six EU member countries (17.9%)—Malta, Slovenia, Greece, Czech Republic, Portugal, and Slovakia. GDP per capita did not exceed the average amount of the EU-28; the amount of GDP per capita amounted to 80.8% of the EU-28 average amount.

The cluster #5 is a group of 8 EU member countries (25.0%)—Estonia, Hungary, Lithuania, Poland, Croatia and Latvia, Romania and Bulgaria. Domestic production of these countries amounted to only 59.1% of the EU-28 average amount.

Model Restrictions:

1. The model that forecasts the amount of public government expenditure on education per pupil/student cannot be used to forecast data for Luxembourg. The reason is the distorted high amount of GDP per capita, which causes that Luxembourg will always be sorted into a segregated cluster.
2. In the case of low involvement of the countries in publishing data on government expenditure on education per pupil there is no possibility to create a desired number of clusters.

3.6.2 Prediction Model of Amount of Government Expenditure on Education Per Pupil/Student

Due to confirmed linear correlation between changes in the amount of government expenditure on education per pupil/student and GDP per capita we can predict future amounts of government expenditure on education based on the regression model. Regression model is formed by using following operation in IBM SPSS Statistics: ANALYZE/Regression/Linear Regression.

Regression Results

To forecast future values of government expenditure on education there is suitable to use linear regression model due to high correlation coefficient $(\rho) = 0.904$ and coefficient of determination $(\rho^2) = 0.818 = 81.8\%$. The correlation coefficient presents a positive correlation between variables and the coefficient of determination interprets what percentage of independent variable (GDP per capita) explains the dependent variable (government expenditure on education).

In order to verify applicability of the linear model we use ANOVA (Analysis of Variance)

$H0$: Linear regression model is not significant (not applicable)
$H1$: Linear regression model is significant (applicable)

Linear regression model is significant based on the fact that the p-value = $0.000 < \alpha = 0.05$ (Table 8).

Table 8 Linear regression model #1

Linear			
Model summary			
R	R square	Adjusted R square	Std. error of the estimate
0.904	0.818	0.815	996.665

The independent variable is GDP per capita in PPPs ($)

ANOVA					
	Sum of squares	df	Mean square	F	Sig.
Regression	276136331.7	1	276136331.7	277.987	0.000
Residual	61587155.32	62	993341.215		
Total	337723487.0	63			

The independent variable is GDP per capita in PPPs ($)

Coefficients					
	Unstandardized coefficients		Standardized coefficients	t	Sig.
	B	Std. error	Beta		
GDP per capita in PPPs ($)	0.257	0.015	0.904	16.673	0.000
(Constant)	−837.148	527.090		−1.588	0.117

Source Processing was carried out in IBM SPSS statistics

The final regression model (RM1) of government expenditure on education per pupil/student:

$$RM1 = -837.148 + 0.257 * \text{GDP per capita}$$

Linear regression model requires the existence of following assumptions:

- **presence of continuous variables**—in the form of the amount of government expenditure on education per pupil/student and GDP per capita
- **linear relationship between variables**—confirmed in Fig. 9 and Table 8
- **no significant extremes**—not seen in Fig. 9
- **verification of model errors and homoscedasticity (constant variance)**

Moreover, model errors should be normally distributed with mean of zero, with constant variance, independent and random.

To detect whether model errors are normally distributed with mean of zero we use IBM SPSS Statistics operation: ANALYZE/Descriptive Statistics/Explore.

We found that average error (Mean) is zero (Table 9).

By tests of normality, we tested the following hypotheses:

$H0$: The errors have normal distribution
$H1$: The errors do not have normal distribution

Test of normality is based on the Shapiro–Wilk test and Kolmogorov–Smirnov test. Based on the fact that the Kolmogorov–Smirnov test is used to test a set of 2000 items or more, we will use Shapiro–Wilk test as there are 64 items ($N = 64$). The resulting p-value is equal to 0.109, which is higher than significance level

Table 9 Mean test #1

			Statistic	Std. error
Error for expenditure per student in PPPs $ with GDP per capita in PPPs $ from CURVEFIT, MOD_1 LINEAR	Mean		0.0000000	123.59042072
	95% confidence interval for mean	Lower bound	−246.9757484	
		Upper bound	246.9757484	
	5% trimmed mean		6.9356539	
	Median		245.7192141	
	Variance		977573.894	
	Std. deviation		988.72336572	
	Minimum		−2466.63335	
	Maximum		2136.07919	
	Range		4602.71254	
	Interquartile range		1519.17295	
	Skewness		−0.325	0.299
	Kurtosis		−0.178	0.590

Source Processing was carried out in IBM SPSS statistics

$\alpha = 0.05$, the hypothesis of normal distribution (H_0) is so not rejected (Table 10; Fig. 14 Normal distribution).

In order to examine whether model errors are with constant variance, independent and random we use the command GRAPHS/Figure Builder/Scatter/Dot in IBM SPSS Statistics. The graph of errors compared to amount of GDP per capita does not show any functional dependence. We can therefore say that the model errors are independent and random. Moreover, based on the fact that the errors are dispersed in the range of −3000 to 3000, we can claim that model errors are with constant variance (Fig. 15).

Table 10 Test of normality #1

Tests of normality

	Kolmogorov–Smirnov[a]			Shapiro–Wilk		
	Statistic	df	Sig.	Statistic	df	Sig.
Error for expenditure per student in PPPs \$ with GDP per capita in PPPs \$ from CURVEFIT, MOD_1 LINEAR	0.128	64	0.011	0.969	64	0.109

[a]Lilliefors significance correction
Source Processing was carried out in IBM SPSS statistics

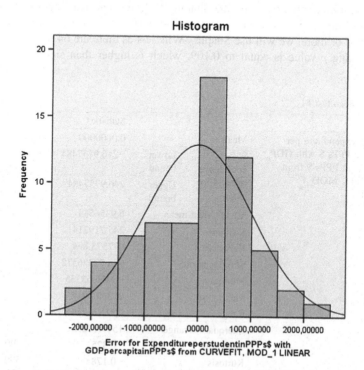

Fig. 14 Normal distribution. *Source* Processing was carried out in IBM SPSS statistics

Fig. 15 Regression model
errors characteristics #1.
Source Processing was carried
out in IBM SPSS statistics

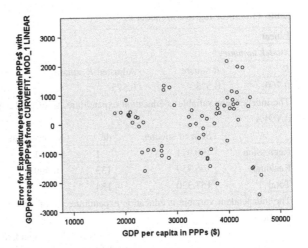

3.6.3   Prediction Model of Amount of Government Expenditure on Education

In this step we will try to predict the amount of total government expenditure on education expressed as % of GDP based on its % of total government expenditure, as there was confirmed positive correlation in Sect. 3.5.3. We will proceed similarly as in Sect. 3.6.2.

Regression Results

In this case we will again use linear regression model to predict future values of government expenditure on education as % of GDP in the view of relatively high correlation coefficient $(\rho) = 0.760$, and coefficient of determination $(\rho^2) = 0.578 = 57.8\%$. Applicability of linear model is also confirmed by ANOVA (Analysis of Variance), based on the fact that p-value $= 0.000 < \alpha = 0.05$ (Table 11).

The final regression model (RM2) of total government expenditure on education as % of GDP:

$$RM2 = 1.061 + 0.378 * \text{government expenditure on education as } \%$$
$$\text{of total gov. expenditure}$$

It is also necessary to test model errors in similar way as in the previous case. Average error of model (Mean) is equal to zero (Table 12).

Using test of normality we tested the following hypotheses:

$H0$: Model errors are normal distributed
$H1$: Model errors are not normal distributed

Table 11 Linear regression model #2

Linear

Model summary

R	R square	Adjusted R square	Std. error of the estimate
0.760	0.578	0.575	0.706

The independent variable is education expenditure, % of total expenditures

ANOVA

	Sum of squares	df	Mean square	F	Sig.
Regression	90.971	1	90.971	182.331	0.000
Residual	66.359	133	0.499		
Total	157.330	134			

The independent variable is education expenditure, % of total expenditures

Coefficients

	Unstandardized coefficients		Standardized coefficients	t	Sig.
	B	Std. error	Beta		
Education expenditure, % of total expenditures	0.378	0.028	0.760	13.503	0.000
(Constant)	1.061	0.340		3.119	0.002

Source Processing was carried out in IBM SPSS statistics

Table 12 Mean test #2

Descriptives

			Statistic	Std. error
Error for education expenditure of GDP with education expenditure of total expenditures from CURVEFIT, MOD_2 LINEAR	Mean		0.000	0.06056604
	95% confidence interval for mean	Lower bound	−0.1197891	
		Upper bound	0.1197891	
	5% trimmed mean		−0.0144632	
	Median		−0.0157778	
	Variance		0.495	
	Std. deviation		0.70371383	
	Minimum		−1.32856	
	Maximum		1.83200	
	Range		3.16056	
	Interquartile range		0.95695	
	Skewness		0.240	0.209
	Kurtosis		−0.270	0.414

Source Processing was carried out in IBM SPSS statistics

Table 13 Test of normality #2

Tests of normality	Kolmogorov-Smirnov[a]			Shapiro–Wilk		
	Statistic	df	Sig.	Statistic	df	Sig.
Error for education expenditure of GDP with education expenditure of total expenditures from CURVEFIT, MOD_2 LINEAR	0.035	135	0.200*	0.986	135	0.193

*This is a lower bound of the true significance
[a]Lilliefors significance correction
Source Processing was carried out in IBM SPSS statistics

Fig. 16 Regression model errors characteristics #2. *Source* Processing was carried out in IBM SPSS statistics

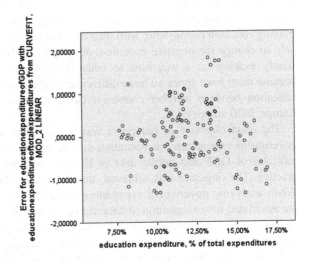

Using Shapiro–Wilk test we found out that model errors are normally distributed based on the fact that p-value equals to 0.193, which is above significance level $\alpha = 0.05$, so the hypothesis of normal distribution is not rejected (Table 13).

Errors are constantly dispersed in the range of −2 to 2. Moreover, we can observe they are independent and random (Fig. 16).

4 Conclusion

In times of crisis, every government has to make a difficult decision about future direction of the country. Every country must seek and select the appropriate instruments of fiscal policy that would improve the economic situation of the country and help it to start growing again. Fiscal policy offers a choice of several tools which, when applied at the right time, can revive the country's economy. At the time of economic downturn it is recommended to use the expansive form of fiscal and monetary policy in the form of increasing of government expenditure, tax cuts, and support of consumption and investments. Management of fiscal policy is more difficult when countries are part of a great community like the EU, where there is no central fiscal policy, and the countries are thus responsible for creating its own fiscal policy taking into account regulations, which stem from EU membership. However, analysis of measures and regulations adopted by the EU in order to reduce public debt, showed us that their application in practice is ineffective due to the fact, member countries failed to meet the requirements and they have not been penalized till now. Thus, the EU will have to find a better solution to break the crisis. The possible solution is to establish a central fiscal policy, but the expert opinions on this issue differ. Most of experts, however, believe in positive effect in the case of its establishment, so we can likely expect it in the near future. However, EU member countries can also participate in fight against the crisis by training educated people who, with their own knowledge and ideas can significantly help to change the negative economic development. The European Union is constantly looking for a way how to make financing of education more effective, because there have appeared huge differences in the amount of invested money into education between member countries. Goals regarding education are set in its Europe 2020 strategy.

The main objective of our paper was to find relation between the amount of government expenditure on education and development of basic macroeconomic indicator of GDP and public debt of EU member countries and find its use in practice. The objective was achieved, thanks to our subgoals which we have set. When analyzing government expenditure on education, we defined problems that are associated with acquisition of data sources needed for the analysis. Comparative analysis provided a comparison of the countries according to the amount of government expenditure on education from different perspectives.

Using comparative analysis we could observe which countries invested in education at most or at least, then where expenditure on education grew at a time of deepening crisis and on the other hand, which countries invested minimum in education. Results of the analysis confirmed significant differences in the amount of expenditure between EU countries. Comparative analysis also allowed us to compare countries regarding GDP. We found which countries are economically developed, and vice versa, the economy of which countries is declining significantly. At the same time we could observe how GDP developed during the economic and debt crisis. Moreover, comparative analysis has been also used in the case of analysis of public debt, where we investigated which countries are in debt at most, and on the other, which countries are successful in the fight against the crisis. Analysis results also showed us which countries exceeded a threshold of public debt, i.e., 60% of GDP, and so they were force to take corrective actions adopted by the EU. By correlation analysis of examined variables we confirmed a positive correlation between the amount of government expenditure on education per pupil/student (in PPPs) and GDP per capita (in PPPs). At the same time, we found a relatively high correlation between (as % of GDP) and (as % of total government expenditure).

Confirmed correlation can be used to create cluster model and linear regression model. Both models allow us to predict the amount of in the future, or to estimate the amount of in the current or prior periods if this information has not been released by member countries or they do not plan to publish it. The models enable a better comparison of between EU countries in a significant advance, with the opportunity of possible adjustment of amount in order to step by step eliminate significant differences between EU member countries.

To achieve the same educational level of EU member countries is a huge challenge, but not impossible. Therefore, let us not forget the famous quote of US entrepreneur Bob Parsons:

Measure everything, because everything that is measured and watched improves.

Appendix 1

Economic Classification of revenue

1	**Revenue**	122	Other social contributions [GFS]
11	**Taxes**	1221	Employee contributions [GFS]
111	Taxes on income, profits, and capital gains	1222	Employer contributions [GFS]
1111	Payable by individuals	1223	Imputed contributions [GFS]
1112	Payable by corporations and other enterprises	**13**	**Grants**
1113	Other taxes on income, profits, and capital gains	131	From foreign governments
11131	Payable by general government	1311	Current
11132	Unallocable taxes on income, profits, and capital gains	1312	Capital
112	Taxes on payroll and workforce	132	From international organizations
113	Taxes on property	1321	Current
1131	Recurrent taxes on immovable property	1322	Capital
1132	Recurrent taxes on net wealth	133	From other general governments units
1133	Estate, inheritance, and gift taxes	1331	Current

(continued)

(continued)

Economic Classification of revenue			
1135	Capital levies	1332	Capital
1136	Other recurrent taxes on property	**14**	**Other revenue**
114	Taxes on goods and services	141	Property income [GFS]
1141	General taxes on goods and services	1411	Interest [GFS]
11411	Value-added taxes	14111	From nonresidents
11412	Sales taxes	14112	From residents other than general government
11413	Turnover and other general taxes on goods and services	14113	From other general government units
11414	Taxes on financial and capital transactions	1412	Dividends
1142	Excise	14121	From nonresidents
1143	Profits of fiscal monopolies	14122	From residents
1144	Taxes on specific services	1413	Withdrawals of income from quasi-corporations
1145	Taxes on use of goods and permission to use goods or perform activities	1414	Property income from investment income disbursements
11451	Motor vehicle taxes	1415	Rent
11452	Other taxes on use of goods and on permission to use goods or perform and activities	1416	Reinvested earnings on foreign direct investment
114521	Business and professional licenses	142	Sales of goods and services
114522	Pollution taxes	1421	Sales by establishments
114523	Radio and television licenses	1422	Administrative fees
114524	Licenses and permits for households	1423	Incidental sales by nonmarket establishments
114525	Other taxes on use of goods and on permission to use goods or perform activities not elsewhere classified	1424	Imputed sales of goods and services
1146	Other taxes on goods and services	143	Fines, penalties, and forfeits
115	Taxes on international trade and transactions	144	Transfers not elsewhere classified
1151	Customs and other import duties	1441	Current transfers not elsewhere classified
1152	Taxes on exports	14411	Subsidies
1153	Profit of exports or import monopolies	14412	Other current transfers not elsewhere classified
1154	Exchange profits	1442	Capital transfers not elsewhere classified
1155	Exchange taxes	145	Premiums, fees, and claims related to nonlife insurance and standardized guarantee schemes

(continued)

(continued)

Economic Classification of revenue			
1156	Other taxes on international trade and transactions	1451	Premiums, fees, and current claims
116	Other taxes	14511	Premiums
1161	Payable solely by business	14512	Fees or standardized guarantee schemes
1162	Payable by other than business or unidentifiable	14513	Current claims
12	**Social contributions [GFS]**	1452	Capital claims
121	Social security contributions [GFS]		
1211	Employee contributions [GFS]		
1212	Employer contributions [GFS]		
1213	Self-employed or nonemployed contributions [GFS]		
1214	Unallocable contributions [GFS]		

Source IMF (2014)

Appendix 2

Economic Classification of expense			
2	**Expense**	**27**	**Social benefits [GFS]**
21	**Compensation of employees [GFS]**	271	Social security benefits [GFS]
211	Wages and salaries [GFS]	2711	Social security benefits in cash [GFS]
2111	Wages and salaries in cash [GFS]	2712	Social security benefits in kind [GFS]
2112	Wages and salaries in kind [GFS]	272	Social assistance benefits
212	Employers' social contributions [GFS]	2721	Social assistance benefits in cash [GFS]
2121	Actual employers' social contributions [GFS]	2722	Social assistance benefits in kind [GFS]
2122	Imputed employers' social contributions [GFS]	273	Employment-related social benefits [GFS]
22	**Use of goods and services**	2731	Employment-related social benefits in cash [GFS]

(continued)

(continued)

Economic Classification of expense			
23	**Consumption of fixed capital [GFS]**	2732	Employment-related social benefits in kind [GFS]
24	**Interest [GFS]**	**28**	**Other expense**
241	To nonresidents [GFS]	281	Property expense other than interest
242	To residents other than general government [GFS]	2811	Dividends
243	To other general government units [GFS]	28111	To nonresidents
25	**Subsidies**	28112	To residents
251	To public corporations	2812	Withdrawals of income from quasi-corporations
2511	Public nonfinancial corporations	2813	Property expense for investment income disbursements
2512	Public financial corporations	2814	Rent
252	To private enterprises	**2815**	Reinvested earnings on foreign direct investment
2521	Private nonfinancial enterprises	**282**	**Transfers not elsewhere classified**
2522	Private financial enterprises	2821	Current transfers not elsewhere classified
253	To other sectors	2822	Capital transfers not elsewhere classified
26	**Grants**	**283**	Premiums, fees, and claims related to nonlife insurance and standardized guarantee schemes
261	To foreign governments	2831	Premiums, fees, and current claims
2611	Current	28311	Premiums
2612	Capital	28312	Fees for standardized guarantee schemes
262	To international organizations	28313	Current claims
2621	Current	2832	Capital claims
2622	Capital		
263	To other general government units		
2631	Current		
2632	Capital		

Source IMF (2014)

Appendix 3

Classification of expenditure by functions of government according to divisions and groups			
7	Total expenditure	706	Housing and community amenities
701	General public services	7061	Housing development
7011	Executive and legislative organs, financial and fiscal affairs external affairs	7062	Community development
7012	Foreign economic aid	7063	Water supply
7013	General services	7064	Street lighting
7014	Basic research	7065	R&D Housing and community amenities
7015	R&D general public services	7066	Housing and community amenities n.e.c.
7016	General public services n.e.c.	707	Health
7017	Public debt transactions	7071	Medical product, appliances, and equipment
7018	Transfers of a general character between different levels of government	7072	Outpatient services
702	Defense	7073	Hospital services
7021	Military defense	7074	Public health services
7022	Civil defense	7075	R&D health
7023	Foreign military aid	7076	Health n.e.c.
7024	R&D defense	708	Recreation culture, and religion
7025	Defense n.e.c.	7081	Recreational and sporting services
703	Public order and safety	7082	Cultural services
7031	Police services	7083	Broadcasting and publishing services
7032	Fire protection services	7084	Religious and other community services
7033	Law courts	7085	R&D recreation, culture, and religion
7034	Prisons	7086	Recreation, cloture, and religion n.e.c.
7035	R&D Public order and safety	709	Education
7036	Public order and safety n.e.c.	7091	Preprimary and primary education
704	Economic affairs	7092	Secondary education

(continued)

(continued)

Classification of expenditure by functions of government according to divisions and groups			
7041	General economic, commercial, and labor affairs	7093	Postsecondary nontertiary education
7042	Agriculture, forestry fishing, and hunting	7094	Tertiary education
7043	Fuel and energy	7095	Education not definable by level
7044	Mining, manufacturing, and construction	7096	Subsidiary services to education
7045	Transport	7097	R&D education
7046	Communication	7098	Education n.e.c.
7047	Other industries	**710**	**Social protection**
7048	R&D economic affairs	7101	Sickness and disability
7049	Economic affairs n.e.c.	7102	Old age
705	**Environmental protection**	7103	Survivors
7051	Waste management	7104	Family and children
7052	Waste water management	7105	Unemployment
7053	Pollution abatement	7106	Housing
7054	Protection of biodiversity and landscape	7107	Social exclusion n.e.c.
7055	R&D environmental protection	7108	R&D social protection
7056	Environmental protection n.e.c.	7109	Social protection n.e.c.

Source IMF (2014)

References

Auer L, Belov E, Kryvinska N, Strauss C (2011) Exploratory case study research on SOA investment decision processes in Austria. In: Mouratidis H, Rolland C (eds) 23rd international conference on advanced information systems engineering (CAiSE-2011). LNCS, vol 6741. Springer, London, UK, pp 329–336, 20–24 June 2011

Engelhardt-Nowitzki C, Kryvinska N, Strauss C (2011) Strategic demands on information services in uncertain businesses: a layer-based framework from a value network perspective. In: The first international workshop on frontiers in service transformations and innovations (FSTI-2011), in conjunction with the second international conference on emerging intelligent data and web technologies (EIDWT 2011), Tirana, Albania, pp 131–136, 7–9 Sept 2011

EurActiv SK (2012) Finančná kríza, viewed 13 Mar 2015

European Commission (2014a) National sheets on education budgets in Europe, viewed 19 Mar 2015

European Commission (2014b) Stability and growth pact, viewed 3 Mar 2015

European Commission (2015) Strategický rámec pre vzdelávanie a odbornú prípravu 2020, viewed 31 Mar 2015

Fauska P, Kryvinska N, Strauss C (2014) Agile management of complex good & service bundles for B2B E-commerce by global narrow-specialized companies. Glob J Flex Syst Manag (Special Issue on Flexible Complexity Management and Engineering by Innovative Services) 15(1):5–23 (Springer)

Gregus M, Kryvinska N (2015) Service orientation of enterprises—aspects, dimensions, technologies. Comenius University in Bratislava

http://ec.europa.eu/economy_finance/economic_governance/sgp/index_en.htm
http://ec.europa.eu/education/policy/strategic-framework/index_sk.htm
http://eacea.ec.europa.eu/education/eurydice/documents/facts_and_figures/National_Budgets.pdf
http://www.euractiv.sk/ekonomika-a-euro/zoznam_liniek/financna-kriza-000227
IMF (2014) GFS manual 2014. IMF, Washington
Kaczor S, Kryvinska N (2013) It is all about services—fundamentals, drivers, and business models. Soc Serv Sci J Ser Sci Res 5(2):125–154 (Springer)
Kryvinska N, Strauss C, Auer L, Zinterhof P (2009) Information technology investment decision-making under uncertainty. In: Fourth IIASA/GAMM workshop on coping with uncertainty (CwU'2009), managing safety of heterogeneous systems, IIASA, Laxenburg, Austria, 14–16 Dec 2009
Kryvinska N, Barokova A, Auer L, Ivanochko I, Strauss C (2013) Business value assessment of services re-use on SOA using appropriate methodologies, metrics and models. Inderscience Publishers, Int J Serv Econ Manag (IJSEM) (Special Issue on Service-Centric Models, Platforms and Technologies) 5(4):301–327
Kryvinska N, Kaczor S, Strauss C, Gregus M (2014a) Servitization—its raise through information and communication technologies. In: 5th international conference on exploring services science (IESS 1.4). Lecture Notes in Business Information Processing (LNBIP 169). Springer, Geneva, Switzerland, pp 72–81, 5–7 Feb 2014
Kryvinska N, Kaczor S, Strauss C, Gregus M (2014b) Servitization strategies and product-service-systems. In: The IEEE fourth international workshop on the future of software engineering FOR and IN cloud (FoSEC 2014), at Hilton Anchorage, Alaska, USA, within IEEE 10th world congress on services (SERVICES 2014), pp 254–260, 27 June–2 July 2014
Kryvinska N, Kaczor S, Strauss C, Gregus M (2015) Servitization—transition from manufacturer to service provider. In: Gummesson E, Mele C, Polese F (eds) Service dominant logic, network and systems theory and service science: integrating three perspectives for a new service Agenda, Naples Forum on Service 2015, Naples, Italy, 9–12 June 2015
Lajčiak R (2013) Míňať alebo šetriť? Fiškálne politiky EÚ". Zahraničná politika 17(2):23–24
Medzinárodné porovnanie výdavkov na vzdelávanie, Bratislava, viewed 31 Mar 2015. https://www.minedu.sk/data/att/4761.pdf
Ministry of Education, Science, Research and Sport of the Slovak Republic 2013
Ministry of Finance of the Slovak Republic 2014. Pakt stability a rast, viewed 3 Mar 2015. http://www.finance.gov.sk/Default.aspx?CatID=99077
OECD (2012) OECD Factbook 2011–2012, OECD Publishing, viewed 31 Mar 2015. http://www.oecd-ilibrary.org/sites/factbook-2011-en/10/02/04/index.html?contentType=%2Fns%2FStatisticalPublication%2C%2Fns%2FChapter&itemId=%2Fcontent%2Fchapter%2Ffactbook-2011-89-en&mimeType=text%2Fhtml&containerItemId=%2Fcontent%2Fserial%2F18147364&accessItemIds=
SITA (2011) Merkelová vidí jediné riešenie ako z krízy von. Spoločnú fiškálnu politiku, viewed 10 Mar 2015. http://spravy.pravda.sk/svet/clanok/241021-merkelova-vidi-jedine-riesenie-ako-z-krizy-von-spolocnu-fiskalnu-politiku
Stoshikj M, Kryvinska N, Strauss C (2014) Efficient managing of complex programs with project management services. Glob J Flex Syst Manag (Special Issue on Flexible Complexity Management and Engineering by Innovative Services) 15(1):25–38 (Springer)
Stoshikj M, Kryvinska N, Strauss C (2016) Service systems and service innovation: two pillars of service science. Elsevier J Procedia Comput Sci (Special Issue on the 7th International Conference on Ambient Systems, Networks and Technologies (ANT-2016)) 83:212–220
Sulík R (2014) Nové rozpočtové pravidlá EÚ sú ignorované, viewed 12 Mar 2015. http://europskaunia.sulik.sk/nove-rozpoctove-pravidla-eu-su-ignorovane/
Uhliarik I (2013) Príčiny dlhovej krízy v eurozóne, viewed 1 Mar 2015. http://www.konzervativizmus.sk/upload/pdf/Uhliarik_ESEJ_2013.pdf
Urikova O, Ivanochko I, Kryvinska N, Strauss C, Zinterhof P (2012a) Exploration of factors affecting the advancement of collaborative eBusiness in the enterprises—research efforts examination. In: First international workshop on inter-clouds and collective intelligence

(iCCI-2012), in conjunction with the 26th IEEE international conference on advanced information networking and applications workshops (WAINA-2012), Fukuoka, Japan, pp 1227–1232, 26–29 Mar 2012

Urikova O, Ivanochko I, Kryvinska N, Zinterhof P, Strauss C (2012b) Managing complex business services in heterogeneous eBusiness ecosystems—aspect-based research assessment. Elsevier J Procedia Comput Sci (Special Issue on the 3rd International Conference on Ambient Systems, Networks and Technologies (ANT-2012)) 10:128–135

Chapter 2
Math Analysis of Informational Factors Affecting State Fiscal Policy in Short-Term Development Prediction

Gabriel Okasa and Mária Bohdalová

Abstract This case study focuses on the usage of mathematical tools within a broader macroeconomic application. The prime objective of the case study is to predict a short-term development of the most important macroeconomic variable, GDP, and to analyze its influence on the state's fiscal policy. As the future GDP development prediction tools serve time series analysis methods, namely moving averages and exponential smoothing. Results are afterward being used in the macroeconomic IS–LM model to identify changes in the goods and money market, respectively. The final outcome reflects fiscal policy behavior based on changes caused by GDP development and policy recommendations for obtaining desired objectives. For the sake of the paper, all the above-stated steps are being applied for data reflecting Germany's and Greece's GDP, as for the best-performing and the worst-performing Eurozone economy. The results show that an established trend in growth and recession will be even more significant.

Keywords GDP · Fiscal policy · IS–LM model · Correlation matrix · Moving averages · Exponential smoothing

1 Introduction

This chapter combines two very close yet different academic disciplines, Mathematics and Economics. It begins with a basic economic concept called fiscal policy. It describes what the purpose of such a concept is and what variables are involved. Furthermore, it clarifies the interdependence of these variables and how

G. Okasa · M. Bohdalová (✉)
Department of Information Systems, Faculty of Management, Comenius University in Bratislava, Odbojárov 10, P.O. BOX 95, 82005 Bratislava 25, Slovakia
e-mail: maria.bohdalova@fm.uniba.sk

G. Okasa
e-mail: okasag@gmail.com

© Springer Science+Business Media Singapore 2018
N. Kryvinska and M. Gregus (eds.), *Agile Information Business*,
Flexible Systems Management, DOI 10.1007/978-981-10-3358-2_2

they affect the economy. As a next step it identifies major factors that can possibly affect the whole fiscal policy and factors that are already integrated and are a part of the fiscal policy concept. It treats these factors as one of the key variables and examines a development of the variables in certain countries in the past. Having all the necessary information from the past about a key indicator, Mathematics starts to play its role. Moving from Economics to Mathematics, the key factor is treated by various mathematic computations and models which show an interdependence and correlations among various countries. Going beyond analyzing interdependence and correlations, the chapter involves using certain time series analysis tools in order to make short-run projections of a development of the key variable. Once the projections are made a focus moves back to Economics. In the chapter, the results are implemented into an economic model, which shows how the development of the key factor influences the country's economy and provides some kind of recommendations and possible scenarios that it could lead to and how to adapt fiscal policy actions in order to reach desired situation on the market.

The main objective of this case study is to analyze factors that can influence a country's fiscal policy. The chapter, however, contains a couple of particular objectives. The first particular objective is a comparison of countries, meaning an analysis of correlations of certain variables. The second particular objective is to provide some kind of recommendations based on a projected development of certain variables. How does it affect the economy, what impact does it have on other key variables, and last but not least what fiscal policy actions should be undertaken to either avoid or emphasize the impact on other key variables?

The meaning of the topic of this chapter is to interconnect Mathematic and Economic knowledge into one complex unit in order to quantify economic decisions. More specifically, to take certain variables from an economic environment then process them using mathematic computations and consequently put them back into the economic environment. The purpose is to find particular relations of the key factor among certain countries, to describe the relation, and to find certain patterns. Furthermore, to forecast a future development of the key factor, so the economy knows what to expect in the future and what steps concerning fiscal policy to undertake in order to achieve desired goals.

The first section includes all the theoretical knowledge necessary for performing a successful practical part of the case study (Kryvinska et al. 2014a; Stoshikj et al. 2014; Urikova et al. 2012a). It explains the basics of fiscal policy, GDP, interest rates, the IS–LM model, correlation matrix, moving averages, exponential smoothing models, and so on.

The second section explains the main objective as well as particular objectives together with the associated working methodology.

The third section contains a description of a concrete environment and an economic situation in involved countries, namely, Slovakia, Austria, Germany, France, Spain, and Greece.

The third section involves a whole practical part of the case study using a programming tool Wolfram Mathematica 9.0 such as figures, tables, correlation matrices, and performing time series analysis methods including moving averages and exponential smoothing, afterward applying results into the IS–LM model.

2 Macroeconomic and Time Series Insight

2.1 Aggregate Output

What does 'aggregate' mean? According to Blanchard (2003), the word aggregate is widely used in economics meaning total. So when we talk about aggregate output we mean total output. In the past, there was no certain measure of a total economic activity. In order to quantify the total economic activity, macroeconomists had no other choice but to collect all kinds of available information such as sales of a car manufacturer or a number of telephones produced at a specific price. This was very long lasting and also inaccurate process. After World War II, product accounts and national income were finally combined into national income accounts and consequently published regularly. Considering that it is an accounting system, first it is crucial to set concepts, and second to come up with measures which correspond to those concepts. It was truly essential to create such a system in order to maintain consistency and precision (Blanchard and Johnson 2009).

2.1.1 Gross Domestic Product

Gross domestic product (GDP) represents the measure of aggregate output within already mentioned national income accounts. What does GDP include and how does it work? Let us take a closer look at it using a basic example:

Consider an island with only two companies.

- Company1 is a flour factory using mills and employs millers who make flour out of wheat. Afterward, Company1 sells the flour to a Company2 for 1000 €. Out of revenue the Company1 pays 600 € to its millers and 400 € are kept as profit (Table 1).
- Company2 is a bakery and buys the flour for 1000 € from Company1 and uses it also for its ovens and bakers to bake bread. The amount of revenue for selling bread amounts to 3000 € of which 1000 € is paid for the flour, 1500 € is a salary for bakers and remaining 500 € is a profit for the Company2 (Table 2).

Table 1 Company1—flour factory, income statement

Revenues	1000 €
Expenses	600 €
Wages	*600 €*
Profit	400 €

Table 2 Company2—bakery, income statement

Revenues	3000 €
Expenses	2500 €
Wages	*1500 €*
Flour purchase	*1000 €*
Profit	500 €

Table 3 Merged company income statement: flour factory + bakery

Revenues	3000 €
Expenses	2100 €
Wages 1	*600 €*
Wages 2	*1500 €*
Profit	900 €

Based on the provided information, Blanchard (2003) identifies three ways how to define GDP at the same time:

1. GDP is the value of the final goods and services produced in the economy during a given period (Blanchard and Johnson 2009).

What is really the most important part of this definition is the word final. Why is the word final so important? Considering our basic example, should both the price of flour which is 1000 € and the price of bread which is 3000 € be included in GDP calculations as well? Or should it only be the price of bread alone? The answer is rather simple. When calculating GDP, only the price of finished products is included. In our example the price of bread is 3000 € because the price of flour is already included there. The flour was used in a production process of baking bread, thus, becoming a so-called intermediate good (Blanchard and Johnson 2009):

- An input to the production of a final good (Arnold 2013).
- There are some goods which can be considered an intermediate good as well as a final good.

Looking at our example, when the flour is used in the production process of the breads it is the intermediate good. But if the flour was sold in a supermarket it would have been the final good, hence contributing to GDP (Kryvinska et al. 2014b; Stoshikj et al. 2016).

Our example could be considered also a little bit differently. Imagine our two companies would merge and thus becoming a single company (Kryvinska et al. 2015; Urikova et al. 2012b). That would mean that the sale of the flour would basically disappear from the income statement and we could see just the revenues in the amount of 3000 €, the expenses on the wages 1500 € + 600 € = 2100 € and the profit reaching 900 €. But what is the most important thing here is that the revenues remained without any change and it should be like that. All can be expressed in Table 3.

To sum it up, one method of calculating GDP is recording and summarizing the production and consequently the prices of final goods. That is basically the system of how GDP is being conducted.

2. GDP is the sum of value added in the economy during a given period (Blanchard and Johnson 2009).

As in the previous definition there was a focus on the word final, here the focus is on a term value added. Blanchard (2003) says that the value added by a company means subtracting a value of intermediate goods used in a production from a value of its production. Considering our basic example, Company1, the flour factory simply does not use any intermediate product, thus the value added by the Company1 is the same as the value of the produced flour and that is 1000 €. Unlike the flour factory, Company2, the bakery uses an intermediate product—the flour. According to the definition, the value added by the Company2 is the value of the produced bread minus the value of the flour which has been used in its production process, 3000 € − 1000 € = 2000 €. A whole value added in the island with our two companies is 1000 € + 2000 € = 3000 € and that equates to the total of GDP in the economy. Bear in mind that the same value added and thus the same GDP would have been conducted if these two companies were merged. In that case, there would not be any intermediate product causing that the total value added and the total GDP, respectively, would be just the value of produced bread, 3000 € (Blanchard and Johnson 2009).

To summarize, as Blanchard (2003) declares, these two definitions provide a point of view on GDP calculation from a production side. The first definition of GDP describes it as a value of final products and services in the economy. The second definition of GDP implies that it is also a total value added by all the companies which are in the economy. However, there is also another point of view on how to look at GDP calculation and that is an income side point of view (Blanchard and Johnson 2009).

3. GDP is the sum of incomes in the economy during a given period (Blanchard and Johnson 2009).

Considering the income side, analysis of the remained revenues of the company after it has purchased and paid all the intermediate products that it had used in the production process:

• One part of the revenues is taken away by the government representing indirect taxes which are basically taxes on sales.
• Another part of the revenue is being used as wages for employees representing labor income.
• The residual revenue remains in the company representing profit income.

Basically, from the income point of view, conducting GDP means that the value added is adding up all indirect taxes, labor income, and profit income (Blanchard and Johnson 2009).

Getting back to our basic example, in this case, indirect taxes amount to zero. The value added by Company1 is 1000 € of which 600 € are wages representing the labor income and the rest, 400 € is the profit income. The value added by Company2 is 2000 € of which 1500 € are wages representing the labor income and the rest, 500 € is the profit income. By adding up the indirect taxes (0 €), the labor income (600 € + 1500 € = 2100 €), and the profit income (400 € + 500 € = 900 €), the total sum is 3000 € which equals to the total value added and also to the value of finals goods, describing a conduction of GDP from the income side.

In this example, the distribution of the income is 70% labor income to 30% profit income which, when no indirect taxes are being considered, more or less corresponds to a real trend in developed economies.

To sum it all up, GDP is the most important macroeconomic variable providing information about aggregate output and it is a key factor in signalizing how good or bad is the economy doing. GDP reflects an actual performance of the economy. The higher the GDP, the greater the performance. GDP can be conducted by focusing either on the production side, meaning an aggregate production or the income side, meaning an aggregate income. Bear in mind that both sides, production and income, are always equal (Blanchard and Johnson 2009)!

2.1.2 Nominal Versus Real GDP

When comparing a level of GDP expressed in units of Money, it can be clearly seen how huge a difference between today's GDP and GDP from the 1970s is. Today's GDP is always several times higher than it was ten, twenty, or even thirty years ago. Although the economy is continually growing, according to Mankiw (2006), the main reason why there are such enormous GDP differences is primarily caused by an increase in prices and not by increase in production. This fact is responsible for a distinction between real and nominal GDP (Mankiw and Taylor 2006):

- Nominal GDP: Nominal GDP uses current prices to place a value on the economy's production of goods and services (Mankiw and Taylor 2006).
- Real GDP: Real GDP uses constant base-year prices to place a value on the economy's production of goods and services (Mankiw and Taylor 2006).

According to the definition, the difference between nominal and real GDP is that real GDP is nothing more than nominal GDP cleaned of inflation. The higher the inflation, the higher the nominal GDP. A growth of nominal GDP is influenced by two main factors:

1. An increase in prices, and
2. An increase in production and services.

A growth of real GDP is only influenced by one main factor:

1. An increase in production and services.

Using constant base-year prices, real GDP provides an answer to a theoretical question: what would products and services produced today be worth, if they had prices which prevailed in a particular year in the past? By giving price tags from a specific year in the past to value today's production, real GDP is an indicator of change in production and services. In other words, base-year prices serve as a basis for a comparison of a product quantity in different years. The only case when nominal GDP is the same as real GDP is in the base year (Mankiw and Taylor 2006)!

Further in this chapter, nominal GDP is used in computations and figures due to more accurate data availability.

2.2 IS–LM Model

The IS–LM model provides a framework to understand how outputs—GDP and interest rate—are defined and interconnected in the short run. The fundamental part of the IS–LM model is a determination of equilibrium in the financial markets and the goods markets as well as characterizing the implications while achieving such equilibrium. The IS–LM model is based on the General Theory written by John Maynard Keynes and its understanding of two-sided economy. There are two major factors which define the IS–LM approach (Dixon and Gerrard 2000):

1. Output is an endogenous variable which is demand-determined.
2. The rate of interest is an endogenous variable and affects both the demand for goods (investment and possibly consumption) and the demand for money (Dixon and Gerrard 2000).

The IS curve displays the interplay between the output level—GDP—and the interest rate which corresponds with equilibrium in the goods market. The LM curve displays the interplay between the output level—GDP—and the interest rate which respond to equilibrium in the financial market (Blanchard and Johnson 2009).

2.2.1 Construction of the IS Curve

In order to construct the IS curve, the determination of output is needed. To reach equilibrium in the goods market, which represents the IS curve, the following condition has to be fulfilled:

- Production = Demand.

Further, the IS relation is defined as follows (Blanchard and Johnson 2009):

- $$Y = C(Y - T) + I(Y, i) + G, \tag{1}$$

where

Y Output—GDP—Income
C Consumption
T Taxes
I Investment
i Interest rate
G Government spending

Let us break the demand side of the equation into smaller pieces and explain what it means.

1. Consumption:

The first part of the right side of the equation, $C(Y - T)$, defines consumption as a function of disposable income, represented by $(Y - T)$. Disposable income is what is left after taxes have been paid (Boyes and Melvin 2012). It is based on an assumption which says that people (consumers) spend more when they have more.
  Basic rules that apply are as follows (Blanchard and Johnson 2009):

- The higher the income, the higher the consumption by constant taxes
- The lower the income, the lower the consumption by constant taxes
- The higher the taxes, the lower the consumption by constant income
- The lower the taxes, the higher the consumption by constant income

2. Investment:

The second part of the right side of the equation, $I(Y+, i-)$, defines an investment as depending on the level of production, Y, and the interest rate, i (Blanchard and Johnson 2009).
  Considering the dependence on production, it derives from the sales level which leads to a series of implications; higher sales lead to increase in the production, for which a company has to buy for instance new equipment or build a whole new building, thus investing more. To put it the other way around, low sales lead to constant or decreasing production; hence, the company has no incentive to invest (Blanchard and Johnson 2009; Engelhardt-Nowitzki et al. 2011; Fauska et al. 2014; Kryvinska et al. 2013).
  Considering the dependence of the interest rate, a company that wants to buy new equipment and needs to take a loan for that is more likely to actually take the loan when the interest rate is low. On the other hand, when the interest rate is higher, it is less attractive to take the loan. If the interest rate is too high, the

company will not buy new equipment due to an insufficient additional profit resulting from the purchase to cover interest payments (Blanchard and Johnson 2009).

Basic rules that apply are as follows (Blanchard and Johnson 2009):

- The higher the production, the higher the investment; hence $Y+$
- The lower the production, the lower the investment; hence $Y+$
- The higher the interest rate, the lower the investment; hence i^-
- The lower the interest rate, the higher the investment; hence i^-.

3. Government Spending:

The third part of the right side of the equation, G, defines government spending as an exogenous variable because it is neither expressed by a function nor by a dependency. Government spending is treated as a given variable due to its inability to predict a government's behavior and its future decisions. The government's behavior does not follow any particular pattern as for instance consumers' behavior and is a subject for various possible decisions and strategies according to a behavior and development of other endogenous variables. Therefore, it is an aim of this chapter to further focus precisely on this topic (Blanchard and Johnson 2009).

Next, when the IS relation is already expressed by the equation, the important question within the IS–LM model is how does the IS relation look drawn? The answer is that the IS relation is represented by the IS curve which is displayed in Fig. 1 with the interest rate on a vertical axis and the output—GDP—on a horizontal axis. The IS curve is a type of a downward-sloping curve.

What can be seen in Fig. 1 is that the IS curve defines the dependency between the interest rate and the output—GDP—income. Obviously, the higher the interest rate, the lower the output. Why is this so?

An increase in interest rate causes a decrease in investment. Consequently, a decrease in investment implies a decrease in output. Moreover, a decrease in output further decreases consumption as well as investment which shift output even lower.

Fig. 1 The IS curve (Lipsey and Chrystal 2011)

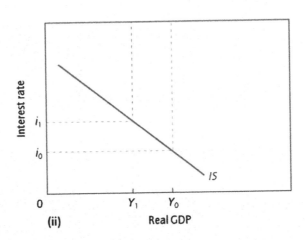

A decrease in interest rate causes an increase in investment. Consequently, an increase in investment implies an increase in output. Moreover, an increase in output further increases consumption as well as investment which again shift output even higher (Blanchard and Johnson 2009).

Shifting the IS curve:

When shifting the IS curve, it is very important to be aware that the IS curve shifts only on a horizontal axis. It can be shifted either left or right. That is, a basic principle of shifting the IS curve. But how can it be shifted? The shifts of the IS curve reflect a change in either the level of taxes, T, or the level of government spending, G, at a given level of interest rate. Generally, based on the IS relation, any factor which influences level of demand and consequently output shifts the IS curve. According to the equation, it could be output, taxes, interest rate, and government spending, but the output and the interest rate are now excluded, due to a fact that the IS curve shows the equilibrium level of GDP associated with each given rate of interest (Blanchard and Johnson 2009), thus cannot be used, while both are endogenous variables, already explained within the model. On the other hand, taxes and government spending are considered exogenous. That is why they influence shifts of the IS curve (Lipsey and Chrystal 2011) (Fig. 2).

Basic rules that apply are as follows (Blanchard and Johnson 2009):

- Any change which causes a level of output to rise at a given rate of interest shifts the IS curve to the right. It can be either a decrease in taxes, T, or an increase in government spending, G.
- Any change which causes a level of output to fall at a given rate of interest shifts the IS curve to the left. It can be either an increase in taxes, T, or a decrease in government spending, G.

Fig. 2 Shifts in the IS curve (Lipsey and Chrystal 2011)

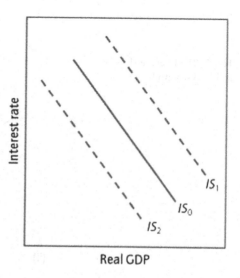

2.2.2   Construction of the LM Curve

In order to construct the LM curve, the determination of money supply is needed. To reach equilibrium in the financial market, which represents the LM curve, the following condition has to be fulfilled:

- Money Supply = Demand for Money.

  Further, the LM relation is defined as follows (Blanchard and Johnson 2009):

$$\frac{M}{P} = YL(i), \tag{2}$$

where

M/P	Real money supply
Y	Real income—GDP—Output
L	Liquidity function
i	Interest rate

Let us break the money demand side of the equation into separate pieces and explain what it means and what effect it has on the real money supply.

1. Real income

The first part of the right side of the equation is represented by real income, Y, and equivalently, level of output and GDP as well. The basic assumption is that when people earn more they want to spend more, for which they need more money. Expressed by the equation, the basic rule that applies is as follows:

- When real income goes up, so does real money demand (Blanchard and Johnson 2009).

2. Interest rate

The second part of the right side of the equation is defined by the function of interest rate, $L(i^-)$. That is very closely connected with a distribution of real income. People do not have to demand just money when their income rises. Another option is to put a part of their income in bonds, because unlike money, bonds actually pay an interest. That means, when people earn something extra, they decide whether to take money to spend their income immediately or to invest it in bonds, not touching that part of the income for a certain period of time but receiving interest. How this distribution of income works explains the negative sign next to the interest rate, i^-. If the interest rate is really high, people will rather give up an immediate use of money, in order to receive high interest. On the other hand, if the interest rate is really low, there is no reason to invest in bonds. It is safer and more convenient to hold the whole income in money. So the basic rules that apply are as follows (Blanchard and Johnson 2009):

- The higher the interest rate, the lower the demand for money; hence i^-
- The lower the interest rate, the higher the demand for money; hence i^-.

When the right side of the equation is clarified, meaning how the variables influence demand for money, it is essential to highlight that in order to maintain equilibrium in financial market, demand for money must be equal to supply of money (Blanchard and Johnson 2009).

Next, when the LM relation is already expressed by the equation, the important question within the IS–LM model is how does the LM relation look drawn? The answer is that the LM relation is represented by the LM curve which is displayed in Fig. 3 with the interest rate on a vertical axis and the output—GDP—on a horizontal axis, same as for the IS curve. The LM curve is a type of upward-sloping curve.

What can be seen from Fig. 3 is that the LM curve defines the dependency between the interest rate and the output—GDP—income as well as the IS curve which is also drawn in Fig. 3. Unlike the IS curve, the higher the output, the higher the interest rate (Lipsey and Chrystal 2011). Why is this so?

An increase in income causes an increase in money demand, but the money supply remains constant. Consequently, the interest rate rises until reaching equilibrium again. In other words, people want more money, but there is not enough money for all of them and that is why their income has to be invested in bonds. To do that, the interest rate must increase in order to make people willing to put their income in bonds rather than in money (Blanchard and Johnson 2009).

- Shifting the LM curve

When shifting the LM curve, it is very important to be aware that the LM curve shifts only on a vertical axis. It can be shifted either up or down. That is, a basic principle of shifting the LM curve. But how can it be shifted? The shifts of the LM curve reflect a change in real money supply, M/P, so either in nominal supply of money, M, or in a price level, P, due to a fact that the LM curve plots combinations

Fig. 3 The LM curve
(Lipsey and Chrystal 2011)

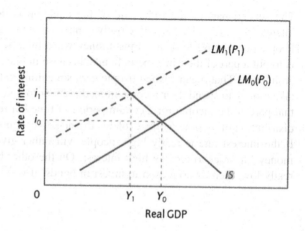

Fig. 4 Shifts in the LM
curve (Lipsey and Chrystal
2011)

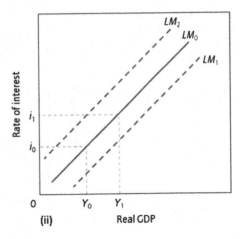

of GDP and the interest rate, for a given nominal money supply and given price
level, that are consistent with the equality of money demand and money supply
(Lipsey and Chrystal 2011) (Fig. 4).

Basic rules that apply are as follows (Blanchard and Johnson 2009):

- Any change which causes a level of real money supply to rise shifts the LM
  curve down. It can be either an increase in nominal money supply, M, or a
  decrease in the price level, P.
- Any change which causes a level of real money supply to fall shifts the LM
  curve up. It can be either a decrease in nominal money supply, M, or an increase
  in the price level, P.

2.2.3 Integration of the IS and the LM Curve

Knowing both, the IS and the LM relation and their curves, we can construct the
completed IS–LM model. What does it tell us?

Any point on the downward-sloping IS curve corresponds to equilibrium in the
goods market. Any point on the upward-sloping LM curve corresponds to equilibrium in financial markets. Only at point A are both equilibrium conditions satisfied (Blanchard and Johnson 2009) (Fig. 5).

In other words, the point A represents, at the corresponding level of interest rate,
i, and output, Y, total equilibrium, meaning the point of equilibrium in both markets, namely goods and financial markets. The IS–LM model shows what consequences have changed in all the variables included in the IS and the LM relation
such as taxes, government spending, money supply on the level of output—GDP—
income and the level of interest rate in the short run (Blanchard and Johnson 2009).

Fig. 5 The IS–LM model
(Blanchard and Johnson
2009)

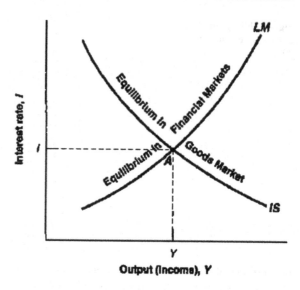

2.3 Fiscal Policy

The word 'fisc' means 'state treasury' and 'fiscal policy' refers to policy concerning the use of 'state treasury' or the government finances to achieve certain macroeconomic goals (Dwiwedi 2010).

Fiscal policy is a government tool to influence macroeconomic factors such as GDP and interest rate in order to fulfill its macroeconomic objectives by changing two main variables, namely, level of taxes, T, and level of government spending, G. When performing fiscal policy, the government can use two techniques depending on what the goal is (Dwiwedi 2010).

2.3.1 Fiscal Expansion

In this case, the government either decreases the level of taxes, T, or increases the level of government spending, G, and thus shifting the IS curve to the right.

- A decrease in taxes, T, leads to an increase in disposable income, hence increasing consumption and ultimately output—GDP.
- An increase in government spending, G, directly leads to an increase in output—GDP.

Both of these actions result in a rise of output—GDP—and so shifting the IS curve to the right. But what happens with the LM curve? Absolutely nothing happens. But what is actually happening within the IS–LM model is that the economy is moving along the LM curve and reaching a new equilibrium with not only higher output but also with higher interest rate. Because of higher output and

Fig. 6 Fiscal expansion
(Blanchard and Johnson
2009)

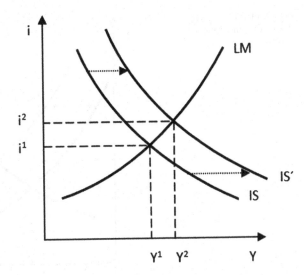

income, demand for money is higher as well, forcing interest rate to go up
(Blanchard and Johnson 2009) (Fig. 6).

Results of the fiscal expansion are as follows (Blanchard and Johnson 2009):

- Higher level of output—GDP
- Higher level of interest rate.

2.3.2 Fiscal Contraction (Consolidation)

In this case, the government either increases the level of taxes, T, or decreases the
level of government spending, G, and thus shifting the IS curve to the left.

- An increase in taxes, T, leads to a decrease in disposable income, hence
  decreasing consumption and ultimately output—GDP.
- A decrease in government spending, G, directly leads to a decrease in output—
  GDP.

Both of these actions result in a decline of output—GDP—and so shifting the IS
curve to the left. Does something happen with the LM curve in this case? Again,
absolutely nothing happens. But the economy is moving along the LM curve in
order to reach a new equilibrium with not only lower output but also with a lower
interest rate. Because of lower output and income, demand for money is lower as
well, forcing the interest rate to go down (Blanchard and Johnson 2009) (Fig. 7).

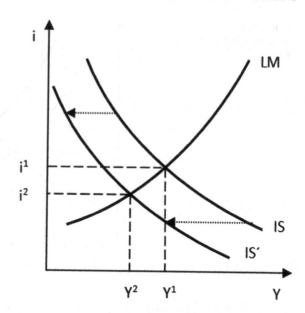

Fig. 7 Fiscal contraction (Blanchard and Johnson 2009)

Results of the fiscal contraction (consolidation) are as follows (Blanchard and Johnson 2009):

- Lower level of output—GDP
- Lower level of interest rate.

2.4 Matrices and Their Properties

2.4.1 Correlation Matrix

A correlation matrix is one of the widely used matrices in math and statistics and this matrix describes correlations among random variables. The correlation matrix is a square symmetric matrix, where components on the i, j positions are the correlations between (i)th and (j)th components of a vector of random variables. Diagonal components of the correlation matrix are the correlations of the same variables and therefore they are always equal to 1 (Bohdalová 2006b).

Definition of the correlation matrix:

The matrix, R, whose (i, j)th component is a number $\rho_{xi, yj}$ is called the correlation matrix of the random variable vector (Bohdalová 2006a):

$$X = (X_1, X_2, \ldots, X_n)^T \tag{3}$$

$$R = \begin{pmatrix} \rho_{X_1,X_1} & \rho_{X_1,X_2} & \cdots & \rho_{X_1,X_n} \\ \rho_{X_2,X_1} & \rho_{X_2,X_2} & \cdots & \rho_{X_2,X_n} \\ \vdots & \ddots & \ddots & \vdots \\ \rho_{X_n,X_1} & \rho_{X_n,X_2} & \cdots & \rho_{X_n,X_n} \end{pmatrix}. \tag{4}$$

The correlation matrix, R, has the following properties (Bohdalová 2006a):

If X and Y are independent random variables with finite mean values, $E(X)$ and $E(Y)$, then

$$E(XY) = E(X) \cdot E(Y). \tag{5}$$

If X and Y are independent random variables with finite second moments, then $\Sigma = 0$, where Σ is a covariance matrix with components cov(X, Y) of the random variables, X and Y.

Vectors, X and Y, are uncorrelated, if their covariance matrix is equal to 0.

2.5 Time Series Analysis

Time series analysis deals with statistical methods for analyzing and modeling an ordered sequence of observations. This modeling results in a stochastic process model for the system which generated the data (Madsen 2007). Data which create a time series are chronologically ordered observations and that is very important.

The major objective of the time series analysis is a construction of a corresponding model. The construction of the model helps not only to obtain an understanding of a mechanism for generating the data but also enables forecasting and monitoring of the future development of a system. The time series analysis is widely used in several fields such as sales forecasting, yield projections, and stock market analysis, but the main application is for economic forecasting (Cipra 1986).

It is essential to highlight the fact that under the term 'time series' is meant 'statistical time series',

$$y_t = \beta_0 + \beta_1 t + \varepsilon_t, \tag{6}$$

where

t time
β_0, β_1 parameters of a linear trend
ε_t random variable (Cipra 1986).

2.5.1 Moving Averages

This method may be considered as an artificially constructed time series in which each periodic figure is replaced by the mean of the value of that period and those of a number of preceding and succeeding periods (Srivastava et al. 2005). Moving averages method is one of the adaptive approaches and these are characterized as approaches which are able to work with various trend components that change their nature globally in time. That is why it is not feasible to use a curve with constant parameters in order to define them. However, it is feasible to define them by a local smoothing of a trend which is often called as the concept of a gradual trend.

The major advantages are as follows:

- its ability to adapt to a current local course of the series while eliminating the trend component and
- flexible responding of a forecast to time changes in a series' character.

When constructing moving averages, it is essential to make an assumption that every function can be approximated by a polynomial, in our case so-called smoothing polynomial. The degree of this polynomial describes the order of moving average. The construction of moving averages itself is basically creating a linear combination of the components of the initial series. When considering time series such as (Cipra 1986)

$$y_t = T_t + \varepsilon_t, \tag{7}$$

where

- T_t represents a trend which can be defined by a function of time, t
- ε_t represents a random error, often referred to a so-called white noise.

An estimated trend component and at the same time a smoothed value of a series in time, t, can be expressed as follows (Cipra 1986):

$$\hat{y}_t = \frac{1}{35}(-3y_{t-2} + 12y_{t-1} + 17y_t + 12y_{t+1} - 3y_{t+2}). \tag{8}$$

This can be also defined as (Cipra 1986)

$$\hat{y}_t = \frac{1}{35}(-3, 12, 17, 12, -3)y_t. \tag{9}$$

Particularly, this smoothed value, $\hat{y}_t$, describes $2m + 1 = 5$ values of the considered time series, $y_{t+\tau}$, with a third-order polynomial and values of time, $\tau = -2$, -1, 0, 1, 2. Generally, we can smooth a series with $2m + 1$ length by rth-order polynomial and thus obtain moving averages of the length, $2m + 1$, and the order, r. The smoothed value, $\hat{y}_t$, in a time, t, and with even, j, is a linear combination of the following expression (Cipra 1986):

$$\sum_{\tau=-m}^{m} \tau^j y_{t+\tau}. \tag{10}$$

As already mentioned before, it is a linear combination of values, $y_{t+\tau}$, with fixed coefficients which represent weighs of the moving average.

Moving averages have the following properties (Cipra 1986):

1. The sum of the weighs of the moving average equals 1.
2. The weighs are about the middle value symmetrical.
3. If the order, r, is an even number, then rth and $r + 1$th-order moving averages with length, $2m + 1$, are the same ones.

Further in the case study we will be working with two main types of trends which can be observed using moving averages method:

1. Linear trend

Linear trend is defined by the line with the following inscription:

$$Tr_t = \beta_0 + \beta_1 t, \tag{11}$$

where $t = 1, \ldots, n$ and a prediction, $\hat{y}_T$, of the future value y_T, is defined as follows:

$$\hat{y}_T = b_0 + b_1 T. \tag{12}$$

In addition, the first differentials of $y_{t+1} - y_t$ are approximately constant (Cipra 1986).

2. Quadratic trend

Quadratic trend is defined by the line with the following inscription:

$$Tr_t = \beta_0 + \beta_1 t + \beta_2 t^2, \tag{13}$$

where $t = 1, \ldots, n$ and a prediction, $\hat{y}_T$, of the future value y_T, is defined as follows:

$$\hat{y}_T = b_0 + b_1 T + b_2 T^2. \tag{14}$$

In the quadratic trend the first differentials of the following expression are approximately constant: $y_{t+2} - 2y_{t+1} + y_t$ (Cipra 1986).

2.5.2 Exponential Smoothing

Exponential smoothing is a method for forecasting trends in unit sales, unit costs, wage expenses, and so on. The technique identifies historical patterns of trend or seasonality in the data and then extrapolates these patterns forward into the forecast period (Hirschey 2009).

Single exponential smoothing has the following properties (Chaman and Malehorn 2005):

1. More weight is given to recent data and less weight to previous data
2. Includes automatic adjustments for errors in current data.

Exponential smoothing method can be defined by the following equation (Chaman and Malehorn 2005):

$$F_{t+1} = \alpha \cdot X_t + (1 - \alpha) \cdot F_t, \tag{15}$$

where

$F_{(t+1)}$ Forecast of the next period
α Smoothing constant
X_t Actual value of the current period
F_t Forecast value of the current period.

The smoothing constant, α, is responsible for error adjustments. The higher the value of the smoothing constant is, the bigger is the error adjustment and vice versa. The question is how to determine it. The basic rule is that the smoothing constant, α, has to be from the following interval: $0 < \alpha < 1$. However, practical experience has shown that for the majority of applications this interval can be reduced to $0.7 < \alpha < 1$. The final determination can be done either using the following formula:

$$\alpha = \frac{M - 1}{M + 1}, \tag{16}$$

where M is a length of a moving average, which has been the most suitable one for smoothing the particular series (Cipra 1986).

Or by iterations, when the smoothing constants from the interval are incrementally examined and the one which provides the most accurate forecast is chosen, i.e., the one with the lowest error, ε, which can be expressed as (Cipra 1986)

$$\varepsilon = \sum_{t=1}^{n} (X_t - F_t(t - 1))^2. \tag{17}$$

3   Objectives and Working Methodology

This part of the case study is focused closely on the main objective as well as particular objectives and the corresponding methodology of how to accomplish them.

3.1 Main Objective

The main objective of this chapter is to analyze factors affecting state fiscal policy, namely GDP, the most important macroeconomic variable, particularly, to analyze GDP development in selected European countries. The goal is to find similarities in the GDP development, to try to project a future development based on a right fit model and ultimately to draw macroeconomic consequences of such a projected development in the short run.

3.2 Particular Objectives

- Topic introduction

The very first objective is to dive into the elaborated topic including macroeconomic and mathematic background, in order to fully be able to proceed with the practical part of performing the analysis itself.

- Analysis of the GDP development and its dependence

Another particular objective is to analyze the GDP development in selected countries, namely Slovakia, Austria, Germany, France, Spain, and Greece, and to identify interdependence of these various GDP developments to find out how strongly these values are correlated.

- Finding an appropriate forecasting model

The next particular objective is to find an appropriate model for forecasting a future GDP development and consequently to perform such a short-run forecast based on the model.

- IS–LM Model interpretation

The last particular objective is to interpret obtained results using the macroeconomic IS–LM model and to identify possible consequences resulting from the fiscal policy strategy. Last but not least, some recommendations based on the IS–LM model as well as the overall macroeconomic situation today shall be provided.

3.3 Methodology

In the case study a very systematic approach of elaboration is used: first to get familiar with the necessary theoretical background and afterward a sequence of analysis resulting in the final outcome. All the computations and analysis within the chapter are made using Wolfram Mathematica 9.0 software which also serves as a source of all the data used in the chapter. However, Wolfram Mathematica 9.0 software is only a tool for obtaining necessary data and right results, and everything what is needed to obtain those results is purely self-made input to this software. The following methods are being used:

- Correlation Matrix

In order to find out the interdependence of selected GDP developments and consequently to quantify the interdependence, the correlation matrix serves as a tool to do so. Further, the coefficient of determination divides the selected GDP developments into two groups, each one with its representative.

- Moving Averages

Once obtaining representatives, moving averages as a time series analysis method is used to describe a trend of GDP development, namely linear and quadratic. After finding an appropriate trend, a short-run forecast is conducted using this method.

- Exponential Smoothing

Next to the moving averages method, the exponential smoothing serves as a second-time series analysis method to describe the trend of GDP development, namely simple exponential smoothing.fvelopment—Germa

- IS–LM Model

After completing the GDP development forecasting, the results are implemented into the macroeconomic IS–LM model in order to identify macroeconomic consequences resulting from the forecasted development.

- Fiscal policy

Lastly, based on the IS–LM model and also on the current macroeconomic situation, a simple deduction is done in order to provide some kind of recommendations for certain fiscal policy measures, considering various types of scenarios that could possibly happen according to a fiscal objective of the state's government.

4 GDP Development in the EU States

On the vertical axis of Figs. 8, 9, 10, 11, 12, and 13, the total amounts of GDP in Slovakia, Austria, Germany, France, Spain, and Greece, respectively, are displayed. On the horizontal axis, the year corresponding to the amounts of GDP on the vertical axis is displayed. Time frame accounts to the data from year 1993 to 2012.

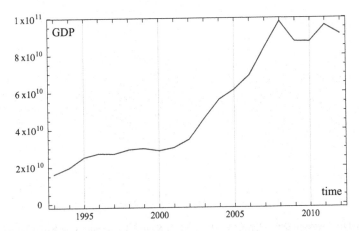

Fig. 8 GDP development—Slovakia, 1993–2012. *Source* Processing was based on data from Trading Economics (2013f)

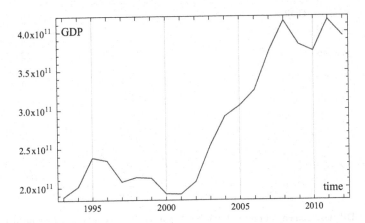

Fig. 9 GDP development—Austria, 1993–2012. *Source* Processing was based on data from Trading Economics (2013a)

4.1 Slovakia

As can be seen from in Fig. 8, although there some fluctuations might be observed, the overall tendency of a trend is increasing.

The highest GDP was reached in 2008 and is estimated at 9.791×10^{10}. Slovakia's GDP amounts to 0.15% of the world economy. Despite some growth fluctuations which have been caused mainly by the crisis, Slovakia ranks to one of the fastest growing European economies, thanks to reforms in social welfare,

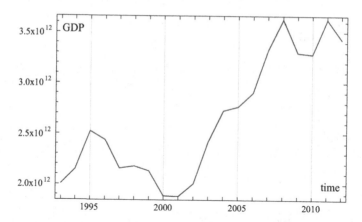

Fig. 10 GDP development—Germany, 1993–2012. *Source* Processing was based on data from Trading Economics (2013b)

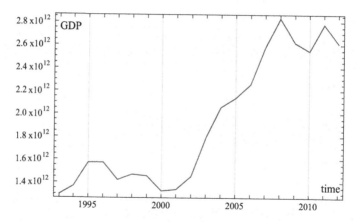

Fig. 11 GDP development—France, 1993–2012. *Source* Processing was based on data from Trading Economics (2013d)

taxation, pensions, etc. Slovakia is a host country to severe foreign investments in the electronic and automotive industry that boosted the expansion (Trading Economics 2013f).

4.2 Austria

As shown in Fig. 9, a slightly more GDP value changes were recognized during the observed period. However, Austria's GDP is more or less steady and the overall trend remains upward sloping.

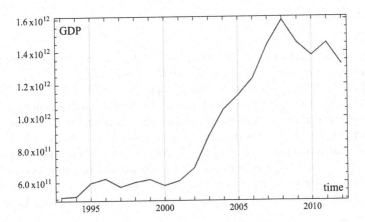

Fig. 12 GDP development—Spain, 1993–2012. *Source* Processing was based on data from Trading Economics (2013c)

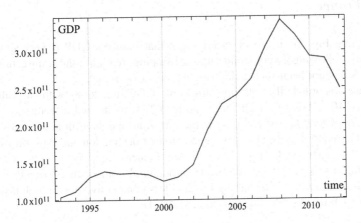

Fig. 13 GDP development—Greece, 1993–2012. *Source* Processing was based on data from Trading Economics (2013e)

According to Fig. 9, Austria's GDP development pattern is more or less the same as can be seen in Fig. 8 for Slovakia. The highest GDP amounts to 4.156×10^{11} recorded in 2011. Austria's GDP accounts to 0.64% of the world economy. The strongest pillar of Austrian economy is the service sector with Vienna becoming a finance and consulting center and a gate to Eastern Europe at the same time (Trading Economics 2013a).

4.3   Germany

As can be seen from Fig. 10, Germany's GDP has a very similar tendency to Austria's one only with higher amounts on the vertical axis.

Germany's GDP reached the all-time high of 3.625×10^{12} in 2011 and recorded really fast resurrection after the crisis. Germany's GDP accounts to 5.48% of the world economy and as Germany is the largest economy in the Eurozone and the fourth largest in the world, many other countries are heavily dependent on Germany's performance. German economic driver is without any doubts the export. Mainly the export of high-added value goods boosted the German economy in the last decades. Moreover, the German economy profits from a highly developed infrastructure, qualified labor, and big capital stock as well (Trading Economics 2013b).

4.4   France

Considering Fig. 11, it can be clearly seen that France's GDP is very similar to Germany, following a very similar upward-sloping trend, but the resurrection after the crisis has not been such a dramatic one as in Germany.

France recorded the all-time high of GDP in 2008 with a value of 2.832×10^{12}. France's GDP accounts to 4.21% of the world economy, representing the second largest economy in the Eurozone and the fifth in the world, right behind Germany. France is a very famous tourist destination and thus almost 79% of GDP is generated by the service sector. French economy is well-diversified, containing a mixture of industrial and agricultural components. Despite rational diversification, France is becoming less and less competitive due to high taxes and inflexible labor laws (Trading Economics 2013f).

4.5   Spain

Unlike the countries above and their GDP development, Spain's GDP development has a bit of a different tendency, mainly after the crisis. After the year 2008 no resurrection has come yet and the trend is downward sloping.

The all-time high of Spain's GDP has been achieved in its economic peak in 2008 with a value of 1.593×10^{12}. Spain's GDP accounts to 2.18% of the world economy. Similar to France, Spain's biggest economic driver is tourism together with huge manufacturing industry. Thanks to an early membership in the Eurozone, Spain has become a host country to several foreign investments. Nevertheless, after the crisis, Spain is still looking for a solution for how to escape from a recession (Trading Economics 2013e).

4.6 Greece

Similar to Spain but even worse is Greece after the crisis. The country reached its economic peak in 2008 and after that, according to GDP values, no sign of improvement in economic performance has been recorded.

Greece has recorded its GDP value the all-time high in 2008 when it was estimated to 3.416×10^{11}. Greece's GDP accounts to 0.40% of the world economy. Greek economy is strongly service based as it is one of the major tourist destinations as well as Spain and France. Its economic expansion has been caused mainly by an early membership in the Eurozone and by access to cheap credit. After it became unsustainable, Greece experienced a huge crisis which it still cannot find a way out of (Trading Economics 2013e).

5 GDP Forecasting and Its Economic Consequences

5.1 Correlation Matrix

First of all, it is very important to find out how and to what extent GDPs are dependent on each other. In other words, we have to find out individual correlations of GDPs in order to identify a linkage among GDP values. The very first indicator showing interdependence among GDP values is undoubtedly displaying these values in a figure. We could already observe some indications that GDP development of a certain country follows more or less the same pattern as the other one. However, to obtain more precise information and also to quantify that interdependence, it is essential to use a correlation matrix. This will provide us with all the necessary information according to correlation coefficients.

To construct this correlation matrix, we will use Wolfram Mathematica 9.0 program which already contains all the necessary parameters and data (Table 4).

Analyzing the correlation matrix given below, it can be identified between which countries GDP values are correlated the most and on the other hand, the least correlated ones.

Table 4 Correlation matrix

	SVK	AT	GER	FR	ESP	GRC
SVK	1	0.985	0.955	0.989	0.990	0.972
AT	0.985	1	0.992	0.998	0.980	0.962
GER	0.955	0.992	1	0.985	0.954	0.937
FR	0.989	0.998	0.985	1	0.990	0.976
ESP	0.990	0.978	0.954	0.990	1	0.993
GRC	0.972	0.962	0.937	0.976	0.993	1

Source Own processing was based on data from Trading Economics

5.1.1 Correlation Coefficient

The highest correlation coefficient can be found between France and Austria GDP values, as stated in the matrix. This correlation coefficient amounts to 0.997809, which is very close to 1, thus almost reaching an absolute correlation. That means that the interdependence between the two GDP values is very high. Thus their economic performance is very similar.

On the other hand, the lowest correlation coefficient can be found between Germany and Greece GDP values, as stated in the matrix. This correlation coefficient amounts only to 0.937, which means that the interdependence between these two GDP values is not so significant. This statement is further confirmed by the economic performance of these two countries when Germany is the best-performing economy within the Eurozone and on the other side Greece the worst one.

However, here it is essential to verify the hypothesis of independence, meaning that these countries have independent GDP developments and thus that their correlation coefficients are equal to zero. The alternative hypothesis would be that GDP developments are dependent. As a proof, such a hypothesis serves the following matrix (see Fig. 14).

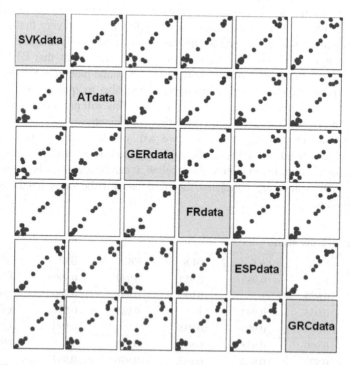

Fig. 14 Test of independence hypothesis. *Source* Own processing was based on data from Trading Economics

The matrix stated bellow illustrates the independence test of GDP developments among selected states. The result confirms that all the correlation coefficients are significant and hence dependent.

In order to further continue in forecasting of GDP development, it is essential to divide all the stated countries and their economic performance into two groups which follow almost the same pattern, i.e., the correlation coefficients among their GDP values are the highest. Doing so, we will create two groups, one representing stronger economies and the other one representing weaker ones. The strongest and the weakest economy (according to its GDP development) out of each group will serve as a representative of the group and will be used for further GDP development forecasting.

5.1.2   Coefficient of Determination

To divide it into two groups will help us to find the so-called coefficient of determination. It will determine the content of each group. Again we will use Wolfram Mathematica 9.0 to obtain the coefficient of determination.

The coefficient of determination matrix shows the R-squared, in other words it shows squared correlation coefficients. As can be seen from the matrix, the highest coefficient of determination is again between Austria and France which amounts to 0.995623. The lowest coefficient of determination is between Germany and Greece as in the previous matrix and amounts to 0.877339 (Table 5).

As a decision rule in order to determine two groups, we will use Germany as the strongest economy according to GDP development values and state the reference value of the coefficient of determination to 0.90, meaning that one group will consist of Germany plus all the countries with the coefficient of determination to Germany higher than the reference value 0.90 and on the opposite side, the other group will consist of all the countries with the coefficient of determination to Germany lower or equal to 0.90. The distribution according to the above-stated criteria is in Table 6.

In the first group are the following countries: Germany, Austria, France, and Slovakia ordered by the highest value of coefficient of determination. In the second

Table 5 Coefficient of determination matrix

	SVK	AT	GER	FR	ESP	GRC
SVK	1	0.970	0.913	0.977	0.980	0.946
AT	0.969	1	0.984	0.996	0.960	0.925
GER	0.913	0.984	1	0.971	0.910	0.877
FR	0.977	0.996	0.971	1	0.980	0.953
ESP	0.980	0.960	0.910	0.980	1	0.986
GRC	0.946	0.925	0.877	0.953	0.986	1

Source Own processing was based on data from Trading Economics

group is Greece and Spain ordered by the lowest value of coefficient of determination.

A graphic illustration is shown in Figs. 15 and 16 of both groups as follows.

As before, on the vertical axis total GDP amounts are displayed and on the horizontal axis the year corresponding to the GDP amounts is displayed. Time

Table 6 Distribution according to the coefficients of determination

First group	Second group
GER	GRC
AT	ESP
FR	
SVK	

Source Own processing

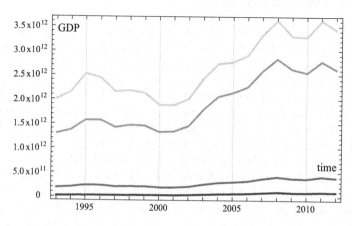

Fig. 15 GDP developments of the first group. *Source* Own processing (Color figure online)

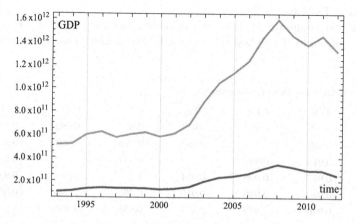

Fig. 16 GDP developments of the second group. *Source* Own processing (Color figure online)

frame accounts to the data from year 1993 to year 2012. The yellow line stands for
Germany, green for France, pink for Austria, and blue for Slovakia.

In Fig. 16, the red line stands for Spain and the blue one for Greece.

Further in this chapter we will work with GER GDP and GRC GDP as representatives of each group due to Germany being considered as the strongest and
Greece as the weakest economy.

5.2 Moving Averages

In order to smooth out fluctuation in Germany's and Greece's GDP development
and thus to define a long-term trend, moving averages method will serve as a time
series analysis tool to do so. But not only defining a long-term trend, smoothing the
trend also provides a basis for a subsequent short-term prediction.

5.2.1 Linear Trend

Let us start with moving averages with a linear trend to recognize to what extent it
can be used as a reliable and accurate method. To find it out, we use Wolfram
Mathematica 9.0 with the following input:

- $T = (-2, -1, 0, 1, 2)$; odd window length
- Y, GER GDP and GRC GDP values for 20 consecutive years
- $ML = 5$, moving length
- $J = (1, 1, 1, 1, 1)$, $J = \text{Table}[1, \{ML\}]$, unit vector
- $A = \{(-2, 1), (-1, 1), (0, 1), (1, 1), (2, 1)\}$; transposed $T, J, 2 \times 5$ matrix
- $AT = \{(-2, -1, 0, 1, 2), (1, 1, 1, 1, 1)\}$; transposed matrix A
- $n = 20$; number of values under Y
- $k = ML - 1$; difference between the last and the first parameter out of the window
- $Yestim$; estimated data of Y, smoothed values
- $m = (k/2)$, number of additionally calculated points
- $Jp = (1, 1)$; $Jp = \text{Table}[1, \{m\}]$, unit vector for two initial estimates, two end estimates
- $Ywindow$; 5 variables out of Y within the window T
- $ParamL$; parameter of the line (Figs. 17 and 18).

At first, it was necessary to obtain an inverse matrix of transposed matrix
A multiplied by matrix A, and then multiply it by transposed matrix A in order to
define a parameter of the line, $ParamL$, which has been calculated as a multiplication of the obtained Matrix and $Ywindow$. Once having $ParamL$ it is possible to
compute inner estimates and consequently initial as well as end estimates of data
Y. To compute inner estimates, we take the middle value $i + m$. To compute initial

```
In[16]:= Matrix = Inverse[AT.A].AT;
         Yestim = Table[0, {n}];
         Jp = Table[1, {m}];
         For[i = 1, i ≤ n - k, i++, {Ywindow = Take[Y, {i, i + k}], ParamL = Matrix.Ywindow,
           (* inner estimates*)Yestim[[i + m]] = ParamL[[2]], (* constant element of the line *)
           (* initial estimates *)
           If[i == 1, {(* spot forecasts in time -2,-1 *) Tp = Take[T, 2], (* -2,-1 *)
             Ap = Transpose[{Tp, Jp}], Yestim[[1]] = Ap[[1]].ParamL, Yestim[[2]] = Ap[[2]].ParamL}],
           (* end estimates *)
           If[i == (n - k), {(* spot forecasts in time 1,2 *)Tp = Take[T, -2], (* 1,2 *)
             Ap = Transpose[{Tp, Jp}], Yestim[[n - 1]] = Ap[[1]].ParamL, Yestim[[n]] = Ap[[2]].ParamL}] }]
         Yestim

Out[20]= {2.1366 × 10^12, 2.1955 × 10^12, 2.2544 × 10^12, 2.2886 × 10^12, 2.2852 × 10^12, 2.1578 × 10^12,
          2.0466 × 10^12, 2.0166 × 10^12, 2.0658 × 10^12, 2.1848 × 10^12, 2.3608 × 10^12, 2.5652 × 10^12, 2.8286 × 10^12,
          3.0686 × 10^12, 3.183 × 10^12, 3.2864 × 10^12, 3.4308 × 10^12, 3.4516 × 10^12, 3.4451 × 10^12, 3.4386 × 10^12}
```

Fig. 17 Linear trend MA—Germany. *Source* Own program code

```
In[12]:= Matrix = Inverse[AT.A].AT;
         Yestim = Table[0, {n}];
         Jp = Table[1, {m}];
         For[i = 1, i ≤ n - k, i++, {Ywindow = Take[Y, {i, i + k}], ParamL = Matrix.Ywindow,
           (* inner estimates *)Yestim[[i + m]] = ParamL[[2]], (* constant element of the line *)
           (* initial estimates *)
           If[i == 1, {(* spot forecasts in time -2,-1 *) Tp = Take[T, 2], (* -2,-1 *)
             Ap = Transpose[{Tp, Jp}], Yestim[[1]] = Ap[[1]].ParamL, Yestim[[2]] = Ap[[2]].ParamL}],
           (* end estimates*)
           If[i == (n - k), {(* spot forecasts in time 1,2 *)Tp = Take[T, -2], (* 1,2 *)
             Ap = Transpose[{Tp, Jp}], Yestim[[n - 1]] = Ap[[1]].ParamL, Yestim[[n]] = Ap[[2]].ParamL}] }]
         Yestim

Out[16]= {1.0592 × 10^11, 1.1478 × 10^11, 1.2364 × 10^11, 1.2994 × 10^11, 1.3434 × 10^11, 1.3312 × 10^11,
          1.3148 × 10^11, 1.3376 × 10^11, 1.4528 × 10^11, 1.6424 × 10^11, 1.8738 × 10^11, 2.1376 × 10^11, 2.4562 × 10^11,
          2.7536 × 10^11, 2.9396 × 10^11, 3.044 × 10^11, 3.0998 × 10^11, 2.9872 × 10^11, 2.7708 × 10^11, 2.5544 × 10^11}
```

Fig. 18 Linear trend MA—Greece. *Source* Own program code

estimates, we take the starting value $i = 1$ and perform spot forecast in time $-2, -1$. To compute end estimates, we take the end value $i = n - k$ and perform spot forecasts on the other side of the vector T, in time 1, 2. Finally, values represented by *Yestim* are estimated data of the original data Y. In other words, they are smoothed values using linear trend moving averages.

Figures 19 and 20 serve as a tool to obtain a better view of how this data is smoothed.

The blue spots in Figs. 19 and 20 are actual values of Germany's GDP and of Greece's GDP. The red line represents the linear trend of averaged smoothed values. As can be seen, the smoothed red line captures the actual trend quite precisely. However, there is too big a distance between the actual and smoothed values, especially at the beginning and at the end of the time span. Due to this reason, a prediction based on this linear trend would not be that accurate. It is therefore necessary to use moving averages with a quadratic trend, in order to obtain more precise prediction.

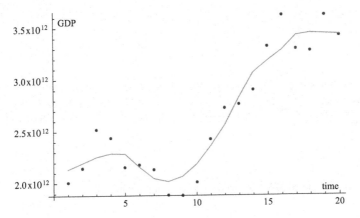

Fig. 19 Plotted linear trend MA—Germany. *Source* Own processing

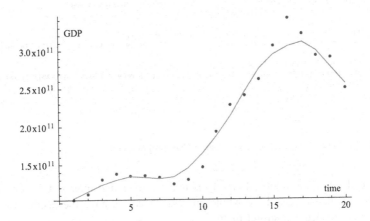

Fig. 20 Plotted linear trend MA—Greece. *Source* Own processing

5.2.2 Quadratic Trend

When implementing the quadratic trend we will use exactly the same procedure as we did for the linear trend, only with the following minor changes:

- $A = \{(-4, -2, 1), (1, -1, 1), (0, 0, 1), (1, 1, 1), (4, 2, 1)\}$; transposed T^2, T, J, 3×5 matrix
- $AT = \{(4, 1, 0, 1, 4), (-2, -1, 0, 1, 2), (1, 1, 1, 1, 1)\}$; transposed matrix A
- Instead of using *ParamL* in the point 2 in the computation, now it is used in the point 3 as a constant element of the line
- The previous formula of the vector Ap has changed from $Ap = \text{Transpose}[\{Tp, Jp\}]$ to $Ap = \text{Transpose}[\{Tp^2, Tp, Jp\}]$ (Figs. 21 and 22).

```
In[53]:= Matrix = Inverse[AT.A].AT;
        Yestim = Table[0, {n}];
        Jp = Table[1, {m}];
        For[i = 1, i ≤ n - k, i++, {Ywindow = Take[Y, {i, i + k}], ParamL = Matrix.Ywindow,
          (* inner estimates *)Yestim[[i + m]] = ParamL[[3]], (* constant element of the line *)
          (* initial estimates *)
          If[i == 1, {(* spot forecasts in time -2,-1 *) Tp = Take[T, 2], (* -2,-1 *)
            Ap = Transpose[{Tp^2, Tp, Jp}], Yestim[[1]] = Ap[[1]].ParamL, Yestim[[2]] = Ap[[2]].ParamL}],
          (* end estimates *)
          If[i == (n - k), {Tp = Take[T, -2], (* 1,2 *)
            Ap = Transpose[{Tp^2, Tp, Jp}], Yestim[[n - 1]] = Ap[[1]].ParamL, Yestim[[n]] = Ap[[2]].ParamL}]}]
        Yestim
```

Out[57]= $\{1.95046 \times 10^{12}, 2.28857 \times 10^{12}, 2.44054 \times 10^{12}, 2.41746 \times 10^{12}, 2.23106 \times 10^{12}, 2.15751 \times 10^{12}, 2.08231 \times 10^{12},$
$1.93289 \times 10^{12}, 1.85794 \times 10^{12}, 2.05551 \times 10^{12}, 2.4018 \times 10^{12}, 2.68263 \times 10^{12}, 2.78074 \times 10^{12}, 2.95374 \times 10^{12},$
$3.33257 \times 10^{12}, 3.5004 \times 10^{12}, 3.37437 \times 10^{12}, 3.36374 \times 10^{12}, 3.40117 \times 10^{12}, 3.52646 \times 10^{12}\}$

Fig. 21 Quadratic trend MA—Germany. *Source* Own program code

```
In[12]:= Matrix = Inverse[AT.A].AT;
        Yestim = Table[0, {n}];
        Jp = Table[1, {m}];
        For[i = 1, i ≤ n - k, i++, {Ywindow = Take[Y, {i, i + k}], ParamL = Matrix.Ywindow,
          (* inner estimates *)Yestim[[i + m]] = ParamL[[3]], (* constant element of the line *)
          (* initial estimates *)
          If[i == 1, {(* spot forecasts in time -2,-1 *) Tp = Take[T, 2], (* -2,-1 *)
            Ap = Transpose[{Tp^2, Tp, Jp}], Yestim[[1]] = Ap[[1]].ParamL, Yestim[[2]] = Ap[[2]].ParamL}],
          (* end estimates *)
          If[i == (n - k), {Tp = Take[T, -2], (* 1,2 *)
            Ap = Transpose[{Tp^2, Tp, Jp}], Yestim[[n - 1]] = Ap[[1]].ParamL, Yestim[[n]] = Ap[[2]].ParamL}]}]
        Yestim
```

Out[16]= $\{1.01177 \times 10^{11}, 1.17151 \times 10^{11}, 1.28383 \times 10^{11}, 1.36826 \times 10^{11}, 1.36526 \times 10^{11}, 1.35077 \times 10^{11}, 1.31066 \times 10^{11},$
$1.26474 \times 10^{11}, 1.27837 \times 10^{11}, 1.51397 \times 10^{11}, 1.90251 \times 10^{11}, 2.24246 \times 10^{11}, 2.41806 \times 10^{11},$
$2.65317 \times 10^{11}, 3.07089 \times 10^{11}, 3.332 \times 10^{11}, 3.22251 \times 10^{11}, 3.00691 \times 10^{11}, 2.78066 \times 10^{11}, 2.53469 \times 10^{11}\}$

Fig. 22 Quadratic trend MA—Greece. *Source* Own program code

Basically, what is done differently is that we extended matrix A by one more column and then repeated the whole process. Once we have the results, Figs. 23 and 24 help to better interpret them.

Figures 23 and 24 confirm our assumption that a quadratic trend could better and more precisely smooth out original values, mainly at the beginning and at the end of the time span, which is crucial for forecasting future values. In these figures, the red line captures the actual trend obviously more rigorously and it is very close to the actual values represented by blue spots throughout the whole time span. Thus it can serve as a reliable basis for future short-term predictions.

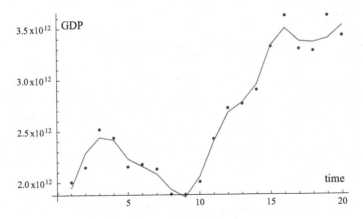

Fig. 23 Plotted quadratic trend MA—Germany. *Source* Own processing

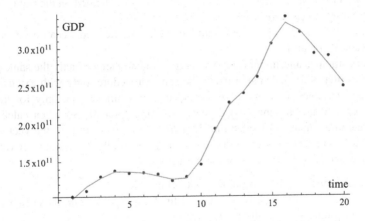

Fig. 24 Plotted quadratic trend MA—Greece. *Source* Own processing

5.2.3   Forecast

When forecasting the GDP development using moving averages, the following statement applies:

- The longer the forecast, the less accurate it is.

Mainly because of this reason it is not worth to try to make long-term projections. In order to make projections as accurate as possible, we will try to forecast the GDP development using moving averages with the quadratic trend for the next two time periods, meaning for the next 2 years. As long as the latest available data we use dates back to 2012, the forecasts will be for the years 2013 and 2014, respectively. In order to calculate those predictions, we will use exactly the same procedure as we did before, only with some additional changes:

```
In[20]:= Matrix = Inverse[AT.A].AT;
        Yestim = Table[0, {n + 2}]; (*plus 2 years of forecasts*)
        Jp = Table[1, {m}];
        For[i = 1, i ≤ n - k, i++, {Ywindow = Take[Y, {i, i + k}], ParamL = Matrix.Ywindow,
          (* inner estimates *)Yestim[[i + m]] = ParamL[[3]], (* constant element of the line *)
          (* initial estimates *)
          If[i == 1, {(* spot forecats in time -2,-1 *) Tp = Take[T, 2], (* -2,-1 *)
            Ap = Transpose[{Tp^2, Tp, Jp}], Yestim[[1]] = Ap[[1]].ParamL, Yestim[[2]] = Ap[[2]].ParamL}],
          (* end estimates *)
          If[i == (n - k), {(* spot forecats in time 1,2,3,4 *)Tp = Take[Tprediction, -4], (* 1,2,3,4 *)
            Ap = Transpose[{Tp^2, Tp, Jpnew}], Yestim[[n - 1]] = Ap[[1]].ParamL, Yestim[[n]] = Ap[[2]].ParamL,
            Yestim[[n + 1]] = Ap[[3]].ParamL, Yestim[[n + 2]] = Ap[[4]].ParamL }]}]
        Yestim
```

$$Out[23]= \{1.95046 \times 10^{12}, 2.28857 \times 10^{12}, 2.44054 \times 10^{12}, 2.41746 \times 10^{12}, 2.23106 \times 10^{12},$$
$$2.15751 \times 10^{12}, 2.08231 \times 10^{12}, 1.93289 \times 10^{12}, 1.85794 \times 10^{12}, 2.05551 \times 10^{12},$$
$$2.4018 \times 10^{12}, 2.68263 \times 10^{12}, 2.78074 \times 10^{12}, 2.95374 \times 10^{12}, 3.33257 \times 10^{12}, 3.5004 \times 10^{12},$$
$$3.37437 \times 10^{12}, 3.36374 \times 10^{12}, 3.40117 \times 10^{12}, 3.52646 \times 10^{12}, 3.7396 \times 10^{12}, 4.0406 \times 10^{12}\}$$

Fig. 25 Forecast Germany—quadratic trend MA

- *Tprediction* = {−2, −1, 0, 1, 2, 3, 4}, a new vector extended on the right side for calculating 2-year forecast
- *Jpnew* = {1, 1, 1, 1}, a new unit vector also extended because of another 2 years of forecast
- Inner estimates and initial estimates are calculated using exactly the same steps. End estimates are calculated using the same procedure, only with extension of certain variables as long as we are calculating estimates not only for the last 2 years but also for the next 2 years, meaning forecast. So when calculating these end estimates, we substitute *Tprediction* vector instead of the vector *T* as well as vector *Jpnew* instead of the vector *Jp*. Naturally, the number of values n is also extended by 2 years of forecast, *n* + 2.

Forecast Germany (own program code) (Fig. 25).

When looking at the last two values of final outcome *Yestim*, those two values are desired predictions for the next 2 years:

- In 2013, Germany's GDP value amounts to 3.7396×10^{12}
- In 2014, Germany's GDP value amounts to 4.0406×10^{12}.

It seems to be a very optimistic prediction as those values of GDP are rising. To obtain a better picture of the forecasting situation, let us take a look at Fig. 26.

In Fig. 26 it can be identified that Germany's GDP will rise quite significantly, as the moving averages method predicts. The forecast reflects an overall rising trend throughout the whole time span and also the latest values that already have a growing tendency. Based on this figure, it seems that Germany's GDP will copy the trend it had in the time span from the year 2002 until the year of the crisis, 2009. That would mean that Germany has already recovered from the crisis and has overcome the deepest recession and is now getting back into a period of economic growth.

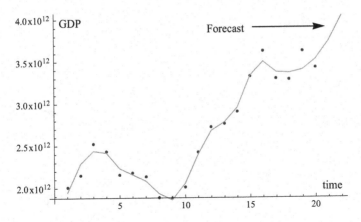

Fig. 26 Plotted forecast Germany—quadratic trend MA. *Source* Own processing

```
In[13]:= Matrix = Inverse[AT.A].AT;
        Yestim = Table[0, {n + 2}];
        (*plus 2 years of forecasts*)
        Jp = Table[1, {m}];
        For[i = 1, i ≤ n - k, i++, {Ywindow = Take[Y, {i, i + k}], ParamL = Matrix.Ywindow,
         (* inner estimates *)Yestim[[i + m]] = ParamL[[3]], (* constant element of the line *)
         (* initial estimates*)
         If[i = 1, {(* spot forecasts in time -2,-1 *) Tp = Take[T, 2], (* -2,-1 *)
           Ap = Transpose[{Tp^2, Tp, Jp}], Yestim[[1]] = Ap[[1]].ParamL, Yestim[[2]] = Ap[[2]].ParamL}],
         (* end estimates *)
         If[i = (n - k), {(* spot forecats in time 1,2,3,4 *)Tp = Take[Tprediction, -4], (* 1,2,3,4 *)
           Ap = Transpose[{Tp^2, Tp, Jpnew}], Yestim[[n - 1]] = Ap[[2]].ParamL, Yestim[[n]] = Ap[[2]].ParamL,
           Yestim[[n + 1]] = Ap[[3]].ParamL, Yestim[[n + 2]] = Ap[[4]].ParamL}]}]
        Yestim
Out[17]= {1.01177 × 10^11, 1.17151 × 10^11, 1.28383 × 10^11, 1.36826 × 10^11, 1.36526 × 10^11,
        1.35077 × 10^11, 1.31066 × 10^11, 1.26474 × 10^11, 1.27837 × 10^11, 1.51397 × 10^11,
        1.90251 × 10^11, 2.24246 × 10^11, 2.41806 × 10^11, 2.65317 × 10^11, 3.07089 × 10^11, 3.332 × 10^11,
        3.22251 × 10^11, 3.00691 × 10^11, 2.78066 × 10^11, 2.53469 × 10^11, 2.269 × 10^11, 1.9836 × 10^11}
```

Fig. 27 Forecast Greece—quadratic trend MA

Forecast Greece (own program code) (Fig. 27).

When looking at the last two values of final outcome *Yestim*, those two values are desired predictions for the next 2 years:

- In 2013, Greece's GDP value amounts to 2.269×10^{11}
- In 2014, Greece's GDP value amounts to 1.9836×10^{11}.

It seems to be a very pessimistic prediction as those values of GDP are falling. To obtain a better picture of the forecasting situation, let us take a look at Fig. 28.

From Fig. 28 it can be identified that Greece's GDP will fall quite significantly as opposed to the German one. The forecast reflects the latest downward-sloping trend as there is no sign of growth at all in comparison with Germany. Since the crisis year 2009, Greece's GDP is constantly lower and lower and thus there are no signs of improvement in the forecasts, too. This means that Greece clearly has not

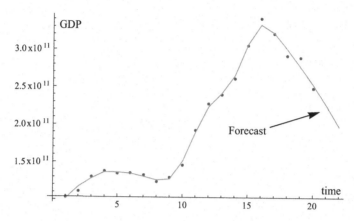

Fig. 28 Plotted forecast Greece—quadratic trend MA. *Source* Own processing

recovered from the crisis yet and that it might have not reached the bottom of the recession yet.

5.3 Exponential Smoothing

Once having a result of the forecasting using moving averages method, we will try to obtain a short-term forecast using another time series analysis method, namely single exponential smoothing. In order to apply this method and to subsequently obtain the short-term forecast in GDP development or if this method is even suitable for such a trend, we will use the Wolfram Mathematica 9.0 software again. The following function expressing single exponential smoothing serves as an input
   where

- *Fnp*; Forecast of the next period
- *Fcp*; Forecast of the current period
- *AV*; Actual values of the current period (either GER GDP or GRC GDP)
- *Alfa*; Smoothing constant in the interval (0.5; 1)
- *t*; Time.

Then it is essential to define *Fcp* as a vector. The length of the *Fcp* vector is extended by 1 as a result of one additional starting value to boost the whole computation. Once obtaining the function and definition of variables, we can begin with starting the computation of single exponential smoothing with the following input:

- *FcpO*; Optimal forecast of the current period
- *AlfaO*; Optimal Alfa for the beginning
- *n*; The length of actual values *AV*

$$Fnp[Alfa\_, t\_] := Alfa * Fcp[[t]] + (1 - Alfa) * AV[[t]]$$

Fig. 29 Single exponential smoothing function

- *np*; Number of points used to calculate the starting value
- *N*; Numerical value of the starting value (mean of first *np* values of the *AV*)
- *Error*; Actual value minus forecasted value
- *MAEO*; Optimal mean of absolute errors
- *YatO*; Optimal total error
- *IaTO*; Optimal error identifier; should be less than 4.

First of all it was necessary to clear *FcpO* value and then to define all the variables as is stated above. Then the starting value is calculated and, according to the Output 36, *Out[36]*, it is equal to 2.2544×10^{12}. Afterward, all the errors (*Out [38]*) for each period are calculated within a cycle based on the *Fnp* function, where the *Fcp* is always one time period ahead, thus $t + 1$. *Error* represents a difference between actual and forecasted value. Additionally, *MAEO*, *YaTO*, and *IaTO* have been calculated as well as it is stated above in Fig. 29. *MAEO* represents an optimal value of a mean of absolute values of all the errors and the value is 2.39467×10^{11}, *Out[39]*. *YaTO* is an optimal value of a sum of all the errors, concretely 2.3813×10^{12} as for *Out[40]*. *IaTO* is an optimal value of the so-called error identifier which is a quotient of *YaTO* and *MAEO*, in this case 9.94417, *Out[41]*. Ultimately, *Out[42]* expresses all the smoothed values as the *FcpO* values are assigned to the *Fcp* (Fig. 30).

However, what really matters here is the value of the error identifier, *IaTO*. In order to obtain reliable smoothed values *IaTO* has to be lower than 4. Unfortunately, in this case *IaTO* exceeds this condition. It means that the smoothing constant *Alfa* is not selected properly and thus a new better-fitting *Alfa* which will secure that *IaTO* will satisfy the condition has to be found. To do so, we will use a method of iterations. We use exactly the same process but instead of optimal values we use actual values, namely *Alfa*, *Fcp*, *MAE*, *YaT*, and *IaT*. Plus we add an If condition in order to perform those iterations. The If condition looks as follows: If *IaT* is lower than 4, then the smoothing constant *Alfa* is chosen properly and it will search for the lowest possible mean of absolute errors, *MAE*. Afterward, it will replace old values with new ones, obtaining a new *Alfa*. On the other hand, when the first condition is not satisfied, meaning *IaT* is higher than 4, it will automatically change the smoothing constant *Alfa* with adding 0.02 within the interval (0.52; 0.98) in order to find the best-fitting *Alfa*. At the beginning of the cycle all the variables have to be cleared in order to get the right results for each iteration. The cycle looks as in Fig. 31.

In Fig. 31 due to capacity reasons only the results for the first and the last value of *Alfa*, namely 0.52 and 0.98, are shown. However, it can be observed that with the initial *Alfa* value, 0.52, the value of the error identifier *IaT* is 10.2594 and by adding 0.02 to the value of *Alfa*, also the value of *IaT* rises proportionally and ends by *Alfa* equal to 0.98 when the *IaT* is 13.9214. Unfortunately, in all of the cases the value of

```
In[31]:=
    Clear[FcpO]
    AlfaO = 0.5 (*Optimal Alfa for the beggining*)
    n = Length[AV]|
    np = n / 4 (*number of points*)
    Fcp = Table[0, {t, 1, Length[AV] + 1}] (*vector*)
    Fcp =
      Table[If[(i > 1), 0, (*starting value,
        mean of the actual values, but just from the first np values*)
          N[Mean[Take[AV, np]]]], {i, 1, n + 1}]
    Do(*cycle*)[Fcp[[t + 1]] = Evaluate[Fnp[AlfaO, t]], {t, 1, n}]
    Error = Table[AV[[i]] - Fcp[[i]], {i, 1, n}] (*Errors*)
    MAEO = Mean[Abs[Error]] (*Mean Absolute Error - Optimal*)
    YaTO = Total[Error] (*Total error - Optimal*)
    IaTO = Abs[YaTO / MAEO] (*Error identifier - Optimal, < 4*)
    FcpO = Fcp (*Assigning,in the fucntion is Fcp instead of FcpO *)
```

Out[32]= 0.5

Out[33]= 20

Out[34]= 5

Out[35]= {0, 0, 0, 0, 0, 0, 0, 0, 0, 0, 0, 0, 0, 0, 0, 0, 0, 0, 0, 0}

Out[36]= $\{2.2544 \times 10^{12}, 0, 0, 0, 0, 0, 0, 0, 0, 0, 0, 0, 0, 0, 0, 0, 0, 0, 0, 0\}$

Out[38]= $\{-2.474 \times 10^{11}, 1.73 \times 10^{10}, 3.8365 \times 10^{11}, 1.05825 \times 10^{11},$
      $-2.27088 \times 10^{11}, -9.25438 \times 10^{10}, -9.32719 \times 10^{10}, -2.91636 \times 10^{11},$
      $-1.50818 \times 10^{11}, 5.0591 \times 10^{10}, 4.42296 \times 10^{11}, 5.23148 \times 10^{11},$
      $3.01574 \times 10^{11}, 2.87787 \times 10^{11}, 5.64893 \times 10^{11}, 5.82447 \times 10^{11},$
      $-3.47766 \times 10^{10}, -3.23883 \times 10^{10}, 3.25806 \times 10^{11}, -3.40971 \times 10^{10}\}$

Out[39]= 2.39467×10^{11}

Out[40]= 2.3813×10^{12}

Out[41]= 9.94417

Out[42]= $\{2.2544 \times 10^{12}, 2.1307 \times 10^{12}, 2.13935 \times 10^{12}, 2.33118 \times 10^{12}, 2.38409 \times 10^{12},$
      $2.27054 \times 10^{12}, 2.22427 \times 10^{12}, 2.17764 \times 10^{12}, 2.03182 \times 10^{12},$
      $1.95641 \times 10^{12}, 1.9817 \times 10^{12}, 2.20285 \times 10^{12}, 2.46443 \times 10^{12},$
      $2.61521 \times 10^{12}, 2.75911 \times 10^{12}, 3.04155 \times 10^{12}, 3.33278 \times 10^{12},$
      $3.31539 \times 10^{12}, 3.29919 \times 10^{12}, 3.4621 \times 10^{12}, 3.44505 \times 10^{12}\}$

Fig. 30 Starting computation of single exponential smoothing using starting value—Germany. *Source* Own program code

```
In[47]:= Do(*cycle*)[{Clear[Fcp, MAE, YaT, IaT, Error],
        Fcp = Table[0, {t, 1, Length[AV] + 1}],
        Fcp = Table[If[(i > 1), 0, N[Mean[Take[AV, np]]]], {i, 1, n+1}]
        Do[Fcp[[t+1]] = Evaluate[Fnp[Alfa, t]], {t, 1, n}],
        Error = Table[AV[[i]] - Fcp[[i]], {i, 1, n}],
        MAE = Mean[Abs[Error]],
        YaT = Total[Error],
        IaT = Abs[YaT / MAE],
        Print(*to show results separately*)[Alfa, "  ", MAE,
          "  ", YaT, "  ", IaT, "       ", Fcp]
        If[(IaT < 4)(*Error identifier has to be lower than 4*),
          If(*if it is true, the lowest MAE values has to be
            found*)[(MAE < MAEO),
            (*and then replace old values with new ones,
             a new alfa*){FcpO = Fcp, AlfaO = Alfa, MAEO = MAE}]]},
      (*if the condition is not satisfied,
      meaning IaT is higher than 4,
      it changes Alfa and continues with adding 0.02 within
        the interval from 0.52 to 0.98*){Alfa, 0.52, 0.98, 0.02}]
```

0.52 2.40973×10^{11} 2.47225×10^{12} 10.2594
$\{2.2544 \times 10^{12}, 2.13565 \times 10^{12}, 2.14158 \times 10^{12}, 2.32466 \times 10^{12},$
$2.37858 \times 10^{12}, 2.27222 \times 10^{12}, 2.227 \times 10^{12}, 2.18092 \times 10^{12}, 2.03936 \times 10^{12},$
$1.96335 \times 10^{12}, 1.9843 \times 10^{12}, 2.19536 \times 10^{12}, 2.45007 \times 10^{12},$
$2.60171 \times 10^{12}, 2.74633 \times 10^{12}, 3.02361 \times 10^{12}, 3.3118 \times 10^{12},$
$3.30518 \times 10^{12}, 3.29453 \times 10^{12}, 3.45316 \times 10^{12}, 3.44108 \times 10^{12}\}$

0.98 5.27523×10^{11} 7.34386×10^{12} 13.9214
$\{2.2544 \times 10^{12}, 2.24945 \times 10^{12}, 2.24742 \times 10^{12}, 2.25293 \times 10^{12}, 2.25662 \times 10^{12},$
$2.25462 \times 10^{12}, 2.25309 \times 10^{12}, 2.25065 \times 10^{12}, 2.24336 \times 10^{12},$
$2.23611 \times 10^{12}, 2.23153 \times 10^{12}, 2.23538 \times 10^{12}, 2.24519 \times 10^{12},$
$2.25561 \times 10^{12}, 2.26855 \times 10^{12}, 2.28966 \times 10^{12}, 2.31635 \times 10^{12},$
$2.33598 \times 10^{12}, 2.35492 \times 10^{12}, 2.38032 \times 10^{12}, 2.40128 \times 10^{12}\}$

Fig. 31 Finding the best-fitting smoothing constant using iterations—Germany. *Source* Own program code

the error identifier *IaT* is way higher than 4 and thus exceeds the limit for proper forecast. This means that all the smoothed values are not reliable due to the unsatisfied condition that *IaT* < 4. As a result of that, the single exponential smoothing method is not a suitable one for analysis of such a trend we have both in Germany's and Greece's development. Forecasts using this method would be far too inaccurate.

Mainly for this reason, we will use forecasts made using quadratic moving averages method as a source of relevant information for application into the IS–LM model.

5.4   IS–LM Model Application

Based on the 2-year predictions of Germany's and Greece's development, we are able to apply these results into the macroeconomic IS–LM model which will show us effects and consequences of such a GDP development. Concretely, we will take a closer look on equilibrium shifts on the goods and money markets and with associated changes in interest rates.

5.4.1   Germany

Considering the forecast obtained by quadratic moving averages method, Germany's GDP should be rising quite significantly within the next 2 time periods, namely 2013 and 2014, copying the trend from the growth period in the beginning of the millennium. This means that Germany's output, Y, should be higher in the next two consecutive periods. Growing output indicates certain fiscal policy measures, in this case assuming fiscal expansion, that causes a change in the equilibrium on both goods and money markets which can be illustrated in Fig. 32.

Figure 32 illustrates the fiscal expansion happening in Germany based on the GDP development predictions. As we can see, the IS curve shifts to the right, symbolizing fiscal expansion conditioned by expected higher output, Y^2. Hence a

Fig. 32 Fiscal expansion in Germany within the IS–LM model. *Source* Own processing

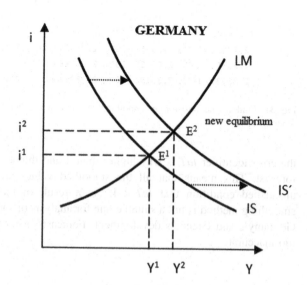

new equilibrium, E^2, is reached. This new equilibrium intersects the LM curve a little bit higher up which indicates a higher interest rate, i^2.

5.4.2   Greece

According to the forecast of further Greek GDP development, it does not seem to be very optimistic as it should be falling quite significantly in the next 2 time periods, 2013 and 2014, and thus will continue in the following today's downward-sloping trend. It basically means that Greece's output, Y, should be even lower than it is now in the next 2 consecutive periods. Decreasing output indicates certain fiscal policy measures, in this case fiscal contraction, caused by mainly austerity measures of the government, that causes a change in the equilibrium on both goods and money markets which can be illustrated in Fig. 33.

Here, Fig. 33 illustrates the fiscal contraction happening in Greece based on the GDP development predictions. As we can see, the IS curve shifts to the left, symbolizing fiscal contraction conditioned by expected lower output, Y^2. Hence a new equilibrium, E^2, is reached. This new equilibrium intersects the LM curve a little bit lower which indicates a lower interest rate, i^2.

5.4.3   Interest Rates Dilemma

In both cases, Germany and Greece, the future change of output triggers, according to the IS–LM model a change in the interest rate. However, interest rates should be

Fig. 33 Fiscal contraction in Greece within the IS–LM model. *Source* Own processing

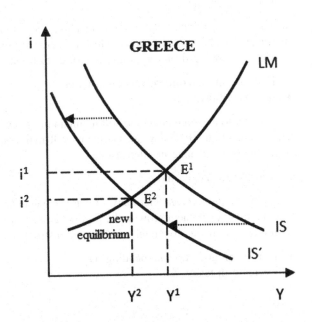

the same within the whole Eurozone as long as ECB takes control over monetary policy of all Eurozone members. The latest monetary policy measure taken by ECB represents a target fixed rate of main refinancing operations to be 0.25% per annum (ECB 2013). This interest rate is valid for all Eurozone members. Thus a policy mix is no longer possible within the Eurozone, i.e., combination of fiscal and monetary policy by each state separately. However, through individual transmission mechanisms of each member state, deposit interest rates differ from state to state. More concretely, as of December 2013, the deposit interest rate in Germany reaches maximally 1.00% and in Greece it is significantly higher, 2.90% (Deposit 2013). This means that except monetary policy remains just fiscal policy as a tool for small fine-tuning measures in interest rates. Considering the forecasts, the interest rate in Germany should slightly increase its value and on the other hand, in Greece it should slightly decrease its value.

5.4.4 Recommendations

Paradoxically, what would be in favor of an interest rate change in both states is exactly opposite. Germany is strictly against any inflation and for Greece a higher interest rate would be beneficial in order to repay debts more easily. In terms of overall economic output though, the growth of GDP is desirable for both countries.

It seems that Germany is already on a good way to boosting its economy as it was before the crisis. The higher GDP growth, however, leads to a higher interest rate according to the IS–LM model. How the fiscal policy should be performed depends on specific goals of Germany's government:

1. Hold interest rates steady

In this case, to prevent an interest rate increase, the overall output should not rise as significantly as the forecast shows. Thus measures of fiscal policy expansion should be a little bit reduced or very slight measures of fiscal contraction either by

- Decrease in government spending, G, or
- Increase in taxes, T.

But only to a certain degree to still maintain the growth, not turning it to a strong fiscal contraction. By doing so, Germany will maintain its economic growth but with little or no change in interest rate.

2. Boost growth even more

According to the forecast, Germany's GDP is expected to grow significantly. But if there is still not sufficient growth, the following fiscal policy measures can boost the economy even more, concretely performing a stronger fiscal expansion:

- Increase in government spending, G
- Decrease in taxes, T.

This would trigger even higher overall output but the price to pay for it would be significantly a higher interest rate which could ultimately lead to a lower investment, I, and thus to a lower growth in the long term. It would work in the short term to stimulate an even higher growth but based on Germany's long-lasting attitude against any increase in interest rate this scenario is rather unlikely.

On the other hand, it seems that Greece has still not recovered from the crisis and continues in declining trend of economic output. It is mainly caused by severe austerity measures Greece had to undertake. Nevertheless, how the fiscal policy should be performed depends again on the Greece government's goals:

1. Stimulating economic growth

In order to immediately boost Greek economy and to attain higher GDP, a radical fiscal expansion would be necessary and that either by

- Increase in government spending, G
- Decrease in taxes, T.

More probably both measures together would be essential in order to really turn around the economic situation. That would mean shifting the IS curve to the right and consequently reaching a higher level of output, Y, and also a higher level of interest rate, i. As already mentioned, paradoxically a higher interest rate would help Greece to repay its debts more easily and next to that, higher GDP and thus economic growth would be reached as well. The problem is that Greece does not have enough resources to finance a huge government spending as well as it has to meet European Union requirements of austerity measures. Moreover, it would be again only a short-term solution as long as really high interest rate would decrease the level of investment in future.

2. Continue in austerity

Based on European Union requirements it is probable that Greece will continue in austerity measures which means fiscal contraction either by

- Decrease in government spending, G
- Increase in taxes, T.

According to the IS–LM model this would lead to further decline in GDP and overall output, Y, but to a decline in the interest rate in the same time which in the long term can stimulate private investment and consequently boost economic growth without having to borrow more money for Greece's government in order to stimulate the growth by government spending, G.

5.4.5 Generalization of Results

Since we divided states into two groups according to their correlations based on GDP development, it can be said that the same analysis applies more or less to the other representatives of the relevant group. Meaning, GDP forecasts of other states should follow a similar pattern as GER GDP and GRC GDP but probably with less unambiguous results of forecasts as long as we analyze the best and worst-performing economy according to GDP development.

In other words, we can expect a positive GDP growth also in all the states included in the first group, namely, Austria, France, and Slovakia. And also the same fiscal policy measure recommendations apply according to specific goals of governments.

On the other hand, we can expect a decline in GDP also in all the states included in the second group, namely, Spain. And also the same fiscal policy measure recommendations apply according to specific goals of government.

6   Conclusions

The first part of this case study described and explained all the essential knowledge and additional information necessary to elaborate the problem (Gregus and Kryvinska 2015; Kaczor and Kryvinska 2013; Kryvinska and Gregus 2014). Concretely, macroeconomic as well as mathematic background were introduced and further clarified. The content of macroeconomic background basically focused on the most important macroeconomic variable, GDP. Then the concept of the IS–LM model was introduced. The chapter explained what the main elements of the IS and LM curve are and how these curves are constructed. Further the fiscal policy theory was presented, including fiscal expansion and fiscal contraction respectively, and how it could be done. In terms of the mathematic background, the basic concept of correlation matrix has been shown together with two time series analysis methods, namely moving averages and exponential smoothing. Both methods were also clarified with algebraic expressions.

The second part of the chapter introduced the main as well as other particular objectives of the case study and presented the working methodology used within the case study as well. All the procedures and methods used for obtaining results were mentioned, too.

The third part of the case study dealt with a concrete description of a researched environment, which was represented by several Eurozone member states: Slovakia, Austria, Germany, France, Spain, and Greece. The concrete GDP development of these states has been shown as well as the substantiation for such a development.

The fourth part of the case study represents the whole practical part and application of knowledge toward the objective of the case study. The following steps have been done in order to meet the main objective of this chapter, i.e., to analyze factors that can influence a state's fiscal policy together with particular objectives, meaning comparison among countries and providing recommendations for fiscal policy measures based on the GDP projections. Thus, the forecasted values of GDP have been used as an input for curve shifts within the IS–LM model. Hence, fiscal expansion and fiscal contraction, respectively, have been recognized and illustrated.

After analyzing macroeconomic consequences of such a GDP development, certain recommendations on possible fiscal policy measures depending on government's goals have been provided.

To conclude, in order to meet the main as well as particular goals of this chapter, it was necessary to construct the correlation matrix with correlation coefficients to identify interdependence of state's GDP developments. The highest correlation has been found between GDP developments of France and Austria. On the other side of the spectrum, the lowest correlation has been found between GDP developments of Germany and Greece, confirming the statement that Germany is the best and Greece the worst-performing economy in the Eurozone. Based on the coefficient of determination, states were divided into two groups. The first group was represented by Germany followed by states with highly correlated GDP development, symbolizing better performing economies and the second group was represented by the rest with Greece having the lowest correlation with Germany, symbolizing worse performing economies. Thus for the purposes of the time series analysis, Germany and Greece were picked. First, using the Wolfram Mathematica 9.0 software, GDP data has been smoothed out by linear trend moving averages. This turned out to be a suitable method except that smoothed values were not accurate enough, especially at the beginning and the end of the time span. Hence, quadratic trend moving averages was used as a method to eliminate this inaccuracy. It has proven to be a suitable method and thus it could serve as a basis for a short-term forecast. For accuracy reasons, only a two-time period forecast has been made and also due to the fact that results were being implemented into the IS–LM model which is a short-run model. The forecast of Germany's GDP showed a very optimistic development, projecting similar growth as it was before the crisis. On the other hand, forecast of Greece's GDP showed rather a pessimistic development, projecting further decline in GDP.

The second forecasting method was single exponential smoothing. Again, a helpful tool to do so was the Wolfram Mathematica 9.0 software. However, it was not possible to find a suitable smoothing constant for obtaining the desired low value of error identifier. As a result of that, a forecast based on single exponential smoothing would not be reliable. Hence the moving averages forecast served as an input for the IS–LM model.

Taking the forecast for Germany's GDP into account, the IS curve has shifted to the right, expressing higher output. New equilibrium on the goods and money market has been reached and as a consequence also a higher interest rate. Recommendation for certain fiscal policy measures depends on the government's goals.

For boosting the growth even higher, fiscal expansion, i.e., higher government spending or lower taxes were decided to be desired measures.

For keeping the interest rate steady, reducing fiscal expansion or even a slight fiscal contraction, i.e., lower government spending or higher taxes, was decided to be desired measures.

Taking into account Greece's GDP forecast, the IS curve has shifted to the left, expressing lower output. New equilibrium on the goods and money market has been reached and, as a consequence, a lower interest rate as well. Recommendation for fiscal policy measures depends again on the government's goals and in this case also on liabilities to the Eurozone.

For stimulating an economic growth, fiscal expansion, i.e., higher government spending together with lower taxes, was decided to be desired measures. However, for Greece it is not possible due to obligation to meet the Eurozone austerity requirements.

For continuation in austerity, fiscal contraction, i.e., even lower government spending or higher taxes were decided to be desired measures. By doing so, Greece will not attain growth in the short run but due to low interest rates it could stimulate investment to boost the economy in the long run.

To sum up, similar results and analysis were expected to be valid for the rest of the states within each group. As a result of that, on one hand a further growth of already recovered economies can be expected and, on the other hand, a further decline of still unrecovered economies can be expected.

References

Arnold R (2013) Macroeconomics. Cengage Learning, South-Western

Blanchard O (2003) Macroeconomics. Prentice Hall Series in Economics

Blanchard O, Johnson DR (2009) Macroeconomics. Pearson, Boston

Bohdalová M (2006a) Random vectors (Náhodné vektory). Online available on https://flurry.dg.fmph.uniba.sk/bohdalova/BohdalovaSubory/NahodneVektory.pdf

Bohdalová M (2006b) Regress models (Regresné modely). Online available on https://flurry.dg.fmph.uniba.sk/bohdalova/BohdalovaSubory/RegresneModely.pdf

Boyes W, Melvin M (2012) Macroeconomics. Cengage Learning, South-Western

Chaman L, Malehorn J (2005) Practical guide to business forecasting. Graceway Publishing Company

Cipra T (1986) Time series analysis with application in economy (Analýza časových řad s aplikacemi v ekonomii). Praha, SNTL

Deposits (2013) Euro deposit rates. Online, available on: http://euro.deposits.org/

Dixon H, Gerrard B (2000) IS-LM and modern macroeconomics. Kluwer Academic Publishers, Dordrecht

Dwiwedi DN (2010) Macroeconomics: theory and policy. Tata McGraw-Hill, New Delhi

Engelhardt-Nowitzki C, Kryvinska N, Strauss C (2011) Strategic demands on information services in uncertain businesses: a layer-based framework from a value network perspective. In: The first international workshop on frontiers in service transformations and innovations (FSTI-2011), in conjunction with the second international conference on emerging intelligent data and web technologies (EIDWT 2011), 7–9 Sept 2011, Tirana, Albania, pp 131–136

European Central Bank (ECB) (2013) Key ECB interest rates. Online, available on: http://sdw.ecb.europa.eu/reports.do?node=100000131

Fauska P, Kryvinska N, Strauss C (2014) Agile management of complex good & service bundles for B2B e-commerce by global narrow-specialized companies. Global J Flex Syst Manag (Special Issue on Flexible Complexity Management and Engineering by Innovative Services, Springer) 15(1):5–23

Gregus M, Kryvinska N (2015) Service orientation of enterprises—aspects, dimensions, technologies. Comenius University in Bratislava

Hirschey M (2009) Managerial economics. Cengage Learning, South-Western

Kaczor S, Kryvinska N (2013) It is all about services—fundamentals, drivers, and business models. J Serv Sci Res (The Society of Service Science, Springer) 5(2):125–154

Kryvinska N, Gregus M (2014) SOA and its business value in requirements, features, practices and methodologies. Comenius University in Bratislava

Kryvinska N, Barokova A, Auer L, Ivanochko I, Strauss C (2013) Business value assessment of services re-use on SOA using appropriate methodologies, metrics and models. Int J Serv Econ Manag (IJSEM) (Special Issue on Service-centric Models, Platforms and Technologies, Inderscience Publishers) 5(4):301–327

Kryvinska N, Kaczor S, Strauss C, Gregus M (2014a) Servitization—its raise through information and communication technologies. In: 5th international conference on exploring services science (IESS 1.4), 5–7 Feb 2014, Geneva, Switzerland. Lecture notes in business information processing (LNBIP 169). Springer, pp 72–81

Kryvinska N, Kaczor S, Strauss C, Gregus M (2014b) Servitization strategies and product-service-systems. In: The IEEE fourth international workshop on the future of software engineering FOR and IN cloud (FoSEC 2014), 27 June–2 July 2014, at Hilton Anchorage, Alaska, USA, within IEEE 10th World Congress on Services (SERVICES 2014), pp 254–260

Kryvinska N, Kaczor S, Strauss C, Gregus M (2015) Servitization—transition from manufacturer to service provider. In: Gummesson E, Mele C, Polese F (eds) Service dominant logic, network and systems theory and service science: integrating three perspectives for a new service agenda. Naples Forum on Service 2015, Naples, Italy 9–12 June 2015

Lipsey R, Chrystal A (2011) Economics. Oxford University Press

Madsen H (2007) Time series analysis. Chapman & Hall/CRC, London

Mankiw NG, Taylor PM (2006) Economics. Thomson Learning, London

Srivastava UK, Shenoy GV, Sharma SC (2005) Quantitative techniques for managerial decisions. New Age International, New Delhi

Stoshikj M, Kryvinska N, Strauss C (2014) Efficient managing of complex programs with project management services. Global J Flex Syst Manag (Special Issue on Flexible Complexity Management and Engineering by Innovative Services, Springer) 15(1):25–38

Stoshikj M, Kryvinska N, Strauss C (2016) Service systems and service innovation: two pillars of service science. J Procedia Comput Sci (Special Issue on The 7th International Conference on Ambient Systems, Networks and Technologies (ANT-2016), Elsevier) 83:212–220

Trading Economics (2013a) Austria GDP growth rate. Online, available on: http://www.tradingeconomics.com/austria/gdp-growth

Trading Economics (2013b) Germany GDP growth rate. Online, available on: http://www.tradingeconomics.com/germany/gdp-growth

Trading Economics (2013c) Spain GDP growth rate. Online, available on: http://www.tradingeconomics.com/spain/gdp-growth

Trading Economics (2013d) France GDP growth rate. Online, available on: http://www.tradingeconomics.com/france/gdp-growth

Trading Economics (2013e) Greece GDP growth rate. Online, available on: http://www.tradingeconomics.com/greece/gdp-growth

Trading Economics (2013f) Slovakia GDP growth rate. Online, available on: http://www.tradingeconomics.com/slovakia/gdp-growth

Urikova O, Ivanochko I, Kryvinska N, Strauss C, Zinterhof P (2012a) Exploration of factors affecting the advancement of collaborative eBusiness in the enterprises—research efforts examination. In: First international workshop on inter-clouds and collective intelligence (iCCI-2012), in conjunction with the 26th IEEE international conference on advanced information networking and applications workshops (WAINA-2012), Fukuoka, Japan, pp 1227–1232, 26–29 Mar 2012

Urikova O, Ivanochko I, Kryvinska N, Zinterhof P, Strauss C (2012b) Managing complex business services in heterogeneous eBusiness ecosystems—aspect-based research assessment. J Procedia Comput Sci (Special Issue on the 3rd International Conference on Ambient Systems, Networks and Technologies (ANT-2012), Elsevier) 10:128–135

Chapter 3
Business Information Consideration for Labour Market Study of the Slovak Republic

Eva Kurdyová and Mária Bohdalová

Abstract This chapter deals with labour market analysis of the Slovak Republic. The first part of the chapter observes the main economic indicators of the labour market, such as gross domestic product (GDP), minimal wage, inflation rate and unemployment rate in the selected Central European counties: Czech Republic, Hungary and Slovak Republic. The influence of GDP to the number of advertised vacant positions on the Slovak labour market and the relationship between vacancies and unemployment rate are analysed. Furthermore in the second part of the paper we evaluated the results of job offer analyses realized on data collected between 2010 and 2013.

Keywords Correlation · Labour market analysis · Statistics · Unemployment · Vacant job positions

1 Introduction

Changing conditions in the labour market as supply and demand, demographic changes, economic conditions, globalization, new laws and government regulations or new trends belong to the most frequent external factors in human resource management (Engelhardt-Nowitzki et al. 2011; Fauska et al. 2014; Gregus and Kryvinska 2015; Kaczor and Kryvinska 2013). As we indicated above, the chapter deals with the development of statistical indicators of labour market such as inflation, unemployment, gross domestic product and minimum wage in the Czech Republic, Hungary and Slovak Republic (Kurdyová 2015). Data for evaluation of

E. Kurdyová · M. Bohdalová (✉)
Faculty of Management, Comenius University in Bratislava,
Odbojárov 10, P.O. Box 95, 82005 Bratislava, Slovakia
e-mail: maria.bohdalova@fm.uniba.sk

E. Kurdyová
e-mail: eva.kurdyova@gmail.com

© Springer Science+Business Media Singapore 2018
N. Kryvinska and M. Gregus (eds.), *Agile Information Business*,
Flexible Systems Management, DOI 10.1007/978-981-10-3358-2_3

the statistical indicators enumerated above were obtained from freely available sources: from the website of the Statistical Office of the European Communities (Eurostat), Organisation for Economic Co-operation and Development (OECD) and Central Office of Labour, Social Affairs and Family of Slovak republic. Significant part of the chapter is devoted to the analysis of advertised free job positions on the Slovak labour market from the online job board of Profesia.sk. The database contained positions on time frame 2010–2013.

2 Development of Statistical Indicators

2.1 Inflation Rate

From the three-dimensional line chart below follows, that inflation rate development in the examined countries (Czech Republic, Hungary and the Slovak Republic) has similar trend. From the countries mentioned above, always Slovak Republic had the highest and Czech Republic the lowest inflation rate. In Slovakia, the development of inflation rate has a downward trend since 2012 which continued till 2014. In 2014, we can talk for the first time about a mild-year deflation in the history of the country. This slim decline in the general price level of goods and services (−0.1% strength deflation) means that for the same money we can purchase a little bit more (Fig. 1).

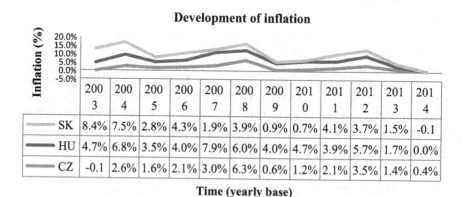

Development of inflation

	2003	2004	2005	2006	2007	2008	2009	2010	2011	2012	2013	2014
SK	8.4%	7.5%	2.8%	4.3%	1.9%	3.9%	0.9%	0.7%	4.1%	3.7%	1.5%	-0.1
HU	4.7%	6.8%	3.5%	4.0%	7.9%	6.0%	4.0%	4.7%	3.9%	5.7%	1.7%	0.0%
CZ	-0.1	2.6%	1.6%	2.1%	3.0%	6.3%	0.6%	1.2%	2.1%	3.5%	1.4%	0.4%

Time (yearly base)

Fig. 1 Development of inflation CZ, SK, HU. *Source* Own processing based on data from Eurostat (Color figure online)

2.2   Unemployment

Similarly, as in the case of inflation, the unemployment indicator says that the Slovak Republic has achieved among the selected countries of CEE region, the worst result since 2003. In 2013, 14.2% of the labour force could not find a valid job. This phenomenon is implicating imbalance between demand and supply in the labour market. From the monitored Central European countries in Czech Republic we are talking about the lowest unemployment rate in value of 7%. In Hungary the unemployment rate rose slightly to 10.2% (Fig. 2).

2.3   Gross Domestic Product

Figure 3 represents the GDP development, where we can recognize the peak of Slovak market in 2007. The financial crisis is mirrored on GDP since 2008/2009. Recovery and growth of GDP in the Czech Republic, Hungary and Slovakia significantly lags compared to the period before the 2009.

2.4   Minimum Wage

The development of the minimum wage in the case of monitored Central European countries is increasing year by year. Comparing the proportional increase of minimum wage with percentage change of inflation, we find that the increase in the minimum wage exceeds the growth of inflation (e.g. Increase in minimum wage in 2013 in Slovakia was around 3% and inflation 1.5%) (Fig. 4).

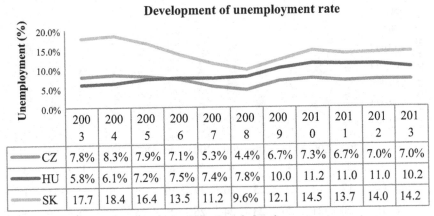

Development of unemployment rate

	2003	2004	2005	2006	2007	2008	2009	2010	2011	2012	2013
CZ	7.8%	8.3%	7.9%	7.1%	5.3%	4.4%	6.7%	7.3%	6.7%	7.0%	7.0%
HU	5.8%	6.1%	7.2%	7.5%	7.4%	7.8%	10.0	11.2	11.0	11.0	10.2
SK	17.7	18.4	16.4	13.5	11.2	9.6%	12.1	14.5	13.7	14.0	14.2

Time (yearly base)

Fig. 2 Development of unemployment rate CZ, SK, HU. *Source* Own processing based on data from Eurostat (Color figure online)

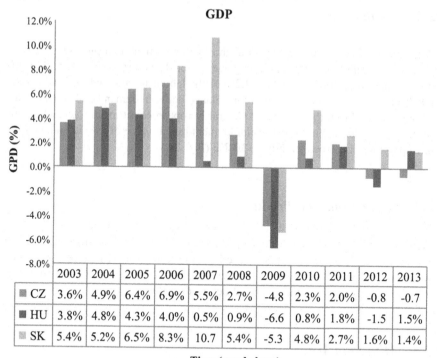

Fig. 3 Development of GDP CZ, SK, HU. *Source* Own processing based on data from Eurostat (Color figure online)

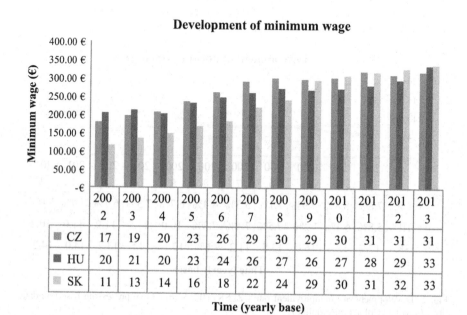

Fig. 4 Development of minimum wage CZ, SK, HU. *Source* Own processing based on data from Eurostat (Color figure online)

3   Predictions of Vacancies in the Slovak Republic

The forecast concerning the number of vacancies for period 2014Q1, 2014Q2, 2014Q3, 2014Q4 and 2015Q1 was realized by time series. Selecting the most convenient tend function we analysed the following alternatives: constant trend, linear trend, quadratic trend and exponential trend function (Fig. 5 and Table 1).

Based on the analysis we have decided to use exponential trend. Contingent on statistical calculation, we assumed the number of vacancies from 2014Q1 to 2015Q1, listed in Table 2.

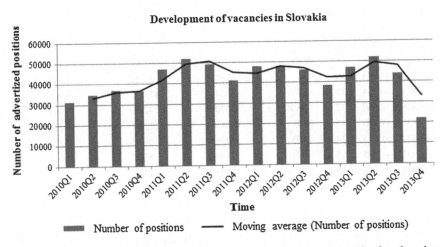

Fig. 5 Development of vacancies in Slovakia from 2010. *Source* Own processing based on data from Profesia spol. s.r.o. (Color figure online)

Table 1 Selection of analytical trend function

Selection of analytical trend function

Time	Number	Time	Constant tread	Linear trend	Quadratic trend	Exponential trend
	$y(t)$	t	1. Absolute difference $\Delta t = y_t - y_{t-1}$	2. Absolute difference $\Delta_t^{(2)} = \Delta_t - \Delta_{t-1}$	3 Absolute difference $\Delta_t^{(3)} = \Delta_t^{(2)} - \Delta_{t-1}^{(2)}$	Growth ration $k_t = \frac{y_t}{y_{t-1}}$
2010Q1	31,305	1	–	–	–	–
2010Q2	34,842	2	3537	–	–	1.113
2010Q3	36,779	3	1937	−1600	–	1.056
2010Q4	36,420	4	−359	−2296	−696	0.990
2011Q1	47,152	5	10,732	11,091	13,387	1.295
2011Q2	52,091	6	4939	−5793	−16,884	1.105
2011Q3	49,215	7	−2876	−7815	−2022	0.945
2011Q4	41,198	8	−8017	−5141	2674	0.837
2012Q1	47,888	9	6690	14,707	19,848	1.162
2012Q2	47,998	10	110	−6580	−21,287	1.002
2012Q3	46,264	11	−1734	−1844	4735	0.964
2012Q4	38,460	12	−7804	−6070	−4226	0.831
2013Q1	47,165	13	8705	16,509	22,579	1.226
2013Q2	51,915	14	4750	−3955	−20,464	1.101
2013Q3	44,005	15	−7910	−12,660	−8705	0.848
2013Q4	22,013	16	−21,992	−14,082	−1422	0.500

Source Own processing based on data from Profesia spol. s.r.o.

Table 2 Predictions of vacancies in the Slovak republic

Time period	Number of anticipated vacancies
2014Q1	42,267
2014Q2	42,387
2014Q3	42,508
2014Q4	42,628
2015Q1	42,749

Source Own processing

4 Analysis of Relationship Between GDP and Number of Vacancies in the Slovak Republic

Quarterly processing of vacant job positions was available from Profesia.sk and we got the quarterly information of Slovak Republic's GDP from online statistics of Organisation for Economic Co-operation and Development. Summary of those indicators is visualized in the following table.

We set up the following hypothesis at the significance level $\alpha = 0.05$.

H0: The number of job vacancies in Slovakia does not depend on the development of GDP.

H1: The number of job vacancies in Slovakia depends on the development of GDP.

The degree of dependence between the two variables, the gross domestic product (independent variable) and the number of advertised job vacancies (dependent variable) were examined by linear Pearson correlation at significance level $\alpha = 0.05$. We tested the correlation value from 2011Q4 to 2013Q4 (Fig. 6).

The correlation rate -0.316 points us a negative rate of leakage, which is within the range <0.3–0.5>. On the other hand, the calculated *p*-value is greater than the considered statistical significance $\alpha = 0.05$. The null hypothesis, according to which the number of advertised job vacancies in Slovakia and GDP are not dependent, we fail to reject. Between GDP and the number of vacant jobs there is no statistically significant correlation (Table 3).

$$p\text{-value} = 0.407$$
$$\alpha = 0.05$$
$$0.407 > 0.05$$
$$P\text{-value} > \alpha$$

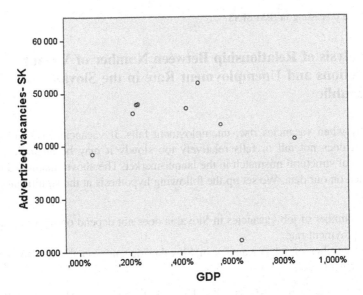

Fig. 6   Correlation between GDP and number of vacant positions. *Source* Own processing in IBMSPSS

Table 3 Correlation analysis (GDP, vacancies)

Correlations

		Advertized vacancies—SK	GDP
Advertized vacancies—SK	Pearson correlation	1	−0.316
	Sig. (2-tailed)		0.407
	N	9	9
GDP	Pearson correlation	−0.316	1
	Sig. (2-tailed)	0.407	
	N	9	9

Source Own processing in IBM SPSS

Table 4 Correlation analysis (vacancies, unemployment rate)

Correlations

		Vacancies	Unemployment rate
Vacancies	Pearson correlation	1	−0.757
	Sig. (2-tailed)		−0.453
	N	3	3
Unemployment Rate	Pearson correlation	−0.757	1
	Sig. (2-tailed)	0.453	
	N	3	3

Source Own processing in IBM SPSS

5 Analysis of Relationship Between Number of Vacant Positions and Unemployment Rate in the Slovak Republic

Normally when vacancies rise, unemployment falls. If vacancies rise and unemployment does not fall or falls relatively too slowly it may be an indication of problems of structural mismatch in the labour market. The above mentioned theory was tested on our data. We set up the following hypothesis at the significance level $\alpha = 0.05$.

H0: The number of job vacancies in Slovakia does not depend on the development of unemployment rate.
H1: The number of job vacancies in Slovakia depends on the development of unemployment rate.

Table 4 shows that between the two variables—vacancies, unemployment rate—has relatively strong negative correlation, −0.757. It means that if number of job vacancies increases the unemployment rate decreases. The calculated *p*-value is greater than the considered statistical significance $\alpha = 0.05$. We reject the null hypothesis, then there is no statistically significant correlation between job vacancies and the number of vacant jobs.

$$p\text{-value} = 0.453$$
$$\alpha = 0.05$$
$$0.453 > 0.05$$
$$p\text{-value} > \alpha$$

5.1 Job Position Survey on the Slovak Labour Market

On time period between 01.01.2010 and 31.12.2013, we analysed 674,710 jobs offers, which included full-time positions, part-time positions, internships and craft contracts (Table 5).

Figure 7 shows the trend of advertised job positions in the Slovak Republic, we can conclude that the number of positions advertised in the months of June, July, August, November and December is generally lower than in other months of the year. This fact can be linked with the holiday season, when the recruitment and selection process is longer based on the fact that the responsible employees—recruiters and managers—are often out of the office consuming vacation time. On the other hand, the job seekers also want to enjoy the summer time and are postponing the job hunt to September. Similar situation occurs on the labour market in November and December when people are preparing for Christmas. They plan to take leave between the public holidays and be with their family. Another fact influencing the beginning of job hunt in January is the annual bonus plan. Majority of international and local companies pay out the part of annual bonuses if the employee works 12 consecutive months and do not quit till 31 December .

Strong annual growth in number of vacant jobs can be identified between 2010 and 2011, especially in 2011, when there were advertised 26.53% more job offers than in the previous year. Changes in 2012 and 2013 have been calmer; the number of positions advertised in 2012 fell only by 5% and in 2013 by 9.4% compared with the previous calendar year.

Table 5 Number of advertised jobs on Profesia.sk

Year	Number of advertised job positions on website Profesia.sk
2010	139,346
2011	189,656
2012	180,610
2013	165,098
Total	674,710

Source Own processing based on data from Profesia spol. s.r.o.

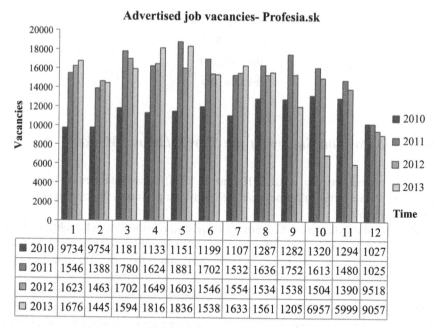

■ 2010	1	2	3	4	5	6	7	8	9	10	11	12
■ 2010	9734	9754	1181	1133	1151	1199	1107	1287	1282	1320	1294	1027
■ 2011	1546	1388	1780	1624	1881	1702	1532	1636	1752	1613	1480	1025
▨ 2012	1623	1463	1702	1649	1603	1546	1554	1534	1538	1504	1390	9518
☐ 2013	1676	1445	1594	1816	1836	1538	1633	1561	1205	6957	5999	9057

Fig. 7 The number of advertised positions from 2010 to 2013 on monthly basis. *Source* Own processing based on data from Profesia spol. s.r.o. (Color figure online)

5.2 Economic Sectors

We revealed that between 2010 and 2013 the highest number of advertised offers were in sectors such as trade (17.48%), information technology (9.54%), administration (9.44%), management (9.12%), economy, finance, accounting (6.39%), transportation and logistics (6.16%), tourism, gastronomy, hotel business (4.57%) and production (4.04%) (Kryvinska et al. 2013; Kryvinska and Gregus 2014). On the other hand, less number of vacant positions was advertised in sectors as water, forestry, environment (0.07%), mining, metallurgy (0.03%), consulting business (0.01%) and research and development (0.01%) (Table 6).

The most significant annual growth between 2012 and 2013 was recorded in the following sectors: security and protection, textile industry, insurance industry, pharmaceutical industry, journalism, arts and culture and education and training. The demand for skilled labour in the field of security has grown by almost 40% (Table 7).

In 2013, they took fewer jobs compared to 2012 in the areas of: human resources, information technology, economics and finance, agriculture, translation and interpretation, wood processing industry and mining. On percentage basis the biggest drop was recorded in mining and metallurgy, up to 75% (in 2012 advertised 35 in 2013 only 20 vacancies). If we examine the number of jobs positions, the

Table 6 Annual increase in vacant jobs on industrial basis (comparing 2012 and 2013)

Economic sector	Number of vacancies 2013	Annual increase (%)
Security and protection	3264	39.12
Textile, leather and clothing industry	476	32.35
Insurance	1472	29.42
Pharmaceutical industry	2401	19.53
Journalism, printing arts and media	875	15.31
Arts and culture	255	11.37
Education, science and research	1589	9.13

Source Own processing based on data from Profesia spol. s.r.o.

Table 7 One-year decline in jobs based on industry (comparison of 2012 and 2013)

Economic sector	Number of vacancies 2013	Annual increase (%)
Human resources	1445	−23.74
Information technology	15,222	−24.39
Economy, finance, accountancy	9450	−29.42
Agriculture	532	−30.08
Translation and interpretation	171	−32.16
Wood industry	609	−55.83
Mining, metallurgy	20	−75.00

Source Own processing based on data from Profesia spol. s.r.o.

largest decline was identified in the field of information technology, where it was advertised about 3712 less jobs than in the previous year, which makes a decrease of −24.39%. Despite the high decrease of vacant jobs in information technology, the industry in 2013 was still seeking a high number of employees. The highest amount of vacancies was advertised in trade and administration, which were followed by information technologies on the third place.

5.3 Companies

Between 2010 and 2013, the majority of jobs were advertised by company INDEX NOSLUŠ s.r.o. in numbers 29,124, representing 4.32% of the advertised positions (Table 8).

As an interesting fact, we identified, that among the top 10 companies with the highest number of advertised vacancies were placed only three companies whose main business is not personal consultancy and recruitment (Accenture, Henkel Slovakia, IBM). The other companies are providers of recruitment solutions, talent management and human resources, thereby facilitating expeditious filling of vacant positions for companies which have no time for preselecting candidates' profiles or

Table 8 Top 20 companies that advertised the most jobs between 2010 and 2013

Rank	Company	Number of vacancies	%
1	INDEX NOSLUŠ s.r.o.	29,124	4.32
2	Grafton Recruitment Slovakia, s.r.o.	27,518	4.08
3	Accenture, s.r.o.	12,899	1.91
4	MANPOWER SLOVENSKO s.r.o.	7127	1.06
5	Lugera & Maklér spol.s r.o.	5460	0.81
6	CPL Jobs s.r.o.	5399	0.80
7	Henkel Slovensko, spol. s r.o.	5201	0.77
8	Trenkwalder, a. s.	4855	0.72
9	ADECCO Slovakia, s.r.o.	4565	0.68
10	IBM	4100	0.61
11	AuJob s.r.o.	4066	0.60
12	R. I. Consultancy Services/Slovakia/, s.r.o.	4053	0.60
13	Tatra banka, a.s.	3862	0.57
14	Všeobecná úverová banka, a.s., Intesa Sanpaolo	3760	0.56
15	TESCO STORES SR, a.s.	3418	0.51
16	AXA Services, s.r.o.	3355	0.50
17	McDonald's Slovakia, spol. s r.o.	3183	0.47
18	KOOPERATIVA, a.s. Vienna Insur. Group	3109	0.46
19	Slovak Telekom, a.s.	3035	0.45
20	ČSOB	2956	0.44

Source Own processing based on data from Profesia spol. s.r.o

just outsource part of the selection process. If we look at the ranking of top 20 companies, we see that apart from recruitment agencies in the rank it dominates also companies from the field of services, banking or insurance.

The job analysis revealed that the ranking of top three companies with the highest number of vacant positions are occupied by the same companies. Grafton Recruitment Slovakia in 2010 advertised 6266 positions, in 2012 7731 positions and in 2013 6294. Company INDEX NOSLUŠ, which always attained the second place, except in 2011, when it advertised even 15,945 jobs, compared with Grafton Recruitment, which acquired the second place in th same year with a total number of positions 7227. The third place belongs to Accenture.

In 2013, in top 20 list appeared new names which up to the present were not placed in top 20, such as recruitment agency McRoy Slovakia or Slovak Telekom.

5.4 Place of Work

During the tracked period of 2010–2013 among 674,710 jobs advertised on Profesia.sk, 654,912 (97.07%) were referred to the place of work inland and 19,799

(2.93%) abroad. Most jobs come from Bratislava (48.34%) and Nitra region (8.25%). In Prešov region was advertised the fewest number of vacancies (4.52%) (Table 9).

Comparing with the previous year, in 2013 there were less vacant positions nationwide. In 2012, on the online job boards of Profesia.sk appeared 180,610 jobs and in 2013 only 165,098. In 2013, the number of offers declined in all regions except Prešov region, where we recorded 15% more offers comparing with the previous year. In Bratislava region in year the 2013 the number of vacancies in field of security (44%), insurance (27%), agriculture (22%), textile industry (61%), customer support (18%) and journalism (23%) increased. In other areas of the Bratislava region, the number of offers we recorded as stable or decline. The most radical decrease in the above-mentioned regions occurred in wood industry (−58%), electronics (−49%), quality management (−42%), engineering (−43%), state government (−131%) and top management (−54%).

Compared to 2012 in the Prešov region we identified increase in number of vacancies in the following areas: auxiliary work (52%), law and legislation (46%), translation and interpretation (62%), education, training, science research (82%), arts and culture (60%) and manufacturing (51%).

From the total number of job vacancies 2.93% were advertised with performance of work abroad. Table 10 shows that vacancies lured the Slovak population mainly to the neighbouring countries such as Austria, Czech Republic and Hungary.

In Austria, the most common offers were related with transport, forwarding, logistics (26.53%), information technology (13.86%) and health and social care (12.35%). In Germany labour force is needed in transport, forwarding, logistics (18.25%) and manufacturing (10.25%) (Auer et al. 2011).

Table 9 Number of vacancies in Slovakia on basis of regions 2010–2013

Region	Number of vacancies	% of vacancies in SK	% of vacancies from total amount of vacancies
Banská Bystrica region	32,729	5.00	4.85
Bratislava region	326,139	49.80	48.34
Košice region	46,119	7.04	6.84
Nitra region	55,644	8.50	8.25
Prešov region	30,489	4.66	4.52
Trenčín region	44,880	6.85	6.65
Trnava region	53,290	8.14	7.90
Žilina region	47,405	7.24	7.03
Slovakia- not specified	18,217	2.78	2.70
Total	654,912	100.00	97.07

Source Own processing based on data from Profesia spol. s.r.o

Table 10 Number of jobs with work performance abroad 2010–2013

Country	Number of vacancies	% of vacancies abroad	% of vacancies from total amount of vacancies
Austria	4941	24.96	0.73
Germany	4187	21.15	0.62
Czech Republic	2211	11.17	0.33
Netherlands	1779	8.99	0.26
Hungary	786	3.97	0.12
Belgium	736	3.72	0.11
Great Britain	709	3.58	0.11
France	597	3.02	0.09
USA	557	2.81	0.08
Abroad—other	3294	16.64	0.49
Total	19,798	100.00	2.93

Source Own processing based on data from Profesia spol. s.r.o

In southern countries such as Greece, Cyprus and Malta jobs were offered in tourism, gastronomy and hotel business (these offers are remarked Abroad—Other).

In the UK, they were most requested specialists in the sectors of health, social care (46.6%) and auxiliary works (14.10%).

In 2013 on job board of Profesia.sk were recorded more jobs with place of work in Finland (95.2%), Cyprus (76.9%), Ireland (75%), Romania (60.5%), Belgium (48.5%), Spain (42.9%) and Hungary (37.6%). On the other hand, the number of jobs in Greece, Iceland, Norway, USA, Switzerland, Ukraine, Luxembourg and Denmark fell by more than 100%.

5.5 Requested Language and Computer Skills

Majority of positions require special language or computer skills: 51.03% jobs require computer skills at user level, 40.72% language skills, and 4.09% computer skills at programmer or administrator level.

Among the analysed positions we can find 130,166 which require knowledge of English, 33,368 German, 5133 Hungarian and 2653 French. In general, we can say that the positions require knowledge of the language at pre-intermediate or advanced level. Least frequently sought-after languages are Estonian, Latvian and Lithuanian. In connection with these languages the basic knowledge was sufficient, for foreign job offers dominated English and German languages at intermediate level.

From an average candidate who responds on a job offer with performance of work in Slovakia the following computer skills are expected at user level: Microsoft Word (22.06%), Microsoft Excel (16.55%) Microsoft Outlook (16.37%), Microsoft PowerPoint (9.49%), Internet (e-mail and WWW 18.05%) or experience with ERP system SAP (2.48%).

In case of programming, experience is expected in SQL (17.64%), C++ (10.60%), Java (10.29%) JavaScript (6.86%), XML (5.35%), (HTML 3.77%), Visual Basic (3.54%), NET (3.25%) and UML (3.06%) at advanced level. Among the rarer sought programming languages we can find C, COBOL, Objective-C, Adobe Flash, ASP.NET, AJAX, Assembler, Delphi, Pascal, Python or Sybase.

Comparing 2012 to 2013, the future employers' expectation increased regarding language skills, e.g. in case of English by 3.47% and German by 2%. The number of jobs with required knowledge and experience with Microsoft Outlook (17.83%), Microsoft Excel (6.73%) and Microsoft Word (3.56%) also increased. Employers take for granted that candidates are familiar with Internet and email usage.

5.6 Driving Licence

Driving licence is a basic requirement in case of 249,758 positions, from positions 231,596 driving category B is essential. Driving licence type B is a prerequisite for job vacancies in field of trade (21.60%), management (14.07%), administration (6.58%), transport, freight forwarding, logistics (6.31%), construction and real estate (5.83%).

Translation and interpreting sector, arts and culture, mining, metallurgy, textile, leather and clothing industry rarely requires entitlement for driving vehicles.

In 2013, the number of positions requesting a driving license type B and simultaneously C (13.84%) as well as the number of jobs requesting driving license type C and E (24.77%) increased.

5.7 Work Experience

The good news for fresh university graduates is that 64.93% of advertised jobs at Profesia.sk between 2010 and 2013 did not require previous work experience in the relevant field.

At positions where experience was an essential condition, we can talk about a 1-year (7.54%), 2-year (12.63%), 3-year (9.35%) or 5-year working experience (4.16%). Requirement of 15 years work experience is not uncommon in marketing or transportation.

Event managers need 2–3 years practice, HR manager 3–5 years' experience, pharmacist 3 years' experience, chief accountant 5 years but an excellent project manager at least 10 years of experience to successfully occupy the position.

Table 11 Years of experience

Years of experience	Vacancies	%
0	438,075	64.93
1	50,894	7.54
2	85,240	12.63
3	63,077	9.35
4	4916	0.73
5	28,048	4.16
6	779	0.12
7	692	0.10
8	488	0.07
9	15	0.00
10	2183	0.32
11	1	0.00
12	86	0.01
15	115	0.02
20	8	0.00
25	9	0.00
Not specified	84	0.01
Total	674,710	100

Source Own processing based on data from Profesia spol. s.r.o

10–20 years' experience is hunted in Bratislava and Trenčín region, on the other hand, the most graduate positions without experience are also advertised in the Bratislava (51.60%), Nitra (7.98%) and Trnava region (7.42%) (Table 11).

Another good news for recent graduates of universities and secondary schools is that the number of jobs that require no experience is still growing. In 2013, there were 67.71% of jobs suitable for graduates without experience, representing a 3.5% increase in comparison with the previous year. For jobs which require one year or two years' experience for the given position we recorded a slight decrease by 0.5%.

6   Conclusion

In this paper, we observed the main economic indicators of the labour market, such as gross domestic product (GDP), minimal wage, inflation rate and unemployment rate in the selected Central European counties: Czech Republic, Hungary and Slovak Republic. Between GDP and the number of vacant jobs we identified no statistically significant correlation. On the other hand strong downhill (negative) linear relationship was realized between unemployment rate and number of vacant position on the Slovak labour market.

For fresh university graduates we recommend to start the job hunt before final state examination, respectively, before June, because at that time there are less free positions on labour market. For people who have to take action quickly and change position as soon as possible, we would recommend to respond for the specific positions during summer months and December, for the reason that people basically do not plan to change the employer during summer holidays and at the end of the year, because of the yearly bonuses, which mean they are less candidates on the market.

For high-school graduates and their parents we suggest considering the selection of field of university studies. Based on the results of statistical data processing of the labour market, we must say that the most stable sectors are: business, information technology and management. During the four years period 2010–2013, these sectors had the highest number of job vacancies in general. Among the other sectors which look stable enough regarding the amount of positions are: management, economics, finance, accounting, transport, forwarding, logistics, tourism, gastronomy, hotel and manufacturing (Kryvinska et al. 2009). Low number of position was identified in forestry, mining, metallurgy or science; alumnus of these studies shall expect longer time while job hunting and difficulties with finding a proper position.

Based on data from the Central Office of Labour, Social Affairs and Family of Slovak republic that relate to fresh graduate job seekers grouped by field of study, we can conclude that the alumnus of the following study programs faced serious difficulties to get employed: graduates of economic area, legal and political sciences, social, historical science and philosophy. These graduates were registered at labour offices in Prešov, Košice, Trenčín and Žilina much longer than their colleagues from other study programs. In terms of length of registration at labour offices, an average graduate is 4–6 months unemployed (69.7% of graduates). Based on the data of the Central Office of Labour, Social Affairs and Family of Slovak republic in November 2014, there were 9593 university graduates jobless countrywide.

Further, we find out that many companies use services of recruitment agencies to obtain a suitable candidate (Stoshikj et al. 2016). If we look at the top 10 companies which advertised the most vacancies over the past 4 years, there results seven agencies out of the ten companies. The highest number of free positions on online platform of Profesia.sk was advertised by Index NOSLUŠ, Grafton Recruitment Slovakia, MANPOWER Slovakia, Lugera & Broker, CLP Jobs, Trenkwalder and ADECCO Slovakia.

For candidates we would recommend improving in foreign languages and computer literacy. 40.72% of jobs positions require specific language skills. From year to year, there increases the number of jobs where good level of English language is a basic requirement, on the other hand number of position with German language is still increasing. We can infer that speaking one foreign language for a dream position in Bratislava region is no longer enough.

Regarding computer literacy, in the case of non-programming positions the number of job offers that require knowledge of Microsoft Outlook, Microsoft Excel or Microsoft Word has increased (Kryvinska et al. 2014a, b; Urikova et al. 2012a).

Information technology demands programmers who have experience with SQL, C++, Java, JavaScript, XML or HTML programming languages (Stoshikj et al. 2014; Kryvinska et al. 2015; Urikova et al. 2012b).

Highest number of vacancies is still in Bratislava region, where almost the half of all vacancies was recorded. In terms of position with work performed abroad, mainly Austria, Czech Republic and Hungary Slovak seek for skilled workforce. On the other hand, we must recognize the fact that in abroad usually lower positions are offered. In Austria there are dominant offers in transportation and health services. In Greece, Cyprus and Malta auxiliary force is demanded in tourism, gastronomy and hotel business, especially during summer time.

The good news for fresh graduates is that half of the advertised positions at Profesia.sk requires no previous work experience or requires only one-year/two-year practice.

References

Auer L, Belov E, Kryvinska N, Strauss C (2011) Exploratory case study research on SOA investment decision processes in Austria. In: Mouratidis H, Rolland C (eds) 23rd international conference on advanced information systems engineering (CAiSE-2011), 20–24 June 2011, London, UK. LNCS, vol 6741. Springer, pp 329–336

Central Office of Labour, Social Affairs and Family of Slovak Republic. Online: http://www.upsvar.sk/statistiky.html?page_id=1247

Engelhardt-Nowitzki C, Kryvinska N, Strauss C (2011) Strategic demands on information services in uncertain businesses: a layer-based framework from a value network perspective. In: The first international workshop on frontiers in service transformations and innovations (FSTI-2011), in conjunction with the second international conference on emerging intelligent data and web technologies (EIDWT 2011), 7–9 Sept 2011, Tirana, Albania, pp 131–136

Fauska P, Kryvinska N, Strauss C (2014) Agile management of complex good & service bundles for B2B e-commerce by global narrow-specialized companies. Springer, Global J Flex Syst Manag (Special Issue on Flexible Complexity Management and Engineering by Innovative Services) 15(1):5–23

Gregus M, Kryvinska N (2015) Service orientation of enterprises—aspects, dimensions, technologies. Comenius University in Bratislava

Kaczor S, Kryvinska N (2013) It is all about services-fundamentals, drivers, and business models. J Serv Sci Res (The Society of Service Science, Springer) 5(2):125–154

Kryvinska N, Strauss C, Auer L, Zinterhof P (2009) Information technology investment decision-making under uncertainty. Fourth IIASA/GAMM workshop on coping with uncertainty (CwU'2009), managing safety of heterogeneous systems, IIASA, Laxenburg, Austria, 14–16 Dec 2009

Kryvinska N, Barokova A, Auer L, Ivanochko I, Strauss C (2013) Business value assessment of services re-use on SOA using appropriate methodologies, metrics and models. Int J Serv Econ Manag (IJSEM) (Special Issue on Service-centric Models, Platforms and Technologies, Inderscience Publishers) 5(4):301–327

Kryvinska N, Gregus M (2014) SOA and its business value in requirements, features, practices and methodologies. Comenius University in Bratislava

Kryvinska N, Kaczor S, Strauss C, Gregus M (2014a) Servitization—its raise through information and communication technologies. In: 5th international conference on exploring services science (IESS 1.4), 5–7 Feb 2014, Geneva, Switzerland. Lecture notes in business information processing (LNBIP vol. 169). Springer, pp 72–81

Kryvinska N, Kaczor S, Strauss C, Gregus M (2014b) Servitization strategies and product-service-systems. In: The IEEE fourth international workshop on the future of software engineering FOR and IN cloud (FoSEC 2014), 27 June–2 July 2014, at Hilton Anchorage, Alaska, USA, within IEEE 10th world congress on services (SERVICES 2014), pp 254–260

Kryvinska N, Kaczor S, Strauss C, Gregus M (2015) Servitization—transition from manufacturer to service provider. In: Gummesson E, Mele C, Polese F (eds) Service dominant logic, network and systems theory and service science: integrating three perspectives for a new service agenda, Naples forum on service 2015, Naples, Italy, 9–12 June 2015

Kurdyová E (2015) Personal marketing and labour market analysis. Master's thesis—Comenius University in Bratislava. Faculty of Management, Department of Information Systems. FM UK, Bratislava, Slovakia, pp 47–73

Organisation for Economic Co-operation and Development (OECD). Online: https://data.oecd.org/gdp/gross-domestic-product-gdp.htm

Profesia.sk. Database of advertised vacant positions in Slovak Republic on time frame 2010–2013

Statistical Office of the European Communities (Eurostat). Online: http://ec.europa.eu/eurostat/data/statistics-a-z/abc

Stoshikj M, Kryvinska N, Strauss C (2014) Efficient managing of complex programs with project management services. Global J Flex Syst Manag (Special Issue on Flexible Complexity Management and Engineering by Innovative Services, Springer) 15(1):25–38

Stoshikj MN, Kryvinska N, Strauss C (2016) Service systems and service innovation: two pillars of service science. J Procedia Comput Sci (Special Issue on The 7th International Conference on Ambient Systems, Networks and Technologies (ANT-2016), Elsevier) 83:212–220

Urikova O, Ivanochko I, Kryvinska N, Strauss C, Zinterhof P (2012a) Exploration of factors affecting the advancement of collaborative eBusiness in the enterprises—research efforts examination. In: First international workshop on inter-clouds and collective intelligence (iCCI-2012), in conjunction with the 26th IEEE international conference on advanced information networking and applications workshops (WAINA-2012), Fukuoka, Japan, pp 1227–1232, 26–29 Mar 2012

Urikova O, Ivanochko I, Kryvinska N, Zinterhof P, Strauss C (2012b) Managing complex business services in heterogeneous eBusiness ecosystems—aspect-based research assessment. J Procedia Comput Sci (Special Issue on The 3rd International Conference on Ambient Systems, Networks and Technologies (ANT-2012), Elsevier) 10:128–135

Chapter 4
Social Financial Benefit Assessment of the Mobile Birth Registration

Thanh van Do, Clark Swafford, Loc H. Khuong and Van Thuan Do

Abstract In this paper, the usability and the usefulness of mobile technologies far beyond personal communication has been demonstrated by the mobile birth registration (MBR) concept. To remove the hindrances like long distances, time-consuming travels, and high costs, MBR makes use of 'gatekeepers', i.e., trusted, reliable, and community-based individuals that carry out birth registration using mobile phones. Mobile technologies have been proven as a technological efficient and scalable supplement to the current fixed infrastructure. It is also shown that MBR brings lots of advantages and conveniences to all parties from the children, parents, government, gatekeepers, and NGOs. A simple Social Benefit assessment reaffirms the social value of MBR. Its financial feasibility is proven by a brief financial feasibility study.

Keywords Mobile identity · mIdentity · Birth registration · Mobile birth registration · Identity establishment · Identity management · Citizen identity

T. van Do (✉)
Telenor Research, Fornebu 1331, Norway
e-mail: thanh-van.do@telenor.com

T. van Do
Oslo & Akershus University College, Oslo, Norway

C. Swafford · L.H. Khuong
Keller Graduate School of Management, DeVry University, Irving, TX 75063, USA
e-mail: cswafford@devry.edu

L.H. Khuong
e-mail: Lkhuong@devry.edu

V.T. Do
Wolffia AS, Haugerudveien 40, Oslo 0673, Norway
e-mail: vt.do@wolffia.no

© Springer Science+Business Media Singapore 2018
N. Kryvinska and M. Gregus (eds.), *Agile Information Business*,
Flexible Systems Management, DOI 10.1007/978-981-10-3358-2_4

1   Introduction

Today, mobile communication is undoubtedly the most popular and successful ICT system in the history and its popularity is reflected by the huge number of mobile phones in circulation, which surpasses by far the number of personal computers. Its extraordinary success is due to the people's appreciation of mobility, i.e., the ability of communicating while moving and changing locations and independently of the location of the telephone (van Do and Audestad 1997; Dekleva et al. 2007; Kryvinska et al. 2003). However, the value brought by mobile communication networks is much beyond personal communication. Indeed, the mobile network is nowadays more ubiquitous than the fixed network (Kryvinska et al. 2009) and in developing countries it constitutes in a great extend a superior and more reliable infrastructure enabling access to numerous services (Bashah et al. 2010, 2012a, b) useful for the social and economic development of the country. To unveil this new potential of mobile networks, the GSMA (GSM Association) with the cooperation of global operators like Telenor (2015), Orange (2014), Telefonica (2015), etc. has initiated a Personal Data program (GSMA 2014) aiming at delivering digital identity solutions to market with scale and low entry barriers (ENISA 2010). In developing countries, where a large portion of the population does still not have an official citizen identity the GSMA works with international organizations like UNICEF (2015), Plan International (2014), etc. in the goal of improving the birth registration by making use of mobile technologies (van Do et al. 2012). Telenor as a major operator in Asia has carried out a few projects in Thailand and Pakistan. This paper presents a recent application of the mobile communication carried out by Telenor called *Mobile Birth Registration (MBR)* in Pakistan, which uses mobile technologies to improve birth registration in Pakistan. The paper will attempt to prove the social value of the MBR application by assessing its social impacts and financial feasibility. The paper starts with a study of the current birth registration in Pakistan, which is based on fixed ICT infrastructure. All the problems both on the citizen's side and on the government's side are identified and explained. Next, the proposed Mobile Birth Registration is introduced and described thoroughly. The value propositions for all the parties, namely, children, parents, government, gatekeepers, and NGOs, are presented. Further, a social benefit assessment is carried out to show the usefulness of the Mobile Birth Registration. A financial feasibility study is provided to justify the introduction of MBR in addition the current fixed birth registration.

2   Current Birth Registration in Pakistan

2.1   Overview

Pakistan has today a population of over 180 million inhabitants with around 86 million children wherein 60 million and an increase of 3 million every year simply cannot prove their legal existence due to the lack of birth registration. National Pakistani statistics show that just over a quarter of births (27%) are registered with 32 and 24% birth registration in urban and rural areas, respectively.

This is mostly unfortunate because these children are hence denied one of the first and fundamental rights—the right to be registered at birth—to have an official identity, a recognized name, and a citizenship (van Do and Jørstad 2008). Children whose births go unregistered are prone to adverse socioeconomic conditions and often illegal and criminal activities (UNICEF 2005). At a more macro level, children who remain uncounted are less likely to be included in state development policies and planning for the provision of social services. Universalisation of birth registration is, therefore, absolutely vital for the future wellbeing of children in Pakistan and the country's sustainable development.

2.2   The Current Birth Registration Process

In Pakistan, the national authority for civil registration and identification is the *National Data base and Registration Authority* (NADRA 2015). However, registration itself is decentralized in Pakistan and under the purview of the respective provincial governments which are further administratively divided into 6550 *union councils (UCs)*. Each municipality is responsible for creating civil registration records for its residents, and the records are then supposed to be eventually stored with NADRA.

At present, the *Civil Registration Management System (CRMS)* managed by NADRA allows births to be registered through local government's basic unit, i.e., *union council (UCs)* offices. While all UCs have been imparted training on the issuance of computerized certificates and the plan was to connect these UCs with the central system of NADRA; however, only 2233 UCs have been made operational with varying degrees of effectiveness. Special certificate issuing paper has been provided to UCs that issue computerized birth certificates in their area of jurisdiction.

A fee of Pakistani Rupee Rs. 100 is payable for all printed certificates while late fee charges and penalties range between lump sum payment of Rs. 500 to Rs. 200 per year that the registration was not made. Unfortunately, the fee is not always charged as per rules or deposited fully with the exchequer. Bureaucratic hurdles and long processing time are also used as tools to force citizens into paying for personal favors in order to expedite the process.

As shown in Fig. 1 the normal process of the registration is as follows:

1. The aspirant goes to the UC office for getting the child birth registered.
2. At the request of concerned a form is issued to the aspirant.
3. The form along with the requisite fees and required documents, which normally include CNIC (Computerized National Identity Card) of the parents, CNIC of the applicant if different than the parents, certificate of birth issued by the

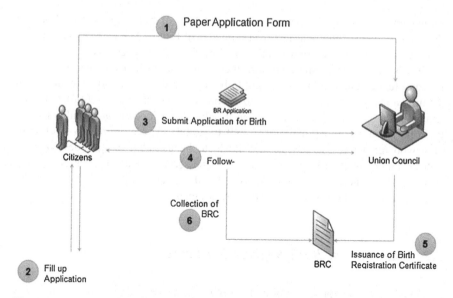

Fig. 1 Current birth registration process in Pakistan (*Source* Telenor/UNICEF)

hospital and/or vaccination card of the child, is then submitted back to the UC office.

4. The UC office after performing due diligence enters the data in its records and also to offline CRMS software provided by NADRA.
5. The UC issues birth certificate using CRMS in cases where UCs are computerized; otherwise, the UC issues a birth certificate using its own format.
6. The aspirant goes back to the UC office to collect the birth certificate.

2.3 Issues and Problems

There are several problems both on the citizen's and government' side, which keep the birth registration low as follows:

On the citizen's side:

- *Lack of Information about the procedure*: There is no central information repository from where the general public could get the information of the birth registration process.
- *Unawareness of birth registration importance*: The general public is not aware of the importance of the birth registration. Most of the persons have some anticipations of its usage in the future but when asked about the importance of birth registration none of them could highlight any.

- *High Traveling cost*: One needs to take several trips to the UC office before obtaining the birth registration certificate and each round trip is quite expensive.
- *Time-consuming process*: Getting a child birth registered and then obtaining a birth registration certificate is a time-consuming process involving number of trips to and from the office of Union council. Using working hours for these trips is a considerable loss of income for the parents.
- *Tedious process for attestations*: Getting the birth certificate is a tedious process that calls for extra effort and cost on the top of the cost of birth registration.
- *Illiteracy of the parents*: Filling the application forms may be a difficulty that prevents parents from getting their children registered. The alternative is to use consultants that charge extra fee.

On the government's side:

- *Capacity shortage*: The offices of Union Council are understaffed and quite often the staff does not receive adequate training to make use of computers. Furthermore, they may be busy with other more prioritized functions. The equipment is unsufficient, e.g., shortage of papers for certificates.
- *Electricity shortage*: Long hours of load shedding and un-scheduled shutdowns of electrical supply seriously hamper productivity of the UC office. Data can only be entered in the time intervals when electricity is available. Similarly taking the printout of the birth registration certificate is again dependent upon the availability of electricity.
- *No standardized fee for birth registration*: Fee is variable not only between provinces but also within a province. Even in a district different Union councils have been found charging different amounts of fee from the aspirants.
- *No defined time limit for the procedure*: Absence of such a limit does increase the vulnerability of the aspirants, resulting in a lower birth registration rate.
- *Difficult late Registration process*: The process becomes extreme tedious, in case someone gets late in getting ones child registered. It needs not only a number of trips to office of the Union council but also requires completion of legal documentation including presentation in front of magistrate to get the birth registered.
- *No defined procedure for orphans and IDPs*: There is no process defined for the orphans or internally displaced persons, making it extremely difficult to get a child birth in such a category registered.

3 Mobile Birth Registration

The fundamental change proposed to driving up birth registration is the introduction of trusted, reliable, and community-based '*gatekeepers*' who make use of mobile phones to carry out birth registration.

These gatekeepers can help leapfrog the natural adoption and acceptance of birth registration as a must practice. While the citizens and households will take a long time to reach the literacy and awareness levels to proactively get births registered among the various societal issues and bias, gatekeepers can help increase birth registration rates.

Two types of gatekeepers are proposed:

- *Mobile gatekeepers* will comprise government officials/field staff that have regular interaction with households in the communities and are well aware of any births happening. The potential primary gatekeepers in this category are as follows:

  - *Lady Health Workers/Supervisors/Visitors* who are the agents of maternal and child health advisory especially in rural areas.
  - *Teachers* who are aware of community dynamics by virtue of their respected role in the social settings and interactions with children in school.
  - *Nikah Registrars* (Marriage Licensing Registrars) who are the only agents registering marriages in a community and are connected to the Union Council as part of their legal authority.

- *Stationary gatekeepers* will serve as an intermediary facilitation improving access of households to get births registered. Instead of interacting with only one UC office, the presence of multiple stationary gatekeepers will not only help reduce the travel time and cost but also streamline the process stages by gate-keepers serving as process facilitators. Typically, private sector partners who have a ready distribution network equipped with technology systems can serve as the ideal fit. Telenor Pakistan, being a partner for this pilot, has offered to use their 'Sahoolat Ghar' distribution network of retailers as stationary gatekeepers.

Gatekeepers will be equipped with handheld devices and a custom application to digitize the standard birth registration application form. As shown in Fig. 2 all inputs necessary for birth registration will now be entered into this mobile application and saved as unique applications. All necessary documents (CNIC, hospital certificate, etc.) will be scanned and/or pictured through the device to serve as an electronic copy. The CNIC details will be verified through NADRA's online/SMS services to ensure the data entered is credible. Once the form has been duly filled, gatekeepers will also collect the stipulated fee and issue a receipt through a pre-printed book.

The digital forms along with supporting digital documents will then be transferred to the respective UC along with the fee collected for onward birth registration through the NADRA CRMS. The mobile application will be designed to shake hands with the NADRA CRMS and enable import of data. The UC Secretary can then review applications address any queries and process the registration. Once registered, the gatekeepers will be issued Birth Registration Certificate (BRC) for their respective households for onward delivery.

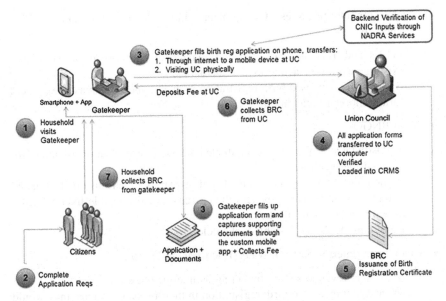

Fig. 2 Mobile birth registration (*Source* Telenor/UNICEF)

In the case of mobile gatekeepers, gatekeepers will be roving agents who will reach out to households and complete the mobile augmented process and deliver the BRC at their doorstep. However, in case of stationary gatekeepers, households will have to visit these kiosks on their own once for application and later for collecting the certificate which can be intimated through a confirmation SMS by the stationary gatekeeper.

4 Value Proposition

The Mobile Birth registration delivers values to the stakeholders as follows:

- Children:
  - Birth Registration means inclusion in the general population and enables identification.
  - Is a pre-requisite for future entitlements such as establishment of bonafide citizenship, school registration, national identity card, etc.
- Parents:
  - Birth registration ensures provision of basic services to their children such as access to education, health, and citizenship.
  - By registering ensures mitigation of adverse risks for their children from illegal and criminal activities.

- Gatekeepers/Intermediaries Government: Lady Heath Workers (LHW), Teachers, etc.

  - LHWs and Teachers can earn additional compensation to augment their existing salaries by acting as intermediaries.
  - By ensuring increased birth registration in their respective areas, they would earn additional recognition.

- NGOs/INGOs:

  - NGOs/INGOs work can be facilitated through identification of areas for targeted interventions.
  - By helping improving the status of birth registration, various other m-health initiatives will ultimately benefit the citizens and also enable INGOs/NGOs to better target their efforts.
  - Build confidence and establish clientele.

- Gatekeepers/Intermediaries Private: Telco franchises, etc.

  - Additional revenue stream by acting as intermediaries.
  - By ensuring increased birth registration in their respective areas, they would earn additional recognition.

- Government Agencies/officials (federal, provincial, and local governments)

  - Birth registration is the right of every child and enshrined in international conventions to which Pakistan is a signatory.
  - As custodians of state interests they have the responsibility to aim for universalization of birth registration.
  - As public officials responsible for facilitating ordinary citizens they can earn respect and trust among people.
  - Increased birth registration will enable better planning and allocation of resources and provision of basic services.

5 Social Benefit Assessment

To show the social benefits brought by the Mobile Birth Registration, a comparison between mobile birth registration and the traditional fixed registration was carried out. The obvious value of Mobile Birth Registration is to increase the registration rate from around 27 to 100%. The project is obviously beneficial since it will bring a better future to a lot of children but the challenge here is how to monetize the outcomes of mobile birth registration and how to prove that it is better than the fixed birth registration (Scholten et al. 2006). In fact it is very difficult or morally impossible to put a value on a child's life. To avoid this, a cost-effectiveness analysis (CEA) (Cellini and Kee 2010; Tuan 2008) is proposed.

The cost-effectiveness is defined as the ratio of cost to outcome. Lower CE will yield high effectiveness:

$$CE_o = \frac{C_o}{27} = \frac{100C_o}{27 \times 100}.$$

According to the Pakistani national statistic, 60 million of children, i.e., around 73%, are not registered.

Let the current birth registration cost be C_o and the outcome be the birth registration percentage.

The current cost-effectiveness is

$$CE_M = \frac{C_o + C_M}{100} = \frac{27C_o + 27C_M}{27 \times 100}.$$

Let C_M be the cost of introducing Mobile Birth Registration and if the goal is to achieve 100% birth registration, the outcome will be 100.

The Mobile Birth Registration Cost-Effectiveness is

$$CE_M = \frac{C_o + C_M}{100} = \frac{27C_o + 27C_M}{27 \times 100}.$$

If Mobile Birth Registration is more beneficial than the current fixed birth registration, we have

$$
\begin{aligned}
CE_M \leq CE_o \quad &\leftrightarrow \quad 27C_o + 27\,C_M \leq 100C_o \\
&\leftrightarrow \quad 27C_M \leq 73\,C_o \\
&\leftrightarrow \quad C_M \leq \frac{73C_o}{27} \\
&\leftrightarrow \quad C_M \leq 2.7\,C_o
\end{aligned}
$$

In general it is difficult to find statistics and we propose to concentrate on the costs for one Union Council instead of the whole country.

According to the figures from The Telenor Mobile Birth Registration pilot project in Pakistan, the total implementation cost of Mobile Birth Registration in two Union Councils in Sindh and two other in Punjab is 30,592,800 Rs.

The average cost for one Mobile Birth Registration is, hence,

$$30{,}592{,}800 \text{ Rs.} : 4 = 7{,}648{,}200 \text{ Rs.}$$

Regarding the cost of the current birth registration we are not able to find any documentation. Since the current birth registration is executed by the Union Councils (UC), we propose to use part of UC's total expenditure, for instance, a quarter of the expenditures as the birth registration cost.

According to Tehsil Municipal Administration Kasur (2015), the total expenditure of Tehsil Kasur in 2012–2013 is 729,546,800 Rs.

The average expenditure of a UC is

$$729,546,800 \text{ Rs.} : 55 \text{ UC in Kasur} = 13,263,487 \text{ Rs.}$$

The estimated birth registration cost is

$$13,263,487 \text{ Rs.} : 4 = 3,315,872 \text{ Rs.}$$

Consequently,

$$C_M = 7,648,200 \text{ Rs.} < 2.7 C_o = 2.7 \times 3,315,872 \text{ Rs.} = 8,952,854 \text{ Rs.}$$

This shows that

$$CE_M < CE_o.$$

This proves hence at Mobile Birth Registration is more beneficial for the society than the current birth registration.

6 Financial Feasibility Study

According to the figures from The Telenor Mobile Birth Registration pilot project in Pakistan, the total implementation cost of Mobile Birth Registration in two Union Councils in Sindh and two other in Punjab is 30,592,800 Rs.

Studies from other countries such as Kenya and other third world countries have shown the cost of birth registration for each child to cost an average $13 USD (labor, fringes benefits, and overhead costs). If we apply this rate to Pakistan, and using an Exchange rate of $1 USD = 61.7 Rs., the cost of each birth registration would equal anywhere from 802 Rs.

At a population of 60 million children and 73% unregistered birth 44.5 million children, the manual cost for 100% manual registration would require a government budget of 2.747 billion Rs. (or $578.5 million USD). This explains the dilemma and budgetary constraint or difficulty for Pakistan to register all of its newborn children with 3 million added each year. The current fixed birth registration is not scalable while Mobile Birth Registration offers the economy of scale.

An investment of initial $100 million USD for an infrastructure (state of the art IT system for a major global company) for a national Mobile Birth Registration system, and using an average $1 to $3 variable cost (using Western Union or MoneyGram companies cost to process their digital financial transactions as a benchmark) to register each child birth using Mobile technology, it would cost ($1 × 44.5 million = $44.5 million USD to $3 × 44.5 million = $133.5 million USD), one can derive the cost–benefit of such investment as follows:

$100 million (initial one time investment) plus $44.5 million USD in variable costs = $144.5 million USD (best case)

$100 million (initial one time investment) plus $133.5 million USD in variable costs = $233.5 million USD (worst case).

The total cost of a Mobile Birth Registration system (best case $144.5 million USD) or (worst case $233.5 million USD) is clearly more scalable and economical when compared to manual system costing $578.5 million USD. This benefit, when combined with other societal benefits of a registered and educated child who could contribute more to the productivity of a country GDP, clearly can add to the justification of a Mobile Birth Registration system for childbirth registration in Pakistan. Funds can be raised by partnering with telecom companies, donation from countries, and revenue sharing concepts. This should be the topics for future feasibility researches.

7 Conclusion

In this paper, the usability and the usefulness of mobile technologies far beyond personal communication has been demonstrated by the Mobile Birth Registration (MBR) concept. Mobile technologies have been proven as a technological efficient and scalable supplement to the current fixed infrastructure. It is shown that MBR brings lots of advantages and conveniences to all parties from the children, parents, government, gatekeepers, and NGOs. A simple Social Benefit assessment reaffirms the social value of MBR. Its financial feasibility is proven by a brief financial feasibility study. A pilot project is now currently executed in two Union councils in Sindh Province and two other in Punjab. So far, the situation looks good and the results of the project will decide the further deployment of MBR in Pakistan. However, independent of the outcome, experiences and findings will be collected and used in other initiatives in other countries such as Thailand, Myanmar, Bangladesh, etc., where Telenor has mobile network operations.

References

Bashah NSK, Kryvinska N, Van Do T (2010) Service discovery in ubiquitous mobile computing environment. In: Emerging research and projects applications symposium (ERPAS 2010), in conjunction with the iiWAS2010, Paris, France, 8–10 Nov 2010. ACM, pp 761–765. ISBN 978-1-4503-0421-4

Bashah NSK, Kryvinska N, Van Do T (2012a) Quality-driven service discover techniques for open mobile environments and their business applications. J Serv Sci Res (The Society of Service Science, Springer) 4(1):71–96. (ISSN: 2093-0720 (print version), ISSN: 2093-0739 (electronic version), Journal no. 12927)

Bashah NSK, Kryvinska N, Van Do T (2012b) Novel service discovery techniques for open mobile environments and their business applications. In: Third international conference on exploring services science (IESS 1.2), Geneva, Switzerland, 15–17 Feb 2012. Lecture Notes in Business Information Processing (LNBIP 103), Springer, pp. 186–200. ISBN 978-3-642-28226-3

Cellini SR, Kee JE (2010) Cost-effectiveness and cost benefit analysis, In: Wholey JS, Hatry HP, Newcomer KE (eds) Handbook of practical program evaluation. Published by Jossey-Bass, A Wiley Imprint 989 Market Street, San Francisco, CA 94103-1741. ISBN 978-0-470-52247-9 (hardback)

Dekleva S, Shim JP, Varshney U, Knoerzer G (2007) Evolution and emerging issues in mobile wireless networks. Commun ACM 50(6):38–43

ENISA (2010) European network and information security agency: mobile identity management. In: Papadopouli M (ed), University of Crete, Greece, 13 Apr 2010

GSMA (2014) E-Estonia Mobile ID. http://e-estonia.com/components/mobile-id. GSMA Personal Data: http://www.gsma.com/personaldata/

Kryvinska N, Lepaja S, Nguyen HM (2003) Service and personal mobility in next generation networks. In: The fifth IEEE international conference on mobile and wireless communications networks (MWCN 2003), Singapore, pp 116–119, 27–29 Oct 2003

Kryvinska N, Strauss C, Zinterhof P (2009) Mobility in a multi-location enterprise network, case study: global voice calls placing. The IEEE wireless telecommunications symposium (WTS 2009), Prague, Czech Republic, 22–24 Apr 2009. ISBN 1-4244-2589-1

NADRA (2015) National Database & Registration Authority. https://www.nadra.gov.pk/

Orange (2014) Orange group. http://www.orange.com

Plan (2014) Plan international. http://plan-international.org/

Scholten P, Nicholls J, Olsen S, Galimidi B (2006) Social return on investment: a guide to SROI analysis, Lenthe publishers. ISBN 90 75458 282

Tehsil Municipal Administration Kasur (2015) http://tmakasur.com/Budget.html

Telefonica (2015) Telefónica. http://www.telefonica.com

Telenor (2015) Telenor ASA. http://www.telenor.com

Tuan MT (2008) Bill & Melinda Gates Foundation—impact planning and improvement measuring and/or estimating social value creation: insights into eight integrated cost approaches—final 12/15/08

UNICEF (2005) The 'rights' start to life: a statistical analysis of birth registration, Feb 2005. ISBN 92-806-3858-0

UNICEF (2015) http://www.unicef.org/

van Do T, Audestad JA (1997) Terminal mobility support in TINA. In: Proceedings of TINA 97 conference, IEEE computer society, Santiago, Chile, pp 38–50, Nov 1997. ISBN 0-8186-8335-X

van Do T, Jørstad I (2008) The ambiguity of identity. Telektronikk, vol 103 No. 3/4 20057, Identity Management. ISSN 0085-7130. Published in Jan 2008

van Do T, Huy NP, Khuong LH (2012) Mobile identity as social economic enabler. In: Proceedings of the 7th international conference on computing and convergence technology 2012 (ICCCT2012), IEEE PDF files ISBN: 978-89-94364-22-3, IEEE DVD version ISBN: 978-89-94364-26-1, IEEE Print version, Seoul, Korea, 3–5 Dec 2012. ISBN 978-89-94364-21-6

Chapter 5
Mobile Banking Services—Business Information Management with Mobile Payments

Katerina Markoska, Iryna Ivanochko and Michal Gregus ml.

Abstract The service sector is closely related with the technology developments and consequently the access to services, their provision, and consumption are optimized. The banking industry is no exception to it. It is strongly influenced by technology developments and tries to meet new challenges and thus to develop further itself. Particularly affected and being put under increasing pressure are the core banking businesses—accounts and payments. Their central element is the money that has experienced a change in its form of existence over time. Money (same as many other goods and services) were being digitized and its value were being transferred to plastic card and lately mobile phones (PPP (paper—plastic—phone) evolution of money). Along with the technological developments comes both the socio-demographic shifts and changes in the legal environment. On the other hand, opportunities for new participants (other than banks) on the (cashless) payment market are opening up and with it the position of the banks on the payment market is threatened. Due to the fact that banks are very much impacted by the developments in technology and they count among the heaviest investors in information technology, this paper will attempt to provide valuable insight into how the banks implement or could implement the new (mobile) technologies and the smartphone. Further, this paper comprises three aspects of our contemporary society: the importance of the tertiary sector of the economy—services in the developed countries, the development of new (mobile) technologies, and the high penetration rate and acceptance of "the device" of the contemporary history—the smartphone. The aim of this work is to translate these three aspects into the banking service sector in Austria (with a focus on the payments).

K. Markoska
School of Business, Economics and Statistics, University of Vienna, Vienna, Austria
e-mail: markoska@gmx.at

I. Ivanochko (✉) · M. Gregus ml.
Faculty of Management, Comenius University in Bratislava, Bratislava, Slovakia
e-mail: irene.ivanochko@gmail.com

M. Gregus ml.
e-mail: michal.gregusml@fm.uniba.sk

© Springer Science+Business Media Singapore 2018
N. Kryvinska and M. Gregus (eds.), *Agile Information Business*,
Flexible Systems Management, DOI 10.1007/978-981-10-3358-2_5

Keywords Mobility · Mobile payments · ICT technologies · Mobile banking services · Smartphone

1 Introduction

There are two undeniable facts about the society we live in. It is dominated by services and consumerism. In the developed counties, services are now the lead contributor in the GDP. Along with their importance for the economy, the notion of fostering "the process of servitization in many companies" (Zolnowski et al. 2014, p. 718) no matter which industry they belong to have raised as well. Services are not only an economic activity upon which a business model is being based, but also for many companies they represent "a key differentiator and therefore a source of sustainable and competitive advantage" (Fasnacht 2009, p. 8). With the advancement of the technology, consumers on the one hand have been included in the early stages of the value creation process. In order to increase the value proposition, many companies now offer their customers additional services such as customization and personalization. You can nowadays desiyour T-shirt or even equip your BMW based upon your needs and wishes. On the other hand, the access to a certain service is being automated. By the means of technology, consumers at the same time initiate, use, and benefit from using the service (the rise of self-service technology (SST)).

Furthermore, through technology advances, the access to a certain service is now completely being automated. "The Internet and the commercial development of the World Wide Web" (Hilton et al. 2013, p. 3), have an enormous impact on the behavior of the people. Nowadays we, the consumers of this world, have the luxury to be at home sitting on the sofa and buy our favorite book, a custom garment or book our holiday. And all of this thanks to the Internet and to the advancement of the technology. Empowered with "the device" of the contemporary history, the smartphone, it has become even easier to purchase goods or services being just a fingertip away of it.

Every trade exchange (of goods or services) has its monetary value, meaning that it is required to be paid for. Money is generally accepted means of payment. "It serves as a means of exchange, value preservation and measurement" (Lerner 2013, p. 1). Due to technology advancement, money has undergone a change in its form of existence. The history of money chronicles a "dematerialization from metal money to e-money" (Kumbhar 2013, p. 66). Money (same as many other goods and services) were being digitized and its value over time was being transferred to plastic card and lately mobile phones (PPP (paper—plastic—phone) evolution of money). With the advancement of the technologies (as one of the most important triggers according to my opinion), the society strives for a cashless economy.

Banking is "a major service category" (Oliveira and von Hippel 2011, p. 806) of the financial services family, dealing with payments and accounts as one of its core business activities. Though it seems rather conservative industry, banks are very much impacted by the developments in technology and over the years banks have adopted a vast amount of SST—from ATM to Internet banking to mobile banking. But, what is next?

The latest trend in the banking industry is the mobile banking, as a complementary service distribution channel to the online and offline (bricks-and-mortar) banking and as a way of improving the value proposition to the customers. On the other hand, in a world "where money is increasingly more digitized" (Lukies 2012, p. 41) there is a great plenty of other players (nonbanking institutions) directly competing with the banks "on multiple fronts for the ownership of the customer transaction, customer relationship and customer experience" (ibid). And yet there is no bank playing the same game. Is mobile banking paving the way for successful mobile payment service offered by the banks? Are banks waiting to catch the right wave?

Due to high data sensitivity and an anticipated little chance of big banks revealing their strategy, this work will represent the current occurrences in the banking industry based on a numerous scientific papers as well as case studies and reports, published by prestigious consulting companies. The focus is set on Austria, for couple of reasons; it is a developed country with a relative conservative banking culture and a birthplace of innovative phenomenons. By means of strategic management tools, such as the Rosenzweig's four types of decisions and Bower and Christensen's model for disruptive technologies, it will attempt to conclude and suggest whether mobile banking is paving the way for a mobile payment service and whether banks in this way are going to extend and defend their role in the payment industry.

2 Self-service Technologies

As discussed by Neu and Brown (2008), "increasing global competition, advances in technology, and the search for attractive market opportunities foster a process of servitization in many industries" (as cited in Zolnowski et al. 2014, p. 718). The advancement in information and communication technologies (ICT) and their ubiquitous character have brought the customers and goods producers/service providers together in a way that they both participate in the value creation process (Auer et al. 2009; Bashah et al. 2012b). This has impacted (and it still does) to a greater extent the service industry, so that the line between the customers and service providers has become blurred—the customers are at the same time initiate, use, and benefit from the service (self-service technology (SST)). In this section, the relationship between and the dependence between services and technology will be discussed, emphasizing the financial services as a distinctive category among the services.

2.1 Services and Financial Services

It may though sound straight-forward and everyone would promptly say that they know what a service is. However, it has obviously made quite difficulties for many scholars and researchers to give a uniform definition for the term service and "the definition of services has never reached consensus" (Parry et al. 2011, p. 20). The catalogue of services includes a wide range of activities. From transportation and storage through accommodation and food service activities, information and communication to activities of extraterritorial organizations and bodies (ISIC, United Nations Statistics Division—Classifications Registry 2016). Imagine if we have a banker, an hotelier, a store manager, an IT, and so on, sitting on the same table. The term service will certainly have a different meaning for every one of them (in terms of whom and how is the service being delivered).

The economy has survived the shift from an industry-driven to a service-driven economy. It is inevitable to admit the fact that we are living in a service society. "Services are a strategically important business activity and a key differentiator and therefore have become the source of sustainable and competitive advantage in a global financial market" (Fasnacht 2009, p. 8). Predominantly in the developed countries, the service sector is the main contributor to the GDP. Austria is one of those countries where the tertiary sector counts for about 70% of the GDP (as of end of 2013; see Fig. 1). This number is roughly the same compared with the whole EU area and the other highly developed economies (US and Japan), where the service sector has the largest share of the total output (73.5, 79.7, and 75.0% respectively) (ECB, n.d.).

For the sake of brevity, the following definition is intentionally chosen:

Service is a type of economic activity that is intangible, is not stored and does not result in ownership (What is Service? definition and meaning 2016).

Fig. 1 Origin of GDP by sectors 2013—% of total value added (own representation based on Wirtschaftskammer Österreich (WKO) (2014)) (color figure online)

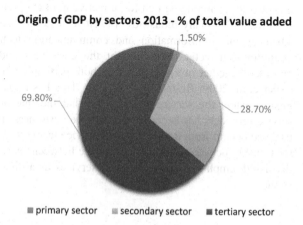

Origin of GDP by sectors 2013 - % of total value added

1.50%

69.80%

28.70%

■ primary sector   ■ secondary sector   ■ tertiary sector

It consists three of the IHIP (intangible, heterogeneous, inseparable, and perishable) characteristics of the services. Namely, the IHIP characteristics "have formed the basis of a consensus in most of the marketing literature" (Parry et al. 2011, p. 21).

According to Pine and Gilmore (1998, p. 97), there are four categories of economic offerings: commodities, goods, services, and experience. If we, for a moment, exclude the last category, experience (suggesting that "the value of experience is a significant intangible characteristic (perishable) of the service itself" (Parry et al. 2011, p. 23)), we can state that concerning the nature of the offering, the intangibility is a feature that distinguishes the services from the commodities and goods (beside the fungibility moment, commodities are yet of tangible nature). And exactly this, the intangibility feature or to be more precise the way of how the service is being delivered, is an important (if not the most important) factor in the value creation process in the service economy. The consumer is a very crucial piece of the service value chain puzzle (See 2.B), due to the fact that the production coincides with the consumption of the service (inseparable) and the fact that a same service is being differently perceived by every single consumer (heterogeneous) (Horn 2009, p. 14).

Services are heterogeneous per se. ISIC (International Standard Industrial Classification of All Economic Activities) among the other economic activities classifies the services into 14 different subcategories (ISIC H-U or 50-99, United Nations Statistics Division—Classifications Registry). A more clear classification of the service sector was proposed by D'Agostino et al. (2006, p. 9). They have differentiated the services into four subcategories: "wholesale, retail trade, restaurants and hotels; transport, storage and communication; finance, insurance, real estate and business services; community, social and personal services. In both ways, banking services fall within the category of financial service industry" (ibid).

"The financial service industry is one of the central pillars of a national economy, in particular for countries in which it makes an important contribution to the gross domestic product" (Fasnacht 2009, p. 6). Fasnacht (ibid) emphasizes the importance of the financial services by stating that "within the last 25 years, firms belonging to the financial services have raised to top global companies, among which the banking industry has the biggest presence out of the global 2,000 largest companies (as of March 2008 according to Forbes)" (Fig. 2).

In order to demonstrate the significance and the importance of the banking services as a representative of the financial services family, two measures significant for the well-being of the economy (GDP—as an indicator of a country's economy health (What is GDP and why is it so important? 2016), employees—as contributors to the GDP) will be pointed out (Table 1).

The focus in this paper is the private banking sector, as "a pure service industry in which the service is performed almost entirely in the presence of the customer" (Horn and Rudolf 2011, p. 173). In particular, it deals with retail banking activities that class among private banking.

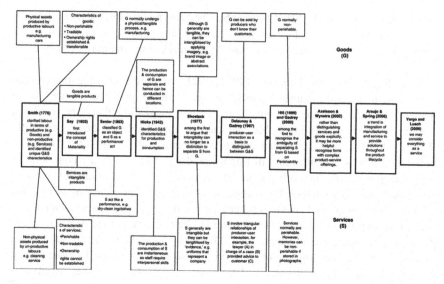

Fig. 2 Defining goods and service: over 230 years and counting (as depicted in Parry et al. 2011, p. 27)

Table 1 Comparing EU and Austria values

	EU-27	Austria
Banking assets as % of GDP	284[a]	~400[b]
Number of bank employee (million)	3[c]	0.237[d]

[a]EBF, International Comparison of Banking Sectors: Data sets for the European Union, euro area, United Kingdom, United States and Japan, as of 2011
[b]Borgioli, Gouveia, Labanca (2013, p. 15)
[c]EBF, International Comparison of Banking Sectors: Data sets for the European Union, euro area, United Kingdom, United States and Japan, as of 2011
[d]Own calculation based on OeNB Statistic; due to consistency 2011 is taken as a comparison year

"Retail Banking ist ein auf den Massenmarkt fokussiertes Privatkundengeschäft. Dieses umfasst den Verkauf standardisierte Finanzprodukte und Finanzdienstleistungen an nicht bis weniger vermögende Kunden, die nur einen geringen bis gar keinen Beratungsbedarf haben. Dabei stehen Basisdienstleistungen wie die Abwicklung des Zahlungsverkehrs, Sparprodukte, Fonds, Kredite, Bausparen und Versicherungen im Vordergrund" (Horn 2009, p. 6).

As clear as the afore-stated definition is, the retail banking includes standardized financial products and services brought on a mass market serving not to less wealthy individuals. If we assumed that not to less wealthy customers are representatives of the younger population that do not dispose of their own financial resources, engaging them into the retail banking as early as possible can lead to a long-term commitment. However, higher customer segments are not excluded from the retail banking services (Horn 2009, p. 6). And as standardized as they could be, the services in their inborn nature pose the heterogenic characteristic.

Following, we will see how and to which extent technology impacts the services, improves customer experience, and with that reinforces the heterogeneity.

2.2 Services + Technology = Self-service Technology (SST)

Referring to the shift of the economy (from industry-driven to service-driven), the paper continues in the same manner comparing the productive processes of goods versus services according to Dhaliwal et al. (2011, pp. 2, 3; see Figs. 3 and 4). Both figures differ in respect to the stage at which the customer is being involved in the process. Though the illustrations are quite helpful, in the course of time with the advancement of the technology the things have changed. Not only in the sense of process by engaging with customers at a much earlier stage in the productive process of goods, "often through using the advantages of automation often through using the advantages of automation offered by the Internet" (Dhaliwali et al. 2011, p. 2); think of customized products, technology has also blurred the lines between *tangible* products and *intangible* services (think of digitalized products).

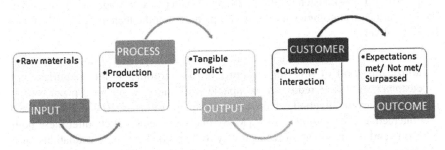

Fig. 3 Productive process of goods (own representation based on Dhaliwal et al. (2011, p. 2))

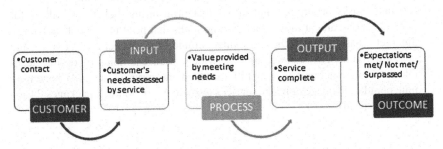

Fig. 4 Productive process of services (own representation based on Dhaliwal et al. (2011, p. 3))

In the process of service delivery there are usually two parties involved: a service user ("firms or individuals that expect to benefit from using a service" (Oliveira and von Hippel 2011, p. 806)) and a service producer ("firms or individuals that expect to benefit from selling a service" (Oliveira and von Hippel 2011, p. 806)). The advancement in the information technologies (IT), with an emphasis on "the Internet and the commercial development of the World Wide Web" (Hilton et al. 2013, p. 3), has brought further enhancement in the service delivery process and has "revolutionized the service landscape" (Lin and Hsieh 2011, p. 194) by increasing the participation of the users themselves. As to that, Vargo and Lusch refer to the term as "the application of specialized competences (knowledge and skills) through deeds, processes, and performances for the benefit of another entity or the entity itself" (2004, p. 2). According to Meuter et al. (2000, p. 50) "self-service technologies (SST) are technological interfaces that enable customers to produce a service independent of direct employee involvement" (as cited in Lin and Hsieh 2011, p. 194). Service-Dominant Logic introduced by Vargo and Lusch (2004) has already suggested the significant role of the consumer of the service in the process of value co-creation, referring at the same time to the inseparable feature of the services (consumer as the initiator and the user of the service) and to "the impact upon customer's perception of whole service experience" (Hilton et al. 2013, p. 3).

Self-service is not something new (Lepaja et al. 2003). It has long existed —"think of do-it-yourself homeowners doing the work of professional contractors, or placing a call by dialing a telephone instead of using telephone operator" (Castro et al. 2010, pp. 1, 4). Hsieh (2005, p. 78) and Meuter et al. (2000, p. 52) categorize the self-service technologies into four groups based on the technology used for the service delivery:

1. "Telephone and interactive voice response (IVR) systems—Many companies utilize this form of SST for customer orders, customer billing inquiries, and customer surveys. Credit card companies, insurance companies, pizza restaurants, and even universities have taken advantage of these" (Hsieh 2005, p. 78).
2. "Interactive freestanding kiosks—Many malls and retail outlets offer these both inside and outside their stores as a way to help you determine availability of a product, as well as to where to locate it in their facility. Some even print coupons. Large discount chains use kiosks in each store to help you determine what size battery or windshield wiper to put on your car, for example. You will also find kiosks at airports and hotels that print airline tickets and allow for quick checkout, and at movie theaters and malls that print movie tickets" (ibid).
3. "Internet based or other on-line connection systems—ATM's and pay-at-the-pump gas stations are two widely used examples of on-line technologies. Internet banking and bill management services are also becoming quite popular. Package delivery services also allow you to track packages 24 h a day now" (ibid).

4. "*Video/DVD/CD based technologies*—This type of SST is typically used for educational purposes. Corporate entities use this media to train their employees, to familiarize sales representatives with new products, and to introduce new products to consumers. Universities have also gotten into the act in the last decade, providing undergraduate, graduate, and continuing education classes by video and CD formats" (ibid).

Castro et al.'s categorization (2010, p. 7) differs slightly from the one mentioned above. However, there are four categories as well, electronic kiosks, the Internet, mobile devices (including smart phones and smart cards), and the telephone, among which the video/DVD/CD-based technologies are not being mentioned. In the same context (being used mainly for educational purposes), no wonder, they were being assimilated into the Internet applications. From Online Health, through Online Banking to access to government services, Internet application gave the self-services a new dimension and "have equipped consumers to take on new roles" (Castro et al. 2010, p. 18) in the service process.

2.3 SSTs Among Banking Services

"The financial services industry is changing rapidly" (Abdullah et al. 2011, p. 542). Many researchers argued about the fact that financial institutions, in our cases banks, are in flux (Arguedas et al. 2014; Oliveira and von Hippel 2011; Wessels and Drennan 2010; Fasnacht 2009). Another inevitable fact is that "the growth of self-service provision is dependent upon technology" (Hilton and Hughes 2013, p. 863). Banks are very much impacted by the developments in technology, so they count among the heaviest investors in ICT (Fasnacht 2009, p. 8; Arguedas et al. 2014, p. 165; Mai 2012, p. 2). But, not only technological advances have contributed "to a rapid growth in IT-enabled self-services" (Castro et al. 2010, p. 3). An increase in labor costs, turbulent market and regulatory environments, customer structure, their sophistication, etc., has over two decades mutually influenced each other and is continuously "forcing financial service institutions to re-evaluate their current business practices" (Hanzaee and Mirvaisi 2011, p. 130) and to "re-examine how they are meeting their customer's needs today and in the future" (Abdullah et al. 2011, p. 542).

As big its importance and significance for the economy, as big is the power of the banking industry to turn over the economy (With great power comes great responsibility—Stan Lee). Banking industry has been considered as a rather conservative and resistant to change. "It used to be a moderate dynamic market for decades due to the stable industry structure, defined boundaries, clear business models, and identifiable players that made change linear and predictable in the past" (Fasnacht 2009, p. 8). Panta rhei. Over the last 20 years things have changed. Stable industry structure with defined boundaries turned into "an industry with ambiguous structure and blurred boundaries" (ibid), where neither the suppliers' (vast numbers

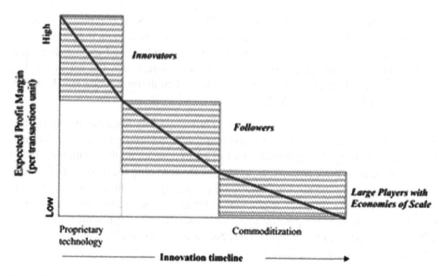

Fig. 5 The innovation timeline (as depicted in Chakravorti and Kobor (2005, p. 32))

of new market entrants) nor the demanders' action and/or reaction to the new challenges can be easily predictable.

Martins, Oliveira, and Popovič argue that "organizations can now profit from the evolution of new technologies and adapt to the emerging ways of interacting with their clients" (2014, p. 2). As a source for profitable growth (Fasnacht 2009, p. 8), innovations are considered as a reasonable response to the fast-changing environment. According to Judt (2006, p. 21) there are "sichtbare" (visible) and "fühlbare" (tangible/noticeable) innovations in the banking industry, that do not always have to be attached to the product or process itself. Thus, he points out innovations referring to "the establishment of new delivery channel (e.g. bank shops), development of a new transaction process (e.g. e-Banking) or launch of a new price system (e.g. all-inclusive account) etc." (Judt 2006, p. 21). The other elements of the marketing mix (product, price, place, promotion, people, process, physical evidence alias 7Ps according to Magrath (1986)) are affected as well. Independent from the type of innovation, Chakravorti and Kobor (2005, p. 12) suggest an innovation timeline (see Fig. 5).

Investing in an innovation "may occur at different points in the evolution of the innovation to commoditized product" (ibid). Depending on the phase companies invest in, different profit margins can be expected. While in the early phases margins are high, investments in new proprietary technology (being a first mover) are high as well. As the innovation matures and "succumbs to commoditization" (ibid), the profit margins decrease and companies can rely on economies of scale (ibid, p. 16).

Dapp (2012, p. 1) argues about the "increasing pressure in one of the financial sector's core business segments: accounts and payments". Their importance hides in the answer of the question: "What is actually a bank?". According to Macho et al.

(1994, p. 31), the monetary intermediation services (taking deposits and granting credits) comprise the core service provision functions. And the only way to provide them is by simply having accounts and by making a payment. Accounts and payments fall into the group of retail banking services. Exactly in this group of services since many years, there have been introduced different types of SSTs although with a smaller amount of IT-enabled self-service at the beginning. ATMs and financial (debit and credit) cards are established and well-known examples after the pioneers of the cashless payments were introduced, such as the check, remittance, and direct debits. And they are enormously being used nowadays.

As it was already mentioned (See 2.B), IT advancement, with an emphasis on "the Internet and the commercial development of the World Wide Web" (Hilton et al. 2013, p. 3), "has further enhanced self-service delivery and revolutionized the service landscape, allowing companies to use variety of SSTs that increase customer participation" (Lin and Hsieh 2011, p. 194). Therefore, many banks have extended their service portfolio by "adding clicks to bricks" (Fernández-Sabiote and Román 2012). Nowadays, "SSTs can be accessed by customers in situ within the operating sites of organizations, …, or remotely, for example through the Internet (Hilton et al. 2013, p. 3) or more recently through their mobile (smart)phones". "Since the mid-1990s, there has been a fundamental shift in banking delivery channels toward using self-service channels such as online banking services" (Pikkarainen et al. 2004, p. 224).

Online banking is another example of a (r)evolution respective the account access or making payment. "Online banking (OLB)[1] provides consumers with a set of information-related benefits, including easy access, responsive systems and the opportunity for the user to control bank account at any time and place and access customized information content enabling customers to make investment and finance-related decisions" (Loureiro et al. 2014, p. 187). Thus, OLB is "an Internet portal, through which customers can use different kinds of banking services ranging from bill payment to making investments" (Pikkarainen et al. 2004, p. 224) "without any interaction with, or assistance from, bank employees" (Loureiro et al. 2014, p. 187).

Eistert, Gordon, Deighton, Ullrich, and Marcu in their study argue that digital banking is not a "hot" topic among the bankers around the world; "it is a necessary part of every bank's agenda as a way to overcome outdated approaches and mismanaged customer relationships" (2013, p. 1). Out of this study, it can be concluded that among the top to high rated countries according to Digital Banking Readiness Index (DiBRix) most of them are from the old continent. DiBRix refers not to "just having the appetite for digital banking" (ibid, p. 16). It comprises the entire banking environment, technology developments, competitive challenges (market dynamics), customer demands, and regulations (ibid, p. 16). Austria is on the 9th place, before Switzerland, France, and Germany (its closest neighbors). Based on the data of

---

[1]Online banking, Internet banking, or electronic banking are used as synonyms throughout the whole paper.

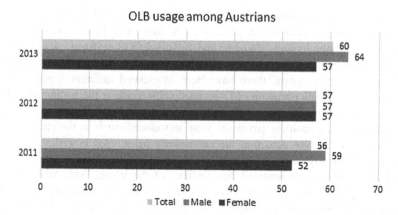

Fig. 6 OLB usage among Austrians (own representation based on Statistik Austria data from the last three years) (color figure online)

Statistik Austria, we can see that besides the other purposes of using the Internet (STATISTIK AUSTRIA—IKT-Einsatz in Haushalten 2016), there is an evident increasing tendency of the OLB usage among Austrians (see Fig. 6).

Innovations are considered not only as a source for profitable growth (Fasnacht 2009, p. 8), but as a source of gaining a competitive advantage and long-term survival on the market (Judt 2006, p. 19). By digitizing the banking services, the banks themselves can easily trace (via data mining tools) and quickly respond to the specific customer wants and needs.

The latest innovation after the evident success of OLB introduction is the mobile banking, as "an emerging facet of electronic banking" (Wessels and Drennan 2010, p. 547). "Mobile banking facility removes the space and time limitations from banking services such as checking account balances or transferring money from one account to another" (Rao 2013, p. 593) meaning that a consumer's account is as mobile as the consumer her-/himself (More about mobile banking in Sect. 3).

As it was mentioned above, the banking industry turned into "an industry with ambiguous structure and blurred boundaries" (Fasnacht 2009, p. 8), where the barriers to entry the market are significantly lower than 20 years ago and where neither the suppliers' (vast numbers of new market entrants) nor the demanders' action and/or reaction to the new challenges can be easily predictable. "As Bar (2005) notes, technology evolves in ways not anticipated by its designers and new applications often result from the accumulated experience of users themselves" (as cited in Maurer 2012, p. 590). Various kinds of competitors are confronting traditional bank with the help of technological developments and web-based applications (Dapp 2012, p. 1) offering alternative banking solutions. Oliveria and von Hippel's "central finding is that user firms often develop and self-provide computerized versions of the services earlier than banks or other types of financial service producers begin to offer them" (2011, p. 806). This raises the question *which of the current alternative payment possibilities will be commercialized by the banks*? Banks should truly consider to extend the horizon of perceiving the smartphones as another service distribution channel (as Gupta (2013, p. 3) suggests) and properly make use of its potential.

3   From e-Commerce Toward mBusiness

Evolution or revolution? The essential element that helps us distinguish the one term from the other is TIME. If the change occurs slower and more gradual it is an evolution (Guedeney 2012, p. 6). If it is quick, sudden, and abrupt we are talking about a revolution (ibid). With the introduction of the Internet, our everyday lives have been revolutionized in many aspects. The way of communication, the way of how information can be acquired, and the way of buying and selling products and services have been transformed. Everything has moved to the virtual environment and the constraints of time and place have been removed. Along with the technological advances and the socio-demographic shifts has come to an extension to the ubiquitous characteristic of the Internet. Thus, to the "anytime, anywhere" paradigm "on any device" has been added due to the high penetration rate and acceptance of the smartphones—the key component of the chain of the next generation of the digital mobility (Becker et al. 2012; Kryvinska et al. 2008b). In this section, it will be discussed the extension of and "the next logical stage in the evolution of the World Wide Web" (Dapp 2013, p. 1) environment.

3.1   Mobility Role in IT Services Support

The advancement in the information technologies (IT), with an emphasis on "the Internet and the commercial development of the World Wide Web" (Hilton et al. 2013; Kryvinska et al. 2011a) has resulted in significant progress toward strategies, requirements, and development of e-commerce applications (Varshney and Vetter 2002, p. 185). The Internet itself has transformed the way people interact with each other, the way they search for information, how they acquire products and services and so on. In addition to that, "the wide-ranging economic developments, e.g. the integration of world economies, have made a significant impact towards increasing the mobility of the people" (Tiwari et al. 2007, p. 3).

During the dot-com fever (late 90s and the beginning of the new millennium), many companies have changed their priorities and strategies by "adding clicks to the bricks". Many others have recognized the potential of the Internet environment and took the challenge of operating and being present only virtually (think of eBay or Amazon for example). In this context, the need of defining the term of e-Commerce is evident. "In its broadest sense, electronic commerce refers to the use of electronic means and technologies to conduct commerce, including within-business, business-to-business, and business-to-consumer interactions"

(Choi et al. 1997, p. 13). Therefore, every action conducted online (including "searching for product information, ordering products, paying for goods and services, customer service, whereas noncommercial activities such as entertainment, communication, filing and paying taxes, managing personal finance, research, and education" (ibid, pp. 9, 13)) with the help of an Internet connection ("the principal vehicle of eCommerce" (Zwass 1996, p. 5)) and a computer is counted in the group of e-Commerce activities.

(As the time goes by and as our society develops) The nature and the structure of the current dynamic fast-changing environment make us (people) more aware of everything that is happening around us. On one hand, we are flooded with information that we want to process as fast as possible and at the end make use of. On the other hand, the time itself is becoming a scarce resource, so what people strive for nowadays is agility, flexibility, quick responsiveness from every point of view. Along with the technological advances and the socio-demographic shifts has come to an extension to the ubiquitous characteristic of the Internet. Thus, to the "anytime, anywhere" paradigm "on any device" has been added.

The next new and big thing in the e-Commerce is the mCommerce. Tiwari et al. refer to it as "an extension of Electronic Commerce to wireless mediums" (2007, p. 3). In its broadest sense, mCommerce includes "any transaction with a monetary value—either direct or indirect—that is conducted via a wireless telecommunication network" (Barnes 2002, p. 92). mCommerce is not a new concept. After the wireless telephone was introduced to the world (Becker et al. 2012), many scholars and researchers (for over a decade) discussed its importance and potential (Barnes 2002; Tiwari et al. 2007).

But, the cornerstone of the mCommerce is the proliferation of the smartphones (not long ago). Smartphones are becoming an indispensable part of our everyday lives (Kryvinska et al. 2010). The telephone itself has long ago exceeded its function of being a device for making a simple phone call. Nowadays when speaking about phones, we think of a device which can literally replace our PC and camera; capable of multitasking; able to connect to the Internet; sending e-mails etc. According to NIST's definition a smart phone is *"a full-featured mobile phone that provides users with personal computer like functionality by incorporating PIM (personal information manager) applications, enhanced Internet connectivity and email operating over an Operating System supported by accelerated processing and larger storage capacity compared with present cellular phones"* (NIST 2010, p. 4). Thus, smartphones being equipped with a sophisticated and an advanced technology (larger storage capacity, faster processors, longer battery life etc.), can literally replace the computers and laptops and "open lucrative opportunities to merchants and service providers" (Dahlberg et al. 2008, p. 165).

According to ITU (International Telecommunication Union) "the number of mobile-cellular subscriptions worldwide is approaching the number of people on earth" (ITU 2014, p. 3). With so high penetration rate (worldwide 96%; ibid, p. 4) and customer acceptance of the smartphones, there cannot be any doubt that mobile commerce is increasingly gaining attention not only by the scholars and researchers, but among the marketers as well. What once was the e-Commerce is nowadays the mCommerce; a new playground with huge potential for conducting business and another step closer to the customers.

"Going "mobile" can be considered as one of the main global trends of the 21st century" (Höhler 2012, p. 5). However scary it may seem, the minute-by-minute rapid advance in technology is undoubtedly making businesses dependent today on technological advances only made available just years ago. This notion of inter dependency between business and technology is stirring up an essential need to always stay vigilant of new things. Hence, the financial industry is not an exclusion and as the other industries are affected by as well and cannot remain immune of it. "Mobile Commerce services in the financial sector are generally known as mobile financial services (MFS) and they comprise of two applications, "Mobile Payment" and "Mobile Banking"" (Tiwari et al. 2007, p. 3).

3.2 Mobile Banking

The banking industry as one of the heaviest investors in information technology has been over the decades using the benefits of the IT. "Not only to run the internal business activities and to promote products, but also to dematerialize the customer relationships" (Martins et al. 2014, p. 2) (in other words to introduce and make full use of SST). On top of it, banks are cutting down on operating expenses and can "act and fight" on different fronts serving and reaching different customer segments through diverse distribution channels.

In an evidently uncertain and fast-changing environment, innovations are considered as a reasonable response to it (as stated above). And as it has been argued (Anyasi and Otubu 2009; Chen 2013; Accenture 2013a) financial institutions failing to introduce innovations or to adapt to and be in step with the new technology trends have less chance to differentiate their products and services and retain their competitive advantage. In the context of new trends and as a result of the technological advances, the importance of the bank branches "as reference points in the distribution process" (Arguedas et al. 2014, p. 167) has been diminished. Consequently, new distribution channels, "such as telephone banking, ATMs, Internet, and mobile phones have become more firmly established" (ibid). And exactly distribution channels and customer interfaces are on the agenda of many bank executives from US and Europe as the main focus areas for innovation, as reported by Sullivan et al. (2014, p. 35).

"Internet banking or online banking (OLB) has emerged as one of the most profitable eCommerce applications over the last two decades" (Lee 2009, p. 130). According to Aladwani (2001) and Yiu et al. (2007) "Internet banking is defined as the use of banking services through the computer network (the Internet), offering a wider range of potential benefits to financial institutions due to more accessibility and user friendly use of the technology" (as cited in Martins et al. 2014, p. 2).

As it was already discussed above, "OLB provides consumers with a set of information-related benefits, including easy access, responsive systems and the opportunity for the user to control bank accounts" (Loureiro et al. 2014, p. 187) by removing the time and space constraints characteristic for the "offline" (in branch) banking.

Advancement of the ICT (Kryvinska et al. 2010b); mobility as one of the main global trends of the twenty-first century (as stated above); high penetration rate and acceptance of the smartphones; mixed altogether they trigger the digital mobility as "the next logical stage in the evolution of the World Wide Web" (Dapp 2013, p. 1). "Technological developments especially in the field of telecommunication have made it possible to offer innovative, location-sensitive services on ubiquitous ("anytime, anywhere") basis to customers on the move" (Tiwari et al. 2007, p. 3). The mobile technology has enriched the "anytime, anywhere" paradigm and "on any device" moment has been added to it. "The exponential growth of wireless and mobile networks has brought vast changes in mobile devices, middleware development, standards and network implementation, and user acceptance" (Varshney et al. 2000, p. 32).

Translated in banking context, along with the technology advances new opportunities have arisen for both banking service users and providers. Thus, besides one of the most established examples of alternative banking the ATM (upgraded with additional functions such as cash recycling) and OLB, "users are nowadays being able to conduct banking services at anyplace and at any time and to connect banking service easily and quickly with mobile devices" (Gu et al. 2009, p. 11605). Given that, mobile banking (mBanking) was born and it has joined the family of alternative[2] banking. Tiwari and Buse (2006) define mBanking as follows:

> Mobile Banking refers to provision and availment of banking and financial services with the help of mobile telecommunication devices. The scope of offered services may include facilities to conduct bank and stock market transactions, to administer accounts and to access customized information (as cited in Tiwari et al. 2007, p. 3).

mBanking is being usually offered in form of a mobile application downloadable in the App Stores available for different operating systems (e.g., Andorid or iOS). In Austria, all of the established and well-known banks (UniCredit Bank Austria, Erste Bank, Raiffeisen Bank, BAWAG etc.) have their own mobile banking application. mBanking differentiates itself from its closely related alternative banking methods, telephone banking, and mBanking as provided at its infancy (banking via SMS), by being completely autonomous SST and by excluding a direct or an indirect bank employee involvement.

Currently the mBanking, as it is consumed and configured, is being perceived as an additional channel of providing the usual services offered in OLB and is adding value to the service delivery process. As argued by Pousttchi and Schurig (2004),

---

[2]Alternative banking as a way of conducting banking services outside a branch.

"the simultaneous and increasing diffusion of mobile phones and especially WAP[3]-enabled devices has made the transformation of banking applications to mobile devices a logical development in electronic banking" (Laukkanen 2007, p. 789). The only difference is the fact that the banking services can be retrieved on the mobile device on the go, and therefore a consumer's account is as mobile as the consumer her-/himself.

As discussed by many information systems (IS) researchers (Herzberg 2003; Kleijnen et al. 2004; Laukkanen 2007; Laukkanen and Lauronen 2005), it has been proposed that "mobile banking can be considered as one of the most significant technological innovation, which is emerging as a key platform for expanding access to banking transactions via mobile or handheld devices, and operating wireless communication technologies" (as cited in Lin 2011, p. 252).

In the development of mobile banking, banks enable users to access account balances, pay bills, and transfer funds through cell phone or other mobile device, instead of visiting banks and internet banking based on computer (Gu et al. 2009, p. 11605). Summed up, "the term mobile banking usually refers to the following three basic applications: mobile account, mobile brokerage (purchase and sale of securities) and mobile financial information services (account balance, securities deposit account, current stock prices, stock alerts, etc.)" (Lerner 2013, p. 4). According to the latest ING International Survey (2014) on how people in Europe are using mobile banking, Austria counts among the top 5 countries (Turkey, Netherlands, Poland and Spain) with the highest mobile banking usage (43% (2014)) and shows a positive tendency in this regard compared to previous year (see Fig. 7).

Among the Austrians (as of ING International Survey 2013), the most used mobile banking service is checking account balance (see Fig. 8).

In this era of Omni-channel service distribution, in which they are "rather complementary and not mutually exclusive" (Arguedas et al. 2014, p. 167), every channel has its own chance. It is a matter of time which one will conquer the other one(s). Undoubtedly, mBanking is gaining more on importance and attractiveness among the users and banks on the one hand and the researchers and scholars on the other. As discussed by Anckar and D'Incau (2002) and Luarn and Lin (2005) mBanking "provides value for consumers, above other banking channels, through ubiquitous access, time convenience, and mobility" (as cited in Wessels and Drennan 2010, p. 548).

Due to the high penetration rate and acceptance of the smartphones, banks can use their potential and "retain existing banking users in providing a new system (mobile banking) into the existing systems and have an opportunity to convert cell

---

[3]Wireless Application Protocol (WAP)—A standard that defines the way in which Internet communications and other advanced services are provided on wireless mobile devices (NIST 2013, p. 214).

Fig. 7 Do you use mobile banking? EU figures based on the ING International Survey "exploring how people in Europe are using mobile banking and new ways to pay" (ING International Survey 2014) (color figure online)

Fig. 8 Mobile banking—usage purposes (*Source* ING International Survey 2013)

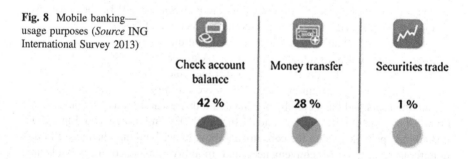

phone users into banking users" (Gu et al. 2009, p. 11605). It is inevitable to state that the "digital technology and rapid-fire changes in customer preferences are threatening to weigh down those full-service banks that limit themselves to products and services that get primarily distributed through physical channels" (i.e., branches) (Accenture 2013a, p. 3).

3.3 Mobile Payments

As it was stated above accounts and payments fall into the group of retail banking services. "Both channels are positively correlated because accounts and payment services often serve as anchor product and there is cross-selling potential" (Dapp 2012, p. 3). In Austria according to figures of OeNB from April 2014, there were 8.2 million transferable overnight deposit accounts, whereas "almost 90% of the Austrian citizens (from the age 15 up) have payment cards" (OeNB 2013, p. 1). Retail payment services are perceived as "stable sources of income, contributing with the fees from payment services (or bank account management) to the non-interest income and helping to attract deposits (and thereby add to interest income)" (Dapp 2012, p. 3).

We live in a consumer society. We buy products, acquire services, and devote ourselves to leisure activities. And for all that it is normally required to pay (the essence of trade[4]), because every trade exchange (of goods or services) has its monetary value. With the advancement of the technologies (as one of the most important triggers according to my opinion), the society strives for a cashless economy. The latest World Payments Report 2013 issued by Capgemini and The Royal Bank of Scotland (RBS) confirms the global trend of cashless payments (see Fig. 9).

The history of money chronicles a "dematerialization from metal money to e-money" (Kumbhar 2013, p. 66). The being of the paper money (initially introduced as paper currency in China in 900 A.D., as depicted by Lerner (2013, p. 3)) and its value were being transferred to plastic card and lately mobile phones (PPP (paper—plastic—phone) evolution). Put it differently, money (same as many other goods and services) were being digitized. And exactly this phenomenon opens opportunities for new participants (other than banks) on the (cashless) payment market.

Among the different types of cashless payments (such as check, remittance and direct debits as the pioneers), ATMs and financial (debit and credit) cards are comprised in this group of payment methods. Financial card market (with the first credit card being introduced in 1958 (according to Lerner (2013, p. 3), more than a half a century ago) besides its high maturity still takes the biggest piece of the noncash market's pie (Capgemini and The Royal Bank of Scotland (RBS) 2013, p. 10). In the course of time, with the commercialization of the Internet (e-Commerce; recently mCommerce as well) not only the way of how we buy has changed, but along with that (mutually dependent) the way of how we pay has also changed. Thus, though slowly but surely (not as anticipated), the cashless market

---

[4]A basic economic concept that involves multiple parties participating in the voluntary negotiation and then the exchange of one's goods and services for desired goods and services that someone else possesses. The advent of money as a medium of exchange has allowed trade to be conducted in a manner that is much simpler and effective compared to earlier forms of trade, such as bartering (*Source* Trade Definition | Investopedia).

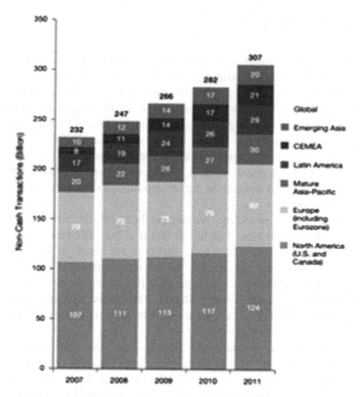

Fig. 9 Number of worldwide noncash transactions by region (Billion), 2007–2011 (as depicted in World Payments Report 2013 (Capgemini and The Royal Bank of Scotland (RBS) 2013, p. 7)) (color figure online)

opens space for new entrants and financial cards (as mostly accepted payment method) will fight on the same front with new competitors—electronic and mobile (e-/m-)payments.

1. Analogous to the fact that mCommerce is "an extension of eCommerce to a wireless mediums" (Tiwari et al. 2007, p. 3), "m-payments are a natural evolution of e-payments" (Kim et al. 2010, p. 310). "E-payments are payments made over the internet, usually in one of these three ways:
2. Making a remote payment card transaction through the internet.
3. Online banking based credit transfers or direct debits under which the payer uses an online banking portal for authentication (currently only operational at domestic level; e.g. Sofortüberweisung or EPS).
4. Payments through e-payment providers, with which the consumer has set up an individual account. Accounts can be funded through 'traditional' payment methods, for example bank transfers or credit card payments" (European Commission 2012, p. 4).

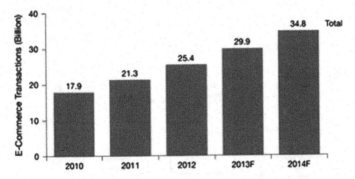

Fig. 10 Number of global e-commerce transactions (Billion), 2010–2014F (as depicted in World Payments Report 2013 (Capgemini and The Royal Bank of Scotland (RBS) 2013, p. 15)

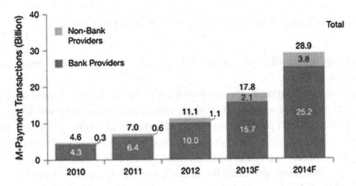

Fig. 11 Number of global m-payments transactions (Billion), 2010–2014F (as depicted in World Payments Report 2013 (Capgemini and The Royal Bank of Scotland (RBS), 2013, p. 15)) (color figure online)

As argued by Ondrus and Pigneur (2006), with the increase in popularity of mCommerce, "m-payment will continue to facilitate secure electronic commercial transactions between organizations or individuals" (as cited in Kim et al. 2010, p. 310). Figures 10 and 11 speak in favor of the new payment methods.

In Fig. 11 two categories have been differentiated—bank and nonbank providers. Exactly this captures the essential difference between mBanking and m-payment (both as subgroups of the MFS), due to the fact that "(m-)payment constitutes an independent business field that does not necessarily involve banks" (Tiwari et al. 2007, p. 3). The category of payment service providers (other than banks) includes payment information or cash processing providers, transaction processing service providers for payment cards and payment terminals (Burger et al. 2009, p. 14; see Fig. 12).

In Fig. 11, two categories have been differentiated—bank and nonbank providers. Exactly this captures the essential difference between mBanking and m-payment (both as subgroups of the MFS), due to the fact that "(m-)payment

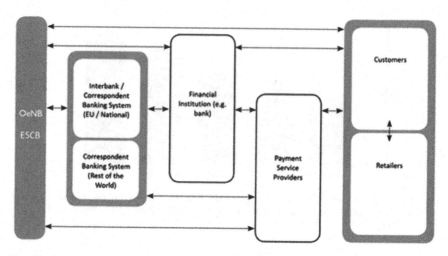

Fig. 12 Payment market participants (as depicted in Burger et al. (2009, p. 14))

constitutes an independent business field that does not necessarily involve banks" (Tiwari et al. 2007, p. 3).

The category of payment service providers (other than banks) includes payment information or cash processing providers, transaction processing service providers for payment cards and payment terminals (Burger et al. 2009, p. 14; see Fig. 12).

Moreover, the definition of m-payments (see below) comprises "mobile payment transactions (remote m-payments) conducted via mobile banking systems" (Mallat 2006, p. 2). This raises the need for making a clear distinction between two concepts of MFS. "Mobile banking services are based on banks' own legacy systems and offered for the banks' own customers" (ibid). "Mobile payments, on the other hand, are offered as a new payment service to a retail market, which is characterized by (1) a multitude of competing providers such as banks and telecom operators, (2) two different and demanding groups of adopters; consumers and merchants, and (3) challenges regarding standardization and compatibility of different payment systems" (ibid).

Same as services, many have tried to define m-payments (Ondrus 2003; Dahlberg et al. 2008; Kim et al. 2010; Kryvinska et al. 2009). Still there is not any commonly accepted definition of mobile payment (as straight-forward as the name suggests). Due to its importance and reputation, the following definition and classification given by the European Commission was chosen:

M-payments are payments for which the payment data and the payment instruction are initiated, transmitted or confirmed via a mobile phone or device. This can apply to online or offline purchases of services, digital or physical goods. Mobile payments can be classified into two main categories (see Fig. 13):

1. Remote m-payments mostly take place through internet/WAP or through premium SMS services which are billed to the payer through the Mobile Network

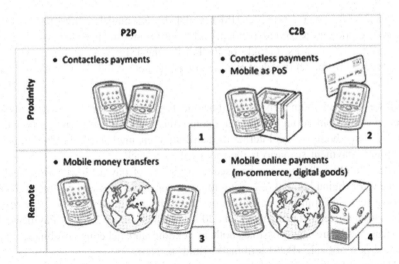

Fig. 13 Mobile payment categories (as depicted in Innopay (2012) report (de Bel and Gaza 2011, p. 14))

Operator (MNO). Most remote m-payments through the Internet are currently based on card payment schemes. Other solutions, based on credit transfers or direct debits, are technically feasible and possibly as secure, efficient and competitive, but seem to have difficulties entering the market.

2. Proximity payments generally take place directly at the point of sale. Using Near Field Communication (NFC), the leading proximity technology at this stage, payments require specifically equipped phones which can be recognised when put near a reader module at the point of sale (e.g. stores, public transport, parking spaces)" (European Commission 2012, p. 5).

The definition and classification of mobile payments show the complex nature of the mobile payments ecosystem, containing various m-payment market participants (including "mobile network operators (MNO's), financial institutions, handset manufacturers or technology providers) providing the payment service through numerous enabling technologies (such as SMS or Unstructured Supplementary Service Data (USSD), NFC, and mobile Internet") depending on "the distance and relation between buyers" (de Bel and Gaza 2011, pp. 16–19). In addition to that, over the last years different viable economic models develop in parallel around the world, i.e.:

- "Bank centric model: a bank is the central node of the model, manages the transactions and distributes the property rights.
- Operator centric model: the same scenario with the operator in the strategic role.
- Collaborative model: financial intermediaries and telephonic operators collaborate in the managing tasks and share cooperatively the proprietary rights.

- Independent service provider (ISP) model: in this model, a third party of confidence operates as an independent and 'neutral' intermediary between financial agents and operators. Google or PayPal are the ISP the most frequently associated to this model (handset manufacturers are not excluded)" (Chaix and Torre 2011, pp. 2, 4).

If we compare both definitions, the one for the e-payments and the one for m-payments (highlighting remote payments), the similarity between them could be noticed, since both use the Internet as distribution channel. The other key player in the mobile payment scenario is the mobile device itself.

Thus, "mobile devices can be used in a variety of payment scenarios, such as payment for digital content (e.g., ring tones, logos, news, music, or games), tickets, parking fees and transport fares, or to access electronic payment services to pay bills and invoices" (Dahlberg et al. 2008; Bashah et al. 2010). "Payments for physical goods are also possible, both at vending and ticketing machines, and at manned point-of-sale (POS) terminals" (ibid, p. 166).

"The proliferation of smartphones, which enable both connection to the Internet and the installation of third-party apps to access new content and services" (Arguedas et al. 2014, p. 175) is opening two horizons for the mBanking; one as a new banking channel (see 3.1) and the other as a direct payment method. Mobile payment is an area with high potential and growth. The emergence of new players in the payment market is shaking the ground and is threatening the banks on their

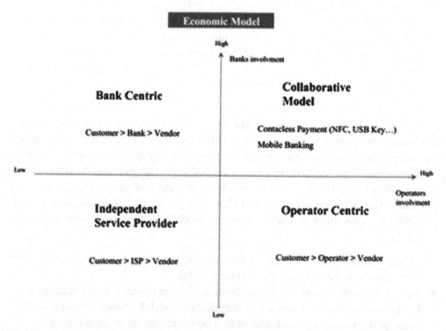

Fig. 14 The four models and the level of implication of partners (as depicted in Chaix and Torre (2011, p. 4))

core financial services. However, one thing is for sure and it is been discussed among many researchers and scholars (Abdullah et al. 2011; Horn and Rudolf 2011; Parry et al. 2011; Keltner et al. 2012): service quality. "Quality in providing payment means quick, reliable and cost-efficient processing of client orders" (Macho et al. 1994, p. 202) (Fig. 14).

In this context the following questions have arisen:

How banks are going to keep the service quality and retain their position on the market?
Are the stakeholders in the banking/payment industry going to remain the same? (change of paradigm)
What are the future prospects of payment industry?
Is mobile banking paving the way for successful mobile payment service offered by the banks?
Are banks waiting to catch the right wave?

4   Alternative Payment Methods

Money is generally accepted means of payment. Lerner (2013, p. 1) refers to money "as a good with a number of special properties and basic functions". "It serves as a means of exchange, value preservation and measurement" (ibid). As it was discussed in the previous section, money undergo a change in its form of existence due to the technology advancement, customers' behavioral shifts and the change of their needs. This has triggered the change of how people make a payment. According to Karnouskos (2004) "payments fall broadly into two categories; payments for purchases and payments of bills/inovices" (as cited in Kim et al. 2010, p. 312). This categorization further on suggests if alternative payments act as a complementary to or compete on the same fronts with already established payment methods. In this section couple of alternative[5] (cashless) payment methods will be presented. Methods, which by their existence, improve the quality of the payment process and establish new innovative ways of making payments and are becoming serious threat to the conventional payment services offered by financial institution.

4.1   Focus—Austria

"The enduringly high and stable intensity of cash usage may simply be a remnant of the past, where cash was the sole means of payment to carry out retail transactions" (von Kalckreuth et al. 2014, p. 1). Nowadays, as previously discussed, we,

---

[5]Alternative to cash payments and in sense of being offered outside the banking industry.

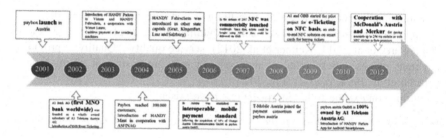

Fig. 15 Paybox timeline (own representation based on paybox—Zahl's mit dem Handy.—M-Commerce und Mobile Payment in Österreich)

the people, have several ways of conducting a payment. We can pay with cash or noncash (with a card or (to a limited extent) with our (smart)phone). According to World Payments Report 2013, Austria counts among the top 10 European noncash payments markets (Capgemini and The Royal Bank of Scotland (RBS), 2013, p. 9). But, compared to the Scandinavian countries, Austria is still considered conservative. Euromonitor International's report (2014a, p. 1) claims that "cash transactions are by far the most common payment method in Austria up to 2013". On the other side, however, as it was already mentioned in Sect. 2.3, Austria counts among the top 10 high rated countries according to the DiBRix.

In Austria there are two examples of alternative payment methods that are worthwhile mentioning; namely paybox and VeroPay. At the same time they are both representatives of the group of m-payments; paybox belonging to remote, while VeroPay to proximity payments. Almost a decade and a half ago, in 2000, "paybox introduced the first mobile service worldwide for a simple, user-friendly and safe payment via a mobile phone" (Punzet 2006, p. 221). paybox's origins come from Germany. One year after its introduction, paybox was launched in Austria (see Fig. 15). "From its outset paybox was designed as an open payment platform and regardless of its ownership structure its service is available for the customers of all Austrian mobile network operators (MNOs)" (ibid). The crucial element in the payment process is the phone number. After entering/specifying the mobile number, the user gets an automatic call (PIN[6] Call) and he/she is being required to enter a 4-digit PIN and press the # key on the keyboard of the phone. Subsequently, the amount for the purchased product or service will be directly debited from the user's bank account (paybox—Zahl's mit dem Handy.—So bezahlen Sie mit paybox 2016).

"Over the years through the cooperation with attractive partners of the domestic economy (such as the municipality of Vienna, ÖBB, ASFINAG, Austrian lotteries, large retail chains etc.), paybox could achieve high market penetration within a few years and with that could expand its offer introducing innovative services" (Punzet 2006, p. 233). Paybox customers could pay in online shops, in stores, in taxi and

---

[6]PIN = Personal Identification Number.

even at the vending machine purchasing parking tickets, tickets for the public transport and for concerts and other events, snacks and drinks, lotto tips, and books using their mobile phones (paybox—Zahl's mit dem Handy.—paybox macht Ihr Handy zur Geldbörse 2016).

In Austria, in 2006, an inter-operable mobile payment standard was established, following the acquisition of 16% of Orange Austria Telecommunication GmbH in paybox austria GmbH (paybox—Zahl's mit dem Handy.—M-Commerce und Mobile Payment in Österreich 2016). Two years later "T-Mobile Austria joined the payment consortium of paybox austria and from that moment, the four largest Austrian mobile operators—mobilkom Austria (currently A1 Telekom Austria AG), ONE (currently Orange Austria Telecommunication GmbH), T-Mobile and tele.ring—rely on paybox as the standard for payment by mobile phone in Austria" (paybox Bank AG | Informationen rund um die paybox Bank AG, die A1 Visa Karte, Paybox und mehr 2016).

There are two crucial milestones in the history of paybox. "After it passed into 100% ownership of A1Telekom Austria AG in 2010, in 2011 paybox Austria GmbH and A1 Bank AG (founded in 2002 as a 100% subsidiary of A1 Telekom Austria) merged into paybox Bank AG" (ibid). The intention of the merger was in order to enable one-stop processing of the financial services and the m-payment services for Austrian mobile operator and other partners (ibid). Thus, according to Chaix and Torre's classification (2011, pp. 2, 4; see 3.3), the business model of paybox Bank AG can be classified as collaborative (financial intermediaries and telephonic operators collaborate in the managing tasks and share cooperatively the proprietary rights).

Paybox austria as a pioneer paved the way for mobile payments in Austria. And better later than never, in September 2012 SECURE PAYMENT TECHNOLOGIES GmbH (founded in 2011) introduced an App, called VeroPay, for mobile payment (VeroPay—Über uns 2016). The App allows payments at POS scanner using Blue Code technology on the smartphone. The Blue Code is actually generated by the App in form of a barcode after entering a PIN code, which is defined by the user itself for accessing the App. The Blue Code does not contain sensitive and personal data. At the POS "the Blue Code is being scanned and then transferred from the supermarket to the Secure Shopping datacenter" (VeroPay— Presse Archiv 1 2016). "Subsequently, the bank transfers the amount from the checking account of the customer to the merchant" (ibid).

VeroPay was initially being offered for customers which have a bank account at Hypo Tirol Bank and buy in the supermarket chain MPREIS, both from the federal province of Tyrol. A year later, after its success at local level, VeroPay was available for customers of any Austrian bank. Following the example of paybox, VeroPay started cooperation with prominent retail chains, such as Billa, Merkur and Hartlauer (VeroPay—Händler 2016). Depending on the provider, a VeroPay user can make purchases of up to 150 euros per day (VeroPay: Bezahl-App aus Tirol startet in ganz Österreich—futurezone.at 2016). Going through the same procedure, VeroPay business model belongs to the group of independent service provider (ISP) model (see 3.3).

Among the other requirements (age limit: over 18 year old and EU citizenship), the users of both m-payment services need to have a valid and an active bank account in Austria. VeroPay and paybox are financial intermediaries and per se are part of the payment system in Austria. "As a rule, payment systems are categorized as follows:

- Large-value payment systems
- Clearing systems
- Correspondent banking arrangements" (Payment Systems—Oesterreichische Nationalbank (OeNB) 2016).

The handling of retail payments counts in the category of clearing systems. "Consumers or companies initiate such retail payments, and banks send files (compilations of payments) to the clearing house, which collects the transactions and, at particular cutoff times, compiles each bank's net settlement position" (Payment Systems—Oesterreichische Nationalbank (OeNB) 2016). "In any event, settlement must be performed by a bank or central bank across whose books the transfers between the participants take place (settlement agent)" (ibid). "In contrast to banks, payment institutions (like VeroPay and paybox) do not have direct access to clearing and settlement systems and are obliged to use the services of a bank to settle payments" (European Commission 2012, p. 10).

4.2 A Transition from Electronic to Mobile

A snapshot of the US market at the end of the 90s: the e-commerce came along with the boom of the Internet. The ubiquitous character of the Internet and thus of the e-commerce, has opened possibilities for "trade between private person" (think of eBay; Feller 2006, p. 237). "The success of the e-commerce is destined by the security, the speed and the ease of use, as the crucial determinants of the systems that support it" (ibid). This new channel of trading required new payment methods that are appropriate for the medium and that need to be adapted to the requirements of the users (ibid). The trade per se has its monetary value and therefore it has to be paid. As discussed by Feller (2006), although credit cards were widely accepted, they were not always an option as a mean of payment in the e-commerce (ibid). "Especially not for many private individuals and small traders, due to the fact that they cannot get from the banks the possibility to directly accept credit cards" (ibid).

The lack of a convenient and an appropriate payment method on the market at that time was recognized by the developers of the PayPal, Peter Thiel and Max Levchin. "They came up with the idea of combining two extremely popular and widely used technologies – the credit card network and the e-mail" (Prashanth 2004, p. 3). "Initially, PayPal was developed as a software for secure money transfer between Palm[7] devices" (Feller 2006, p. 238). Within short time PayPal attracted the attention of prominent investors (Nokia Ventures, Deutsche Bank and Goldman, Sachs & Co.), which financially contributed in the development of PayPal or more precisely in its changeover into an Internet-based payment system (ibid) and in November 1999 was introduced on the market (History—PayPal 2016). The Internet spread at a lighting speed and along with its spread came along the rapid popularity and acceptance of PayPal. Within short period of time, in 2000, PayPal reached 1 million users (ibid). "In 2002 eBay Inc. acquired PayPal, combining the strength of the world's largest online marketplace with the web's leading payment system" (ibid).

Nowadays:

> PayPal make life better for over 152 million active registered accounts by helping people and businesses receive and make payments in more than 100 currencies in 203 markets. As an eBay Inc. (Nasdaq: EBAY) company, PayPal is the faster, safer way to pay and get paid. Giving people simpler ways to send money without sharing financial information, and with the flexibility to pay using their account balances, bank accounts or credit cards, PayPal processes 9.3 million payments every day for its customers (About PayPal 2016).

PayPal is being an established e-payment method. However, if we for a moment go by the fact that mCommerce is "an extension of eCommerce to a wireless mediums" (Tiwari et al. 2007, p. 3), analogously "m-payments are a natural evolution of e-payments" (Kim et al. 2010, p. 310). Thus, "in restructuring its future business, PayPal is guided by two principles: simplicity and mobile first" (Accenture 2014b, p. 6). After introducing on the US market, PayPal should be brought in Europe as well (PayPal Beacon startet Anfang 2014 in den USA—futurezone.at) (Fig. 16).

In its recent study, Accenture (2014a) surveyed retail banking customers in the US and Canada. Among the other findings, many of the interviewees have declared, that they are willing to bank with a nonfinancial institution with which they do business and PayPal found between them (ibid, p. 5).

According to the latest Euromonitor (2014b, p. 2) report "fewer than 10% of internet shoppers pay for their goods using mobile payment schemes or services such as PayPal". Though cultural and lifestyle differences do have an influence on the social habits regarding the acceptance of mobile payments, it is however a very crucial moment in the Internet (and along with that in the mobile) environment is reaching the critical mass—network externalities (as mentioned in Sect. 5.1). My point is to stress the fact which suggests that if PayPal is so widely accepted as a convenient and trustworthy payment method, it could become a serious threat and a direct and nearest competitor to the financial institutions.

---

[7]Personal Digital Assistance (PDA) developed by Palm Inc. (PDA (handheld computer)—Encyclopedia Britannica).

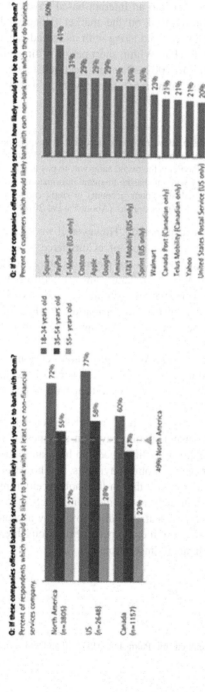

Fig. 16 The likelihood of banking with nonfinancial institutions (US and Canada) (as depicted in Accenture (2014a, p. 5))

4.3 Perspective Near-Field Communications

It is inevitable to accept the fact that nowadays we have the luxury to be at home sitting on the sofa and buy our favorite book, a custom garment or book our holiday. And all of this thanks to the Internet and to the advancement of the technology. Empowered with "the device" of the contemporary history, the smartphone, it has become even easier to purchase goods or services being just a fingertip away of it. "The rapid growth in digital commerce—both online and mobile—is driving wholesale renewal in merchant acquiring technology and operating models" (Accenture 2012, p. 20). On the other side, "as mobile technology becomes more sophisticated, new forms of payment have since emerged within the mobile payment theme" (Tan et al. 2014, p. 292).

In Sect. 3.3 and in the introductory part of this section, different categorization of mobile payments were shown, depending on the distance and relation between buyers, on the enabled technologies and on the purpose of the payment. Regarding this, a new payment method can act as a complementary to or compete on the same fronts with already established payment methods. "The innovation within m-payment has grown rapidly over the last decade with the introduction of various payment methods such as Wireless Application Protocol (WAP), Unstructured Supplementary Service Data, SMS, and General Packet Radio Service (GPRS)" (ibid). In the course of time, "with the advancement in short-range wireless technologies such as Near Field Communication (NFC), Bluetooth, Infrared Data Association (IrDA) and Radio Frequency Identification (RFID)" (Leong et al. 2013, p. 5604) and the looking for a more flexible, more convenient and more user-friendly payment method, brought all the technologies together and integrate into the mobile phones. In this way, it is easier to facilitate the uptake of m-payment due to the fact that they are already "installed in the current customer base" (Ondrus and Pigneur 2007, p. 43) and they can be used promptly by the users themselves.

"Payments via NFC are an increasingly important area of m-payments" (Accenture 2012, p. 10). "Totally unknown just a few years ago, NFC is now increasingly establishing itself as one of the most promising forward-looking technologies for wireless data exchange over short distances" (Lamedschwandner and Bammer 2013, p. 189). "NFC technology enables simple and safe two-way interactions between electronic devices (usually at a distance of 4 cm or less), allowing consumers to perform contactless transactions, access digital content, and connect electronic devices with a single touch" (About the Technology | NFC Forum 2016). A contactless payment transaction "does not require a physical connection between the consumer payment device and the POS terminal" (Pasquet et al. 2008, p. 121). "Contactless payment was firstly developed on credit cards and an important implementation of that type of contactless payment is the PayPass program of VISA and MasterCard" (ibid).

"NFC's 'birthplace' is in Austria (in the town of Gratkorn near Graz) and it is being invented by chip manufacturers NXP Semiconductors and Sony in 2002" (Lamedschwandner and Bammer 2013, p. 190). After several pilot projects, the extensive market introduction of contactless payment in Austria happened mid-2013 (Card Payments—Current-Trends—Oesterreichische Nationalbank (OeNB) 2016) and ever since then several large Austrian banks (in chronological order: Erste Bank und Sparkasse, Volksbank, Raiffeisen Bank, UniCredit Bank Austria and BAWAG (upon customer request)) (Kontaktloses Zahlen: Banken starten NFC Bankomatkarten—Telekom—derStandard.at > Web 2016) issue debit cards in the wake of the general exchange cards with contactless technology. "At the same time began the roll-out of the corresponding terminals at major retail chains" (Card Payments—Current-Trends—Oesterreichische Nationalbank (OeNB) 2016). Exactly this moment, "the infrastructure constraints in terms of handset and acceptance, have kept developments slow" (Pratz et al. 2013, p. 8).

"At the end of 2013 there were approximately three million of these cards were in circulation, and almost the same amount of NFC enabled cards should be issued by the end of 2014" (Kontaktlos bezahlen, kontaktlos stehlen << DiePresse.com 2016). "By the end of 2015, the entire ATM card stock in Austria will be equipped with the new function" (ibid). NFC-enabled card are a fast and convenient way of payment for purchases below certain amount (up to 25 euros) without any authorization requirements (PIN code or card holder's signature), whereas for all other payments exceeding the certain amount an authorization is required (Pasquet et al. 2008, p. 122). According to the latest OeNB's survey about the means of payment in Austria from the third quarter in 2013 (2013, p. 2), it has been shown that 58% from the respondents do not know about the NFC function. The information asymmetry increases with age and the level of education (ibid).

However, the potential of the NFC technology is being recognized by the big players in the payment industry in Austria. On the one side, "in September 2013 companies such as Austria Card, Card Complete, Drei, Erste Bank und Sparkassen, First Data Austria, MasterCard, Nexperts, PayLife Bank, T-Mobile and Visa with joint forces have created the 'Mobile Wallet Initiative Austria'" (Startschuss für nationale NFC-Initiative—futurezone.at 2016). Though coming from different industries, initiative's common goal is to create "an open nationwide standard for NFC mobile wallets" (Austrian companies plan national NFC wallet standard—NFC World 2016). As being reported, with the launch and the distribution by the MNOs of a "special NFC-enabled SIM card" (ibid) the highest security on the mobile phone will be ensured when making contactless payments. On the other side, "domestic banks in Austria want to make more and more use of the NFC enabled cards and thus plan to introduce NFC-ATM for more convenient and faster cash withdrawal" (Banken planen Einführung von NFC-Bankomaten—Innovationen—derStandard.at > Web 2016).

"Making contactless payments via mobile phones or smart cards is widespread in the U.S.A. and in Asia compared to Europe, where it has not been introduced on a large scale" (Card Payments—Current-Trends—Oesterreichische Nationalbank (OeNB) 2016). "The combination between the global popularity of mobile devices and the speed and ease of NFC applications (whether they are used for payments, transit or access control) has the potential to significantly expand the already wide range handsets' capabilities" (de Bel and Gaza 2011, p. 28). "Growing numbers of manufacturers are starting to produce NFC-enabled phones, and major NFC payments propositions—such as Google Wallet—are being introduced" (Accenture 2012, p. 10). The fusion of the ubiquitous character of the mobile phone (exceeding its function of being just a device for making a simple phone call), its wide acceptance and the convenience of the NFC technology making possible offering "additional features, such as loyalty programs, couponing and targeted marketing" (de Bel and Gaza 2011, p. 9), could bring bright future for making payments using the NFC technology.

5 Influential Framework and Factors

As it was discussed in the previous sections, the financial service industry is changing rapidly and new innovations and technologies are constantly being introduced. "Payment services are a special market with strong network effects, specific roles, niches and rules" (Hartmann 2006, p. 8). "It is also highly regulated, since closely related with money and finance" (ibid). "In general, adoption of mobile financial services is context-driven; this means that a 'one size fits all' approach does not work" (de Bel and Gaza 2011, p. 10). Put it differently, mobile payment service providers shall consider many aspects containing "the context" when introducing new service. In context of contingency theory[8] and as suggested by Dahlberg et al. (2008) in this section, three typical contingency factors will be discussed: technological, legal and social. "These contingency factors have significant impacts on the mobile payment services market, but are outside of the influence and control of the market" (Dahlberg et al. 2008, p. 169) itself.

5.1 Enabling Technologies

As a source for profitable growth (Fasnacht 2009, p. 8), innovations are considered as a reasonable response to the fast-changing environment. Another common metric measuring the innovation performance is an increase in customer satisfaction (Efma and Infosys 2013, p. 17). As argued by Edgar Dunn and Company (2007), "companies in the mobile payment business perceive consumer acceptance as the greatest barrier to mobile payment adoption" (as cited in Mallat 2007, p. 414). Accordingly, customer-centricity is on any market participant's agenda.

Technology advancement has a huge influence on our needs, wants, and on our habits (Do et al. 2014). Thus, launching any new product or service on the market

---

[8]Contingency theory suggests that "an organizational outcome is the consequency of a fit or match between two or more factors" (Van de Ven and Drazin 1984). In other words "there is no single best way to manage or organize or make a decision" (Dahlberg et al. 2008, p. 167) and many factor should be taken into consideration.

"demands deep knowledge of individuals to enhance the customer experience" (Capgemini and Efma 2013, p. 20) and to warrant (to a certain extent) its acceptance.

Two crucial elements in the mobile payment process are the mobile device (e.g., smartphone) and the mobile payment enabling technologies. The proliferation of m-payments and their importance in today's society is mainly due to the high penetration rates of mobile (smart)phones (96% worldwide; 82%[9] in Austria) and the customer acceptance. Inductively, all that is possible due to the advancement of the technology and its application (in diverse fields) in our everyday life. M-payments are not a novelty on the payment market (see Sect. 4). But, still their acceptance rate is not at the level at it was anticipated by many.

Many researchers and scholars have invested in proposing common theories and models in order to somehow predict the acceptance of new technologies. A very well-known and the most cited model for predicting IT acceptance is the Technology Acceptance Model (TAM) suggested by Davis (1989), "in which perceived usefulness and perceived ease of use are the main determinants of the attitudes" (as cited in Martins et al. 2014, p. 2). The model "predicts end-user acceptance of information systems within organizations" (Mallat 2007, p. 415). According to Mallat (ibid), the diffusion of innovations theory introduced by Rogers (1995) is more suitable when it comes to m-payments acceptance, since the end-users are consumers. "The theory determines five innovation characteristics that affect adoption: relative advantage, complexity, compatibility, trialability, and observability" (ibid). As argued by Tornatzky and Klein (1982), only three of them (relative advantage, complexity, compatibility) "provide the most consistent explanation for the adoption of information system" (as cited in ibid). Mallat (ibid) expands the model "with constructs of network externalities (Economides 1996; Van Hove 1999), trust and security (Gefan et al. 2003; Jarvenpaa et al. 2000) and situational factors (Lee et al. 2005)" for the purposes of her study.

While the continuous advancement of (mobile) technology per se contains the three above-mentioned constraints, trust and security will always be the main concerns for the consumers (especially in the early stages of a new technology introduction). Dewan and Chen (2005) discussed about "consumers' concerns about the privacy and security of mobile payments, which are commonly related to authentication and confidentiality issues as well as to concerns about secondary use and unauthorized access to payments and user data" (as cited in ibid, p. 417). In mobile payment context, these concerns prevail due to the data sensitivity (e.g., personal financial data, credit card number etc.).

Various technologies, such as SMS or USSD, NFC, and mobile Internet, enable the mobile payment process. Depending on the distance and the relation between buyers (see Fig. 12), different technologies have been used. As stated in the definition of m-payments (see 3.C), remote m-payments mostly take place through

---

[9]According to the latest Mobile Communications Report 2014 from the Mobile Marketing Association Austria (2014, p. 24).

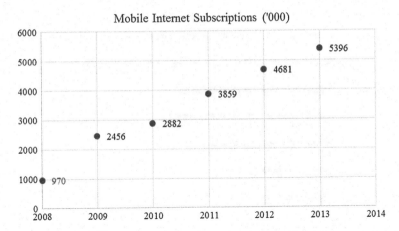

Fig. 17 Mobile Internet subscriptions in Austria ('000) (own representation based on Euromonitor (2014a))

internet/WAP or through premium SMS services which are billed to the payer through the Mobile Network Operator (MNO). SMS as a technology is well known, mature and highly accepted. Over time, the Internet as a technology has changed. If once upon a time surfing the Internet meant sitting in front of the computer and using broadband connection, nowadays we can access the Internet with our smartphones anytime and anywhere we want. Along with the technological advances and the socio-demographic shifts, it has come to an extension to the ubiquitous characteristic of the Internet. Thus, to the "anytime, anywhere" paradigm "on any device" has been added (Fig. 17).

"The Austrian mobile segment is one of the most advanced in Western Europe, with the highest household mobile penetration in the region" (Euromonitor International 2014b, p. 1). "In March 2012, A1 Telekom Austria became the first telecom operator to launch 4G LTE in major urban centers including Vienna, Bregenz and Eisenstadt and in 2013 expanded its 4G services to a number of rural regions, which were not covered either by 3G or 4G networks" (ibid, p. 3). The number of mobile Internet subscriptions shows a positive trend since 2008 according to the latest numbers delivered by Euromonitor (2014a).

The recent report of the Mobile Marketing Association Austria (Mobile Communications Report 2014) gives interesting facts about the users' behavior of mobile phones in Austria. Among the facts it is of essential importance to mention that a huge amount of the interviewees (79.3%, see Fig. 18) surf the Internet at home, even though they probably dispose of another device (such as PC or laptop) with a bigger screen.

Payment services are a special market with strong network effects (Hartmann and Monika 2006, p. 8), "because payment technologies exhibit indirect network externalities" (Economides 1996; Van Hove 1999; as cited in Mallat 2007, p. 417). This applies for both mobile payment categories: remote and proximity payments.

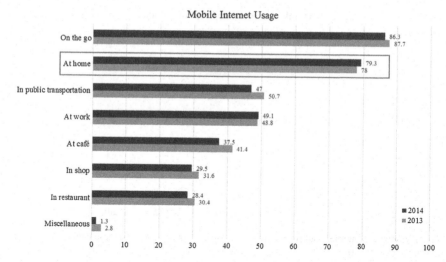

Fig. 18 Mobile Internet usage in Austria (own representation based on Mobile Communications Report 2014 (Mobile Marketing Association Austria 2014, p. 55)) (color figure online)

"A consumer's decision to adopt the network is significantly affected by the amount of merchants using it, since that amount determines the opportunities for consumers to use the new payment service" (ibid). "New consumers adopting the network indirectly increase the value of the network for all consumers because they attract new merchants to join the network" (ibid).

With a high penetration rate of smartphones, their huge acceptance among the consumers, and a technically advanced environment, we can predict a bright future for a successful implementation and growth of mobile payments in Austria.

5.2 Legal Environment Framework

"Economic growth and stability are two very important aspects in the development of every national economy" (Huch 2013, p. 141). And in a world, which is to a large extent dependent on a continuous technological advancements and thus on people's behavioral shifts, "the promotion and the nurturing of these both aspects can be induced by regulatory driven transformation" (ibid). As already discussed, financial sector (with an emphasis on the banking sector) as one of the main contributors to the national GDP is being highly impacted by the IT advancement and lately it is being put under increasing pressure in one of the financial sector's core business segments: accounts and payments. "Payment services, since closely related with money and finance, are highly regulated" (Hartmann 2006, p. 8).

Technology and legal environment are mutually dependent. As technology evolved it has contributed (and it still does) to the "dematerialization from metal money to e-money" (Kumbhar 2013, p. 66). This phenomenon has further on attracted the attention of the policy makers. And as soon as the market is being regulated, the basis for further technical and legal improvements is being established. As argued by Huch (2013, p. 141), a sustainable growth and stability can be also reached by reducing the heterogeneity and establishing less fragmented, but highly standardized market.

"Market observers regard Europe as the market with the greatest potential for m-payments from the year 2015" (Lerner 2013, p. 15). Compared with the other markets, such as US, Japan or even one of the developing markets, "market penetration of m-payments in the EU still has considerable unrealized potential" (European Commission 2012, p. 6). The issue for "the slower market take-up in Europe is being addressed to the highly fragmented mobile payment market" (ibid). But, European legislation does not stay passive in solving this problem. There is a series of directives and acts that regulate the payment services across European Union (EU). In this context, some crucial milestones of the EU legislative are going to be discussed. Each one of these contributes in the establishment of an integrated Single Market for payment services.

The emergence of the Internet has attracted the attention of the policymakers and in 1997 the European Commission with the 97/489/EC (2016): Commission Recommendation has started discussing the increased importance "concerning transactions by electronic payment instruments and in particular the relationship between issuer and holder". Out of the Recommendation were born the both Directives, Directive 2000/28/EC (2016) and Directive 2000/46/EC (2016), dealing with the phenomenon of electronic money ("its issuing and the establishment of a technology-neutral legal framework that harmonizes the prudential supervision of electronic money institutions (EMIs)"). Besides credit institutions, EMI include nonbanks companies for which the issuance of electronic money is the sole business as well as mobile operators (European Commission 2004, p. 5). Later on, alongside with the technology advancement, Directive 2000/46/EC was repealed by the Directive 2009/110/EC (2016). The new E-Money Directive (2009/110/EC) (EMD) on the taking up, "pursuit and prudential supervision of the business of electronic money institutions, aims to:

- enable new, innovative and secure electronic money services to be designed
- provide market access to new companies
- foster real and effective competition between all market participants" (E-money —European Commission 2016).

The last, but the most important milestone of the payment market integration process is the Single European Payment Area (SEPA) project. "The introduction of the euro in 2002 as the single currency triggered the common effort to create a single payment area covering cashless payments as well" (STUZZA—About SEPA 2016). "The SEPA project covers the key retail payment instruments: credit transfers, direct debits and payment cards and is considered as a springboard to creating a competitive and innovative European payments market in two ways"

(European Commission 2012, p. 2). "The first concerns the ever-growing proportion of on-line or internet payments (e-payments) and mobile payments (m-payments)" (ibid). "Secondly, the existing standards and rules developed under SEPA could be re-applied to payment instruments in non-euro currencies, thereby taking the boundaries of a Single Market for payments beyond euro-denominated transactions" (ibid). In order to be in tune with the payment innovations, "the Eurosystem sees a genuine need for secure and efficient online and mobile payment solutions to be offered throughout SEPA" (eSEPA—Oesterreichische Nationalbank (OeNB) 2016). The innovative payment solutions "that are currently available have a purely national focus and eSEPA naturally envisages SEPA-wide innovative solutions" (ibid). eSEPA concept includes innovative payment-related services that are being provided by advanced information and communication technology (e.g., Internet and mobile technology).

The legal foundation for the SEPA is the Directive on Payments Services (PSD). "The PSD aims at establishing a modern and comprehensive set of rules applicable to all payment services in the European Union and seeks to improve competition by opening up payment markets to new entrants, thus fostering greater efficiency and cost-reduction" (Directive on Payment Services (PSD)—European Commission 2016). As stated in SEPA Regulation EC 260/2012 (2016), "the success of SEPA is very important economically and politically". "SEPA is fully in line with the Europe 2020 strategy which aims at a smarter economy in which prosperity results from innovation and from the more efficient use of available resources" (ibid).

Due to the fact that the EU law is a supranational law (European law—Encyclopedia Britannica 2016), Austria's national law (as a member state) is being harmonized in compliance with the EU directives and regulations. "The transposition of the PSD into the Austria's national law (Zahlungsdienstegesetz ZaDiG)" took place in July 2009 (STUZZA—About SEPA 2016). "In March 2013 Regulation No 260/2012 came into effect establishing technical and business requirements for credit transfers and direct debits in euro and stipulated 1st February 2014 as the end date for migration to SEPA credit transfers and SEPA direct debits in the euro area" (ibid). EMD was adopted in December 2010 (E-Geldgesetz 2010).

The mobile payments ecosystem is complex due to the fact that various participants coming from different industries with different interests act on the same market and thus it is of a great importance "where and how each of the participants fit into the ecosystem" (Kemp 2013, p. 176). "The lack of a concrete European framework addressing main concerns, such as technical standards, security, inter-operability, and the cooperation between market participants, risks perpetuating a fragmented m-payments market in Europe" (European Commission 2012, p. 6). "Furthermore for both e- and m-payments, (potential) market participants seem reluctant to invest as long as the legal situation regarding scope for applying collective fee arrangements, such as for payment cards, has not been settled" (ibid). Additionally, "the right legislative framework must be in place to encourage development, especially when we refer to a global payment service" (Karnouskos 2004, p. 55).

5.3 Cultural and Demographic Factors

Human intelligence is defined as a mental quality that consists of the abilities to learn from experience, adapt to new situations, understand and handle abstract concepts, and use knowledge to manipulate one's environment (human intelligence (psychology)—Encyclopedia Britannica 2016). Newell and Simon (1972) define human intelligence as "the adaptive system that can shape them into environment". Thus, our intelligence and reasoning differentiate us humans from the other species and that makes us adaptive and responsive to new circumstances.

"Mobile is a vibrant and evolving industry at the heart of everyday life for a growing proportion of the world's population" (GSMA and A. T. Kearney 2013, p. 4). As stated above (see 3.1), "going 'mobile' can be considered as one of the main global trends of the twenty first century" (Höhler 2012; Kryvinska et al. 2003, 2008a). As the ubiquity of mobile phones grows and as their multifunctional capabilities expand, the appetite of the consumers grows. "Empowered by smartphones and tablets, savvy consumers have come to expect immediacy at their fingertips—they want everything, everywhere, now" (Accenture 2013b, p. 14).

As discussed by Dahlberg et al. (2008, p. 170) there are "distinguishable payment cultures in various countries". In this context, I found two works from Loureiro et al. (2014) and Yang (2007). Though at first impression they deal with issues in two different areas (online banking and mobile payment, respectively), there is something that connects both. Comparing two different markets, it can be concluded that depending on the demography (e.g., technophilia 2016[10]) as well as on the technological environment there are different behavioral (from user perspective) and implementation (from provider perspective) intentions for introducing innovative services.

The mobile-cellular penetration in developing countries is significantly lower than the one in the developed (90 and 121%, respectively; ITU 2014, Bashah et al. 2012a). On the other side, there is a "low penetration of formal financial services" (Capgemini and The Royal Bank of Scotland (RBS), 2013, p. 13). Coupled these things together, inspire the governments in the developing countries (led by Middle East and Africa countries) to force mobile payments in order to "increase bank reach to rural areas" (ibid, p. 29). "The adoption rates of mobile payments in the emerging (developing) markets are far greater than those in most mature (developed) markets" as reported by Accenture (2013b, p. 11). As previously discussed (see 5.B), market penetration of m-payments in the EU still has "considerable unrealized potential" (European Commission 2012, p. 6), but it is considered "as the market with the greatest potential for m-payments from the year 2015" (Lerner 2013, p. 15).

---

[10]Enthusiasm for new technology (technophilia—definition of technophilia by The Free Dictionary).

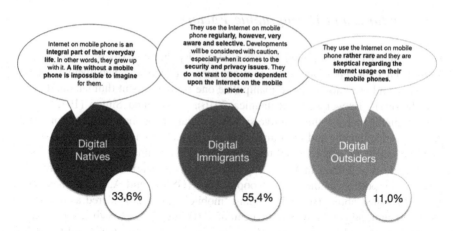

Fig. 19 Types of mobile Internet users—descriptive (as depicted in Mobile Communications Report 2014 (Mobile Marketing Association Austria 2014, p. 49))

Demography and lifestyle characteristics have an impact of the adoption of m-payments (Dahlberg et al. 2008, p. 170). "The growth of smartphones alongside the enhancements of their capabilities makes people more open towards mobile payments" (de Bel and Gaza 2011, p. 26). Generation Y, or often referred to it as Millennials or Digital Natives as well, is the generation born in the late 80s and early 90s. Among the common characteristics of this Generation count their tech-savviness, Internet dependency (24/7) and their mobile lifestyle. It is very often argued that the introduction of new technologies is being dependent of the user's age, due to the familiarity factor. In other words, the sooner the user is being confronted and used to a new technology, the more confident and familiar she or he become in using it.

But, the more the various technologies are becoming indispensable part of our everyday lives; the higher is the notion of their acceptance by everyone (not only the new generation). The Mobile Marketing Association Austria in its latest report classifies the users in three groups, depending on their Internet usage frequency on their mobile phones (see Fig. 19). Subsequently, in Fig. 20 we can see that different age groups are included in every categorization.

Panta rhei, and we, people, are gifted with the ability to adapt and to respond to the new circumstances and face challenges. If we, for a moment (in the context of the paper), regard the current circumstances, we can say that there is an increased familiarity with and usage of mobile technologies. On the other side, new payment methods mature, are becoming widely accepted and bring advantages to the consumers. Under these circumstances, it could be foreseen a bright future for the mobile payments in Austria. But, still, we should never forget the only certain and most probable constant in the whole equation (our environment)—the change.

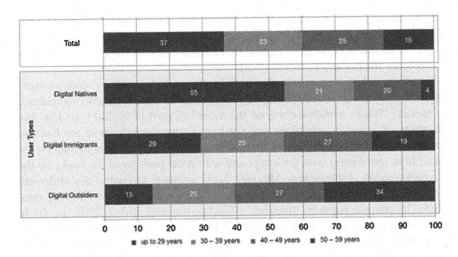

Fig. 20 Types of mobile Internet users—statistically (as depicted in Mobile Communications Report 2014 (Mobile Marketing Association Austria 2014, p. 51))

Fig. 21 Four types of decisions (as depicted in Rosenzweig (2013))

6   Conclusion

In life, whether private or business, we are daily confronted with making decisions. Depending on the situation, the approach of making a decision is surely different. Rosenzweig (2013) suggests four types of decisions varying along two dimensions: "control and performance" (see Fig. 21). Control refers to our ability to reshape the situation when we are making decisions in terms of are we choosing among options already available, or we shape those options and what happens once we have chosen the options (ibid). Performance measures our decision-making differing between our aim to do well, no matter what anyone else does (absolute), or our aim to do better than others (relative) (ibid).

In this paper, it was mainly and heavily discussed how banks' core business segments, payments, and accounts, are being put under pressure due to coincidence of factors. "Banks worldwide are on the move" (Eistert et al. 2013, p. 13). The advances of (mobile) technology and the loosen entry boundaries in the banking industry have opened possibilities for nonfinancial service providers to fight on the same front (payments) with the banks and with it the position of the banks on the payment market is threatened. Although banks continue to control the settlement process, "profit opportunities are shifting to value-added services allowing non-banks to provide payment solutions" (Chakravorti and Kobor 2005, p. 2). In Sect. 3.3 (as argued by Chaix and Torre 2011, pp. 2, 4), we saw that over the last years different viable economic models develop in parallel around the world. In this way, not only banks can have a piece of the payment pie. Offering innovative payment solutions and identifying market segments (not or not properly served by the banks), "these emerging competitors operate and adapt more quickly than banks, creating new tools and services that quickly become the industry standard" (Accenture 2013a, p. 5). MNOs can benefit by creating additional revenue streams, while ISPs—by using their startup position as a first mover (Kryvinska et al. 2011b).

On the other side, banking services and technology are highly correlated. Banking industry has been considered as a rather conservative and resistant to change. It used to be a moderate dynamic market for decades due to the stable industry structure. However, over the last 20 years things have changed. Stable industry structure with defined boundaries turned into "an industry with ambiguous structure and blurred boundaries" (Fasnacht 2009, p. 8), where neither the suppliers' (vast numbers of new market entrants) nor the demanders' action and/or reaction to the new challenges can be easily predictable. Innovation is considered as "the single most important factor driving sustainable top- and bottom-line growth in banking" (Sullivan et al. 2014, p. 35) and as a logical answer to the changing environment in which banks operate. It has been also argued that "companies that fail to innovate and adjust to industry disruptions will miss key opportunities for growth" (Accenture 2013a, p. 5) and survival on the market. Over the years, banks have established new distribution channels for providing their core services (payments and accounts) such as telephone banking, ATMs, Internet, and mobile banking as a way to sustain their competitive advantage and position on the market and as way to improve the service quality (as discussed "quality in providing payment means quick, reliable and cost-efficient processing of client orders" (Macho et al. 1994, p. 202)).

In Sect. 2.3, the innovation timeline introduced by Chakravorti and Kobor (2005, pp. 12–16) was presented. In this sense, banks have three possibilities when making decisions regarding extending their payment service portfolio:

- they can lead the market by heavily investing in new payment innovations and expecting high profit margins and insecurity whether the innovation is going to be accepted or not;
- they can follow and invest in a proven technology (ibid, p. 14), that sooner or later has the chance to become a standard in the industry and needed to be implemented by other players on the market;
- or wait until a new technology succumbs to commoditization and use their (still) superior position and acquire companies providing the new technology and adopt and implement it in their existing service portfolio (big fish eats little fish).

If we take into consideration the four categories of decisions suggested by Rosenzweig (2013), the decisions that banks need to make belong in the upper part of the diagram. Placing competitive bets introduces a competitive dimension in the decision-making process, meaning that decision-maker's success depends on and is determined by the decisions of the others (ibid). "The terms of the game" in such decision-making environment are predetermined and cannot be changed by the "players". If we translate this to what it was discussed in this paper, we can argue the following: The contingency factors discussed in Sect. 5—technological, legal, cultural and demographic environment—have significant impacts on the mobile payment services market, but are outside of the influence and control of the market itself. There are other players that compete with and try to outperform banks in the payment services. Thus, the banks in Austria when making decisions should observe and anticipate the moves of their competitors (in our case paybox and VeroPay) and recognize the right time to grab the chance of introducing their own mobile payment service.

In this context, the model for disruptive technologies introduced by Bower and Christiansen (1995) should also be mentioned, as commonly accepted model in strategic innovation theories. In a nutshell, the model deals with the way of how already established leading companies fail "to stay at the top of their industries when technologies or markets change" (ibid). The main message this model delivers is "catching the right wave"—when it is the right time to let the mainstream business die and focus on doing something new or join the ones that have already introduced it, because "if the corporation does not kill the old-fashioned business itself, competitors will" (ibid). In the payment industry it is not about introducing disruptive innovations. For a long time, we are witnessing a coexistence of different payment methods (cash, financial cards, e- and m-payments) complementary to each other. In the first section, it was also argued, that many firms often "develop and self-provide computerized versions of the services earlier than banks or other types of financial service producers begin to offer them" (Oliveria and von Hippel 2011, p. 806). In the case of VeroPay, there is a strong connection with the Tyrolean bank—Hypo Tirol Bank. Assumably, the application paves the way for extending the bank's service portfolio with its own mobile payment application and test the acceptance among the customers. "Reaching a wide enough initial adopter base of consumers and merchants (a critical mass) is a crucial success factor for m-payments" (Mallat 2006, p. 3), due to the fact that "payment systems exhibit network externalities" (ibid; see 5.A).

With the advancement of the mobile technology new players aggressively enter the payment market. However payment service providers other than banks are still "unable to compete with banks on an equal basis as they are obliged to use the services of a bank to settle payments" (European Commission 2012, p. 10). Additional strategic asset of the banks are the bank accounts. "Bank accounts can be plugged and integrated directly with the payment solutions in order to facilitate the settlement of payment" (Gaur and Ondrus 2012, p. 174). As discussed in Sect. 4, the presented alternative payment method examples were directly connected with the user's bank account. "Bank accounts are specific and cannot be easily replicated by other players in the mobile payment ecosystem" (ibid). Having this privilege and luxury of still holding a unique position in the mobile payment ecosystem, banks should use their strategic assets by sustaining their competitive advantage.

Holding this position and having an ace up their sleeve (controlling and owning the key element in the payment process—accounts), banks should seriously consider their future moves. In this manner, we are moving upwards in the upper right corner of the Rosenzweig's diagram. Managing for strategic success means that the outcome of the decision made can be influenced by the decision-maker her-/himself and with it the rivals can be outperformed. In our case scenario, though the environment remains volatile and out of control, banks can rely on their long banking experience and presence on the market and can "take advantage of their large and diverse customer base and the breadth of the products that they offer" (Chakravorti and Kobor 2005, p. 9). In terms of banking, an increase in customer satisfaction can be achieved by the enhancement of the customer experience through the enhancement of the quality of the provided services and products. The evolution of the mobile channel contributes in the enhancement of the customer experience. This has been confirmed in the Capgemini and Efma's (2013) World Retail Banking Report.

In order to sustain their competitive advantage and enhance service quality and with it the customer experience, banks in Austria should consider providing mobile payment services. The terrain is prepared. Although the cash is still the most preferable means of payment among the Austrians, we saw that there is positive tendency and consumers' willingness to use mobile banking functionalities (see 3. B). Policymakers are creating the laws in favor of cashless payments and big players in Austria (such as Austria Card, Card Complete, Drei, Erste Bank und Sparkassen, First Data Austria, MasterCard, Nexperts, PayLife Bank, T-Mobile and Visa) have recognized the potential of the technologies that enable m-payments. Moreover, the smartphone acceptance (the device through which the payment is conducted) in Austria is high (see 5.A). By going this way, banks should truly consider to extend the horizon of perceiving the smartphones as just another service distribution channel (as Gupta (2013, p. 3) suggests) and properly make use of its potential.

References

97/489/EC (2016) Commission recommendation. http://eur-lex.europa.eu/legal-content/EN/ALL/?uri=CELEX:31997H0489. Retrieved on 01 Aug 2016

Abdullah F, Suhaimi R, Saban G, Hamali J (2011) Bank service quality (BSQ) index: an indicator of service performance. Int J Qual Reliab Manage 28(5):542–555

About PayPal (2016) PayPal. https://www.paypal-media.com/about. Retrieved on 30 July 2016

About the Technology | NFC Forum (2016) http://nfc-forum.org/what-is-nfc/about-the-technology/. Retrieved on 31 July 2016

Accenture (2012) Accenture payment services for financial institutions. Bridging communities, enabling commerce. 2012, 1–26. http://www.accenture.com/SiteCollectionDocuments/PDF/FinancialServices/Accenture-Payment-Services.pdf. Retrieved on 30 July 2016

Accenture (2013a) Banking 2020. As the storm abates, North American banks must chart a new course to capture emerging opportunities, October 2013, 1–15. http://www.accenture.com/SiteCollectionDocuments/PDF/Accenture-Banking-2020-POV.pdf. Retrieved on 01 July 2016

Accenture (2013b) Mobile web watch 2013: the new persuaders. June 2013, 1–15. http://www.accenture.com/SiteCollectionDocuments/PDF/Technology/accenture-mobile-web-watch-2013-survey-new-persuaders.pdf. Retrieved on 21 July 2016

Accenture (2014a) The digital disruption in banking. Demons, demands, and dividends. April 2014, 1–15. http://www.accenture.com/SiteCollectionDocuments/PDF/Accenture-2014-NA-Consumer-Digital-Banking-Survey.pdf. Retrieved on 30 July 2016

Accenture (2014b) Mobile payments. Who is winning the race to a better user experience? February 2014, 1–7. http://www.accenture.com/SiteCollectionDocuments/PDF/Accenture-Fjord-Mobility-Payments.pdf. Retrieved on 30 July 2016

Anyasi FI, Otubu PA (2009) Mobile phone technology in banking system: its economic effect. Res J Inform Technol 1(1):1–5

Arguedas R, Pra I, Reina MD (2014) Mobile banking: challenges and opportunities for the financial sector. In: Liébana-Cabanillas F, Muñoz-Leiva F, Sánchez-Fernández J, Martínez-Fiestas M (eds) Electronic payment systems for competitive advantage in e-commerce. Business Science, Hershey, pp 164–185

Banken planen Einführung von NFC-Bankomaten—Innovationen—derStandard.at > Web (2016). http://derstandard.at/2000003524352/Banken-planen-Einfuehrung-von-NFC-Bankomaten. Retrieved on 01 Aug 2016

Auer L, Kryvinska N, Strauss C (2009) Service-oriented mobility architecture provides highly-configurable wireless services. IEEE, pp 1–1

Austrian companies plan national NFC wallet standard—NFC World (2016). http://www.nfcworld.com/2013/09/18/325959/austrian-companies-plan-national-nfc-wallet-standard/. Retrieved on 01 Aug 2016

Barnes SJ (2002) The mobile commerce value chain: analysis and future developments. Int J Inf Manage 22(2):91–108

Bashah NSK, Kryvinska N, van Thanh D (2010) Service discovery in ubiquitous mobile computing environment. ACM Press, p 763

Bashah NSK, Kryvinska N, van Thanh D (2012a) Novel service discovery techniques for open mobile environments and their business applications. In: Snene M (ed) Exploring services science. Springer, Berlin, pp 186–200

Bashah NSK, Kryvinska N, van Thanh D (2012b) Quality-driven service discovery techniques for open mobile environments and their business applications. J Serv Sci Res 4:71–96. doi:10.1007/s12927-012-0003-4

Becker A, Mladenow A, Kryvinska N, Strauss C (2012a) Aggregated survey of sustainable business models for agile mobile service delivery platforms. J Serv Sci Res 4:97–121. doi:10.1007/s12927-012-0004-3

Becker A, Mladenow A, Kryvinska N, Strauss C (2012b) Evolving taxonomy of business models for mobile service delivery platform. Procedia Comput Sci 10:650–657. doi:10.1016/j.procs. 2012.06.083

Borgioli S, Gouveia AC, Labanca C (2013) Financial stability analysis: insights gained from consolidated banking data for the EU (No. 140). European Central Bank

Bower JL, Christensen CM (1995) Disruptive technologies: catching the wave. Harvard Bus Rev

Burger C, Habacht R, Oppitz M, Pammer M, Pieber C, Radakovits S, Schneeberger D (2009) Zahlungsverkehrsbericht 2009. Oesterreichische Nationalbank, Wien

Capgemini and Efma (2013) World retail banking report. http://www.capgemini.com/resource-file-access/resource/pdf/wrbr_2013_0.pdf. Retrieved on 01 Aug 2016

Capgemini and The Royal Bank of Scotland (RBS) (2013) World payments report (WPR). http://www.capgemini.com/wpr13. Retrieved on 10 July 2016

Card Payments—Current-Trends—Oesterreichische Nationalbank (OeNB) (2016). http://oenb.at/en/Payment-Processing/Card-Payments/Current-Trends.html. Retrieved on 01 Aug 2016

Castro D, Atkinson R, Ezell S (2010) Embracing the self-service economy. Available at SSRN 1590982

Chaix L, Torre D (2011) Four models for mobile payments. University Nice Sophia-Antipolis, JEL Classification: E42, O33, February 2011, 1–25

Chakravorti S, Kobor E (2005) Why invest in payment innovations. J Payment Sys L 1:331

Chen C (2013) Perceived risk, usage frequency of mobile banking services. Manag Serv Qual 23 (5):410–436

Choi SY, Stahl DO, Whinston AB (1997) The economics of electronic commerce. Macmillan Technical Publishing, Indianapolis

D'Agostino A, Serafini R, Ward ME (2006) Sectoral explanations of employment in Europe: the role of services (No. 2257). IZA Discussion Papers

Dahlberg T, Mallat N, Ondrus J, Zmijewska A (2008) Past, present and future of mobile payments research: a literature review. Electron Commer Res Appl 7(2):165–181

Dapp TF (2012) The future of (mobile) payments. New (online) players competing with banks. Deutsche Bank DB Research, 1–32. http://www.dbresearch.com/PROD/DBR_INTERNET_EN-PROD/PROD0000000000298950/The+future+of+%28mobile%29+payments%3A+New+%28online%29+players+competing+with+banks.pdf. Retrieved on 01 July 2016

Dapp TF (2013) Pay wars—attack of the internet giants. Deutsche Bank DB Research, 1–3. http://www.dbresearch.com/PROD/DBR_INTERNET_EN-PROD/PROD0000000000301712/Pay+Wars+%E2%80%93+Attack+of+the+internet+giants.PDF. Retrieved on 01 July 2016

Davis FD (1989) Perceived usefulness, perceived ease of use, and user acceptance of information technology. MIS Q, 319–340

de Bel J, Gaza M (2011) Mobile payments 2012—my mobile, my wallet? Innopay, September 2011, 1–100. http://www.mobiltarca.com/media/documents/mobey-forum-mobile-payments-2012-innopay-2011.pdf. Retrieved on 10 July 2016

Dhaliwal JS, Macintyre M, Glenn P (2011) Understanding services and the customer

Directive 2000/28/EC (2016). http://eur-lex.europa.eu/legal-content/EN/ALL/?uri=CELEX:32000L0028. Retrieved on 01 Aug 2016

Directive 2000/46/EC (2016). http://eur-lex.europa.eu/legal-content/EN/ALL/?uri=CELEX:32000L0046. Retrieved on 01 Aug 2016

Directive 2009/110/EC (2016). http://eur-lex.europa.eu/legal-content/EN/ALL/?uri=CELEX:32009L0110. Retrieved on 01 Aug 2016

Directive on Payment Services (PSD)—European Commission (2016). http://ec.europa.eu/internal_market/payments/framework/index_en.htm. Retrieved on 26 July 2016

Do TV, Hallingby HK, Khuong LH, Kryvinska N (2014) A disruption analysis of mobile communication services using business ecosystem concept. Int J Serv Econ Manage 6:248. doi:10.1504/IJSEM.2014.064299

EBF, International Comparison of Banking Sectors: Data sets for the European Union, euro area, United Kingdom, United States and Japan. (n.d.). http://www.ebf-fbe.eu/publication/

international-comparison-of-banking-sectors-data-sets-for-the-european-union-euro-area-united-kingdom-united-states-and-japan/. Retrieved on 28 May 2016

EC 260/2012 (2016). http://eur-lex.europa.eu/legal-content/EN/ALL/?uri=CELEX:32012R0260. Retrieved on 26 July 2016

ECB, Structure of the euro area economy. (n.d.). https://www.ecb.europa.eu/mopo/eaec/html/index.en.html. Retrieved on 28 May 2016

Efma and Infosys (2013) Innovation in retail banking—simplify technology to innovate. September 2013, 5th annual edition. http://www.infosys.com/finacle/resources/industry-reports/Pages/innovation-retail-banking.aspx. Retrieved on 01 Aug 2016

Eistert T, Gordon F, Deighton J, Ullrich M, Marcu S (2013) Banking in a digital world. A.T. Kearney, October 2013, 1–23. http://www.atkearney.at/documents/10192/3054333/Banking+in+a+Digital+World.pdf/91231b20-788e-41a1-a429-3f926834c2b0. Retrieved on 01 July 2016

E-money—European Commission (2016). http://ec.europa.eu/internal_market/payments/emoney/index_en.htm. Retrieved on 26 July 2016

eSEPA—Oesterreichische Nationalbank (OeNB) (2016). http://oenb.at/en/Payment-Processing/SEPA/eSEPA.html. Retrieved on 26 July 2016

Euromonitor (2014a) Smartphones could lead to more advanced M-payments. Datagraphic. May 2014

Euromonitor (2014b) Consumer lifestyles. attitudes toward payment methods. May 2014

Euromonitor International (2014a) Financial cards and payments in Austria. February 2014

Euromonitor International (2014b) Technology, communications and media: Austria. April 2014

European Commission (2004) Application of the E-money directive to mobile operators. Consultation paper. European Commission, Directorate General Internal Market, Brussels, 1–18. http://ec.europa.eu/internal_market/payments/docs/emoney/2004-05-consultation_en.pdf . Retrieved on 01 Aug 2016

European Commission (2012) Green paper. Towards an integrated European market for card, internet and mobile payments. Brussels, 1–25. http://eur-lex.europa.eu/legal-content/EN/TXT/PDF/?uri=CELEX:52011DC0941&from=EN. Retrieved on 26 July 2016

European law—Encyclopedia Britannica (2016). http://www.britannica.com/EBchecked/topic/1443520/European-law. Retrieved on 26 July 2016

Fasnacht D (2009) Open innovation in the financial services. Springer, Berlin. Oliveira P, von Hippel E (2011) Users as service innovators: the case of banking services. Res Pol 40(6): 806–818

Feller FM (2006) PayPal—Globales Zahlungssystem mit Kompetenz für lokale Zahlungsmärkte. In Handbuch E-Money, E-payment and M-payment. Physica-Verlag, HD, pp 237–247

Fernández-Sabiote E, Román S (2012) Adding clicks to bricks: a study of the consequences on customer loyalty in a service context. Electron Commer Res Appl 11(1):36–48

Gaur A, Ondrus J (2012) The role of banks in the mobile payment ecosystem: a strategic asset perspective. In: Proceedings of the 14th annual international conference on electronic commerce. ACM, pp 171–177

GSMA and A. T. Kearney (2013) The mobile economy 2013. February 2013, 1–98. http://www.gsmamobileeconomy.com/GSMA%20Mobile%20Economy%202013.pdf. Retrieved on 21 July 2016

Gu JC, Lee SC, Suh YH (2009) Determinants of behavioral intention to mobile banking. Expert Syst Appl 36(9):11605–11616

Guedeney H (2012) Private banking in the new era. A.T. Kearney, 1–48. http://www.atkearney.com/documents/10192/640771/2012-07-19+Private+Banking+Report+-+Electronic+%28final%29.pdf/f9d3baf2-96d7-4e92-b85f-583ceb6911b1. Retrieved on 01 July 2016

Gupta S (2013) The mobile banking and payment revolution. Euro Fin Rev, 3–6

Hanzaee KH, Mirvaisi M (2011) Customer orientation of service employees: a case study of Iranian Islamic banking (Based on COSE Model). Int J Mark Stud 3(4):130–145

Hartmann A, Monika E (2006). E-Payments evolution. In: Handbuch E-money, E-payment and M-Payment. Physica-Verlag, HD, pp 7–18

Hilton T, Hughes T (2013) Co-production and self-service: the application of service-dominant logic. J Market Manage 29(7–8):861–881

Hilton T, Hughes T, Little E, Marandi E (2013) Adopting self-service technology to do more with less. J Serv Mark 27(1):3–12

History—PayPal (2016). https://www.paypal-media.com/history. Retrieved on 30 July 2016

Höhler G (2012) Mobile money—the future of the payments market. BearingPoint, 1–55. http://www.bearingpoint.com/en-uk/7-5317/mobile-money-the-future-of-the-payments-market-white-paper/. Retrieved on 01 July 2016

Horn C (2009) Qualitätsmessung im Private Banking: Eine Analyse der Dienstleistungsqualität und deren Auswirkungen (vol 3). BoD–Books on Demand

Horn C, Rudolf M (2011) Service quality in the private banking business. Fin Markets Portfolio Mgmt 25(2):173–195

Hsieh CT (2005) Implementing self-service technology to gain competitive advantages. Commun IIMA 5(1):77–83

Huch S (2013) Die Transformation des europäischen Kartengeschäfts: Auswirkungen der Liberalisierung und Harmonisierung des EU-Zahlungsverkehrs. Springer, Berlin

Human Intelligence (Psychology)—Encyclopedia Britannica (2016). http://www.britannica.com/EBchecked/topic/289766/human-intelligence. Retrieved on 21 July 2016

ING International Survey (2013) Digitales Banking verdrängt Filialen. ING DiBa Austria, September 2013. https://www.ing-diba.at/ueber-ingdiba/presse/pressemeldungen/2013/digitales-banking-verdraengt-filialen. Retrieved on 01 July 2016

ING International Survey (2014) Cash no longer king! Mobile banking still rising. May 2014. http://www.ing.com/Newsroom/All-news/NW/Cash-no-longer-king-Mobile-banking-still-rising.htm. Retrieved on 01 July 2016

Trade Definition | Investopedia (2016). http://www.investopedia.com/terms/t/trade.asp. Retrieved on 10 July 2016

ISIC, United Nations Statistics Division—Classifications Registry (2016) https://unstats.un.org/unsd/cr/registry/regcst.asp?Cl=27. Retrieved on 28 May 2016

ITU (International Telecommunication Union) (2014) The World in 2014—ICT facts and figures. April 2014, 1–8. http://www.itu.int/en/ITU-D/Statistics/Documents/facts/ICTFactsFigures2014-e.pdf. Retrieved on 01 July 2016

Judt E (2006) Zahlungsverkehrsinnovationen im Wandel der Zeit und ihre Vermarktung. In: Handbuch E-money, E-payment and M-payment. Physica-Verlag, HD, pp 19–34

Karnouskos S (2004) Mobile payment: a journey through existing procedures and standardization initiatives. Commun Surv Tutorials IEEE 6(4):44–66

Keltner B, Finegold D, Team LY (2012) Adding value in banking: human resource innovations for service firms. Image

Kemp R (2013) Mobile payments: current and emerging regulatory and contracting issues. Comput Law Secur Rev 29(2):175–179

Kim C, Mirusmonov M, Lee I (2010) An empirical examination of factors influencing the intention to use mobile payment. Comput Hum Behav 26(3):310–322

Kontaktlos bezahlen, kontaktlos stehlen << DiePresse.com (2016). http://diepresse.com/home/meingeld/verbraucher/1514831/Kontaktlos-bezahlen-kontaktlos-stehlen. Retrieved on 01 Aug 2016

Kontaktloses Zahlen: Banken starten NFC Bankomatkarten—Telekom—derStandard.at > Web (2016). http://derstandard.at/1363708001840/Kontaktloses-Zahlen-Banken-starten-NFC-Bankomatkarten. Retrieved on 01 Aug 2016

Kryvinska N, Lepaja S, Nguyen HM (2003) Service and personal mobility in next generation networks. World Scientific, pp 231–234

Kryvinska N, Auer L, Zinterhof P, Strauss C (2008a) Architectural model of enterprise multiservice network maintaining mobility. IEEE, pp 1–22

Kryvinska N, Strauss C, Collini-Nocker B, Zinterhof P (2008b) A scenario of voice services delivery over enterprise W/LAN networked platform. ACM Press, p 332

Kryvinska N, Strauss C, Zinterhof P (2009) Mobility in a multi-location enterprise network, case study: global voice calls placing. IEEE, pp 1–7

Kryvinska N, Strauss C, Auer L (2010a) Next generation applications mobility management with SOA—a scenario-based analysis. IEEE, pp 415–420

Kryvinska N, Strauss C, Collini-Nocker B, Zinterhof P (2010b) A scenario of service-oriented principles adaptation to the telecom providers service delivery platform. IEEE, pp 265–271

Kryvinska N, Strauss C, Collini-Nocker B, Zinterhof P (2011a) Enterprise network maintaining mobility—architectural model of services delivery. Int J Pervasive Comput Communk 7: 114–131

Kryvinska N, Strauss C, Thanh DV, Zinterhof P (2011b) Managing global calls placing in mash-upped enterprise. Int J Pace-Based Situated Comput 1:244

Kumbhar VM (2013) An empirical study on alternative banking and its impact on customers satisfaction: a case study of Public and Private Sector Banks in Satara City, pp 55–92

Lamedschwandner K, Bammer M (2013) NFC-Aktivitäten in Österreich. e & i Elektrotechnik und Informationstechnik 130(7):189–190

Laukkanen T (2007) Internet vs mobile banking: comparing customer value perceptions. Bus Process Manage J 13(6):788–797

Lee MC (2009) Factors influencing the adoption of internet banking: an integration of TAM and TPB with perceived risk and perceived benefit. Electron Commer Res Appl 8(3):130–141

Leong LY, Hew TS, Tan GWH, Ooi KB (2013) Predicting the determinants of the NFC-enabled mobile credit card acceptance: a neural networks approach. Expert Syst Appl 40(14): 5604–5620

Lepaja S, Lila A, Kryvinska N, Nguyen HM (2003) A framework for end-to-end QoS provisioning in mobile internet environment. World Scientific, pp 86–89

Lerner T (2013) Mobile payment. Springer, Berlin

Lin HF (2011) An empirical investigation of mobile banking adoption: the effect of innovation attributes and knowledge-based trust. Int J Inf Manage 31(3):252–260

Lin JSC, Hsieh PL (2011) Assessing the self-service technology encounters: development and validation of SSTQUAL scale. J Retail 87(2):194–206

Loureiro SMC, Kaufmann HR, Rabino S (2014) Intentions to use and recommend to others: an empirical study of online banking practices in Portugal and Austria. Online Inform Rev 38(2): 2–2, 186–208

Lukies A (2012) Separating hype from reality in the world of mobile money. How companies can win the battle against disintermediation. n > genuity, Fall 5(4):39–43. http://www.tsys.com/ Downloads/upload/fall-ngenuity-journal-2012.pdf. Retrieved on 05 June 2016

Macho R, Pater K, Seyffertitz M (1994) Zahlungsverkehrsmanager: bankinterne Abläufe besser verstehen; Ausschöpfung der Kostensenkungspotentiale; Nutzung der Electronic Banking-Angebote. Wirtschaftsverl. Ueberreuter, Wien

Magrath AJ (1986) When marketing services, 4 Ps are not enough. Bus Horiz 29(3):44–50

Mai H (2012) IT in banks: what does it cost? High IT costs call for an eye on efficiency. Deutsche Bank DB Research, 1–6. http://www.dbresearch.com/PROD/DBR_INTERNET_EN-PROD/ PROD0000000000299039/IT+in+banks%3A++What+does+it+cost%3F+High+IT+costs+call +for+an+eye+on+efficiency.PDF. Retrieved on 01 July 2016

Mallat N (2006) Exploring consumer adoption of mobile payments—a qualitative study. In: Proceedings of Helsinki mobility roundtable. Sprouts: Work Papers Inform Syst 6(44):1–16

Mallat N (2007) Exploring consumer adoption of mobile payments—a qualitative study. J Strateg Inf Syst 16(4):413–432

Martins C, Oliveira T, Popovič A (2014) Understanding the internet banking adoption: a unified theory of acceptance and use of technology and perceived risk application. Int J Inf Manage 34(1):1–13

Maurer B (2012) Mobile money: communication, consumption and change in the payments space. J Develop Stud 48(5):589–604

Meuter ML, Ostrom AL, Roundtree RI, Bitner MJ (2000) Self-service technologies: understanding customer satisfaction with technology-based service encounters. J Market 64(3):50–64

Mobile Marketing Association Austria (2014) Mobile communications report 2014. Juni 2014, 1–146. http://www.mmaaustria.at/html/img/pool/Mobile_Communications_Report_2014.pdf. Retrieved on 01 Aug 2016

Newell A, Simon HA (1972) Human problem solving. Englewood Cliffs, NJ: Prentice-Hall, vol 104, No 9 (summary paper)

NIST (2010) Smartphone tool specification. April 2010, 1–8. http://www.cftt.nist.gov/documents/ Smart_Phone_Tool_Specification.pdf. Retrieved on 01 July 2016

NIST (2013) Glossary of key information security terms. May 2013, 1–222. http://nvlpubs.nist. gov/nistpubs/ir/2013/NIST.IR.7298r2.pdf. Retrieved on 01 July 2016

OeNB (2013) Ergebnisse der OeNB Zahlungsmittelumfrage. OeNB-Zahlungsmittelumfrage—3. Quartal 2013, 1–4. http://www.oenb.at/Publikationen/Zahlungsverkehr/Zahlungsmittelumfrage. html. Retrieved on 01 July 2016

Ondrus J (2003) Mobile payments: a tool kit for a better understanding of the market. Universidade de Lausanne

Ondrus J, Pigneur Y (2007) An assessment of NFC for future mobile payment systems. In: International conference on the management of mobile business, 2007. ICMB 2007. IEEE, pp 43–43

Parry G, Newnes L, Huang X (2011) Goods, products and services. In: Service design and delivery. Springer, US, pp 19–29

Pasquet M, Reynaud J, Rosenberger C (2008) Secure payment with NFC mobile phone in the SmartTouch project. In: International symposium on collaborative technologies and systems, 2008. CTS 2008. IEEE, pp 121–126

Paybox Bank AG | Informationen rund um die paybox Bank AG, die A1 Visa Karte, Paybox und mehr (2016). http://www.payboxbank.at/54.htm. Retrieved on 10 July 2016

Paybox—Zahl's mit dem Handy.—paybox macht Ihr Handy zur Geldbörse (2016). http://www. paybox.at/6193/Privat/Bezahlen/Was-ist-paybox. Retrieved on 10 July 2016

Paybox—Zahl's mit dem Handy.—M-Commerce und Mobile Payment in Österreich (2016). http://www.paybox.at/7291/Ueber-uns/Geschichte. Retrieved on 10 July 2016

Payment Systems—Oesterreichische Nationalbank (OeNB) (2016). http://oenb.at/en/Payment-Processing/Payment-Systems.html. Retrieved on 01 July 2016

PayPal Beacon startet Anfang 2014 in den USA—futurezone.at. http://futurezone.at/produkte/ paypal-beacon-startet-anfang-2014-in-den-usa/40.125.747. Retrieved on 30 July 2016

Pikkarainen T, Pikkarainen K, Karjaluoto H, Pahnila S (2004) Consumer acceptance of online banking: an extension of the technology acceptance model. Internet Res 14(3):224–235

Pine BJ, Gilmore JH (1998) Welcome to the experience economy. Harvard Bus Rev 76:97–105

Prashanth K (2004) PayPal.com's business model. ICFAI Center for Management Research (IMCR), 1–19

Pratz A, Bloos JW, Engebretsen O, Gawinecki M (2013) Winning the growth challenge in payments. European payments strategy report. A.T. Kearney, 1–16. http://www.atkearney. com/documents/10192/1448080/Winning+the+Growth+Challenge+in+Payments.pdf/ b9da93a5-9687-419e-b166-0b25daf585ff. Retrieved on 30 July 2016

Punzet J (2006) Paybox Austria—eine M-Payment Erfolgsgeschichte. In: Handbuch E-Money, E-Payment & M-Payment. Physica-Verlag, HD, pp 221–247

Rao RS (2013) Trends, challenges and future functionalities in mobile banking. Int J 1(5):593–602

Rogers EM (1995) Diffusion of innovations, 4th edn. Free Press, New York

Rosenzweig P (2013) What makes strategic decisions different. Harvard Bus Rev, November 2013

Response. In: Service design and delivery. Springer, US, pp 1–18

Paybox—Zahl's mit dem Handy.—So bezahlen Sie mit paybox (2016). https://www.paybox.at/ 6192/Privat/Bezahlen/Wie-bezahlen. Retrieved on 10 July 2016

Startschuss für nationale NFC-Initiative—futurezone.at (2016). http://futurezone.at/b2b/ startschuss-fuer-nationale-nfc-initiative/27.090.230. Retrieved on 01 Aug 2016

Statistik Austria—IKT-Einsatz in Haushalten (2016). http://www.statistik.at/web_de/statistiken/ informationsgesellschaft/ikt-einsatz_in_haushalten/index.html. Retrieved on 01 July 2016

STUZZA—About SEPA (2016). http://www.stuzza.at/12430_EN.htm. Retrieved on 26 July 2016

Sullivan B, Garvey J, Alcocer J, Eldridge A (2014) Retail banking 2020. Evolution or revolution? PWC, 2014, 1–41. http://www.pwc.com/en_GX/gx/banking-capital-markets/banking-2020/assets/pwc-retail-banking-2020-evolution-or-revolution.pdf. Retrieved on 01 July 2016

Tan GWH, Ooi KB, Chong SC, Hew TS (2014) NFC mobile credit card: the next frontier of mobile payment? Telematics Inform 31(2):292–307

Technophilia—definition of technophilia by The Free Dictionary (2016). http://www.thefreedictionary.com/technophilia. Retrieved on 28 July 2016

Tiwari R, Buse S, Herstatt C (2007) Mobile services in banking sector: the role of innovative business solutions in generating competitive advantage. Technology and Innovation Managment Working Paper, 48

Van de Ven AH, Drazin R (1984) The concept of fit in contingency theory (No. SMRC-DP-19) [Abstract]. Minnesota Univ Minneapolis Strategic Management Research Center

Vargo SL, Lusch RF (2004) Evolving to a new dominant logic for marketing. J Market 68(1):1–17

Varshney U, Vetter R (2002) Mobile commerce: framework, applications and networking support. Mobile Netw Appl 7(3):185–198

Varshney U, Vetter RJ, Kalakota R (2000) Mobile commerce: a new frontier. Computer 33(10): 32–38

VeroPay: Bezahl-App aus Tirol startet in ganz Österreich—futurezone.at (2016). http://futurezone.at/b2b/veropay-bezahl-app-aus-tirol-startet-in-ganz-oesterreich/33.188.020. Retrieved on 28 July 2016

VeroPay—Händler (2016). http://veropay.com/mainmenu/akzeptanzstellen.html. Retrieved on 10 July 2016

VeroPay—Presse Archiv 1 (2016). http://veropay.com/submenu/Presse_archiv_1.html. Retrieved on 10 July 2016

VeroPay—Über uns (2016). http://veropay.com/submenu/ueber_uns.html. Retrieved on 10 July 2016

von Kalckreuth U, Schmidt T, Stix H (2014) Choosing and using payment instruments: evidence from German microdata. Empirical Economics 46(3):1019–1055

Wessels L, Drennan J (2010) An investigation of consumer acceptance of M-banking. Int J Bank Market 28(7):547–568

What is GDP and why is it so important? (2016) http://www.investopedia.com/ask/answers/199.asp. Retrieved on 28 May 2016

What is Service? Definition and meaning (2016). http://www.investorwords.com/6664/service.html. Retrieved on 28 May 2016

Wirtschaftskammer Österreich (WKO) (2014). Statistical yearbook 2014. Retrieved on 28 May 2016

Yang Un-Il (2007) Mobile payment providers services—the case of South Korea and Austria. Diplomarbeit. Technische Universität, Wien

Zolnowski A, Weiss C, Bohmann T (2014) Representing service business models with the service business model canvas–the case of a mobile payment service in the retail industry. In: 47th Hawaii international conference on system sciences (HICSS), IEEE, 2014, pp 718–727

Zwass V (1996) Electronic commerce: structures and issues. Int J Electron Commer 3–23

Chapter 6
Organizational Service Management as an Umbrella for Information Business

Jana Hanudelova and Lenka Prochazkova

Abstract In this chapter we intend to address different aspects of service management and business in relation to service science. With the shift from goods to service(s), and from manufacturing to service economy, a need for the new discipline called service science has arisen. The growth of service sector and its relevance for businesses, as we now live in service-based economy, has resulted in the need for many organizations to adjust their everyday operations to enable them to respond more quickly to changing market conditions, and to be more efficient and effective in the application of services. Thus, the main aim of our work is to perform recherché, examination, and systematization of different aspects of service management and business in relation to the service science. A partial goal is to provide the reader with an overview of the need for the discipline called service science to emerge. Another partial goal is to analyze the importance for businesses to create service innovations. And also an objective is to analyze the need for properly educated professionals and tools to apply the principles of service science. While writing this work we combine the study of literature, mostly scientific literature, with our own analytical proposal, and recommendation capabilities.

Keywords Service science · Service management · Business · IT · Innovation

1 Introduction

For the last 100 years there has been a significant shift from the primary and secondary sectors to the tertiary sector in industrialized countries. This sector is mainly characterized by producing services instead of end products.

J. Hanudelova (✉) · L. Prochazkova
Faculty of Management, Comenius University in Bratislava, Bratislava, Slovakia
e-mail: mis@fm.uniba.sk

L. Prochazkova
e-mail: Lenka.Prochazkova@fm.uniba.sk

© Springer Science+Business Media Singapore 2018
N. Kryvinska and M. Gregus (eds.), *Agile Information Business*,
Flexible Systems Management, DOI 10.1007/978-981-10-3358-2_6

For example, agricultural employment today is less than 5% in forward economies, while a century ago, most people worked on farms, although there is enough food even a surplus. This is possible because the productivity of agriculture increased due to the shift of people out of agriculture into knowledge-intensive, specialized industries that support agricultural productivity. This shift of people into knowledge-intensive service industries is also a result of the rise of information and communication technologies that improve automation and connect us to global labor markets (Kryvinska et al. 2014a).

This chapter deals with different aspects of service management and business in relation to the service science. The main aim of it is to perform recherché, examination, and systematization on the different aspects of service management and business in relation to the service science.

The service science emerged as a discipline relatively recently; this chapter enables readers to understand its importance in today's service-based world. It provides the reader with a view on the topic from different authors and their mutual analysis and comparison.

In Sect. 1 we define the term service and we describe the differences between goods and services. In Sect. 2 we describe how the discipline service science emerged, its importance, and concepts giving the views from different authors. Section 3 deals with service management, IT service management, frameworks for aligning IT services with the needs of business, and it also deals with the need for service science professionals. In Sect. 4 we discuss outsourcing as it can provide several benefits for business. Section 5 discusses the business processes, and tools and technologies in this sphere that can enhance and enact business processes. In concluding sections we summarize the results of the research, analyze and compare with works of different authors, and contemplate of further development and research.

1.1   What Is Service?

The term 'service' has many explanations (Kaczor and Kryvinska 2013). Dictionary definitions include:

- an act of helpful activity,
- the supplying or supplier of utilities or commodities, as water, electricity, or gas, required or demanded by the public,
- the organized system of apparatus, appliances, employees, etc., for supplying some accommodation required by the public,
- the supplying or a supplier of public communication and transportation (Dickinson),
- the performance of duties or the duties performed as or by a waiter or servant,

- employment in any duties or work for a person, organization, government, etc.,
- the duty or work of public servants,
- something made or done by a commercial organization for the public benefit and without regard to direct profit (free dictionary) and many others.

For the purpose of this document, we will refer to 'service' as a means of delivering value to customers by facilitating outcomes customers want to achieve without the ownership of specific costs and risks. Service is a type of economic activity that is intangible, is not stored, does not result in ownership and it is consumed at the point of sale. In this type of activity the client and the provider exchange information and adopt differing roles (Katzan 2008a, b). Services are one of the two key components of economics, the other being goods.

There are many types of services that are offered by different organizations, companies, private agencies, or by the government sector. Some of the services are: education, communication, transportation, trade, healthcare and medical services, real state, foodservice, utilities, dispute resolution and prevention services, beauty care, construction, entertainment, and others.

To differentiate between services we can use a classification of services. There are at least five classification's criteria: service process, service nature, service delivery, service availability, and service demand where the major factor is a qualitative concept, "*service nature.*" A qualitative concept consists of service object and results, where the service object retain the roles of the service provider and service client and indicate whether the service is rendered on a person, a possession, or information (Katzan 2008a, b).

1.2 Services Versus Goods

In this subchapter we are going to describe differences between products and services. Probably the most obvious difference is that product is an artifact, something you can see or touch, while a service results in something worthwhile which is a change in a person or possession, not the creation of something (Katzan 2008a, b). In short, products are tangible and services are intangible.

Another difference is that a product is storable and services are not. Any product can be stored, but you cannot save services. When the service is provided, it is done and repeating the service is another service event.

Perishability is another characteristic of services. It means that services are produced and consumed during the same period of time.

Inseparability means the service provider and service consumer are indispensable for service delivery. The service consumer is involved in service delivery from requesting up to consuming the provided benefits and the service provider must immediately generate and provide the service to the requesting consumer.

Inconsistency refers to the characteristic that each service is unique. It can never be exactly repeated at the same point in time, location, conditions, circumstances, resources, and each service is modified for each consumer and situation.

The customer's participation in the service delivery process is also an important characteristic called involvement which means that a customer is able to get the service varied according to his requirements.

The term service and its modern usage has roots in the 1930s' U.S. Department of Commerce's Standard Industrial Classification (SIC) codes where this term referred to a residual category for activities that did not fit into agriculture or manufacturing (Chesbrough and Spohrer 2006). Today, the term 'services' is explained by Ted Hill (1997), an influential scholar, by the following definition: "*A service is a change in the condition of a person or good belonging to some economic unit, brought about as the result of the activity of some other economic entity, with the approval of the first person or economic entity.*"

In our economy services have the leading and significant role. Many business-to-business enterprises, e.g., IBM and GE, business-to-consumer enterprises, such as, Lowe's, Kodak, Apple, and also entire companies have noticed that services are the fastest growing parts of their business.

Now, in most developed countries more than 70% of economic activities are in service sector. Also most of the workforce is employed in services and services are a cornerstone of most business nowadays.

In Fig. 1, we can see the list of most developed countries and their share of the service sector to total GDP. Notice, that China's service sector accounted only 44.6% of GDP in 2012, while the world average represents 63.6%, thus there is a huge space for growth.

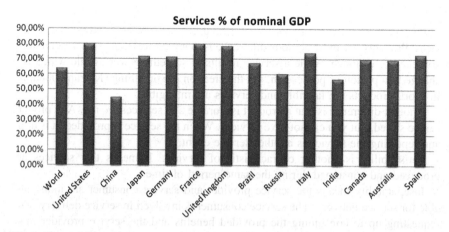

Fig. 1 Share of the service sector to total GDP (*Source* Author own processing according to data gathered from cia.gov)

2   A Short Excursus into Service Science Evolution

For the last 100 years there has been a rise of services and service sector become a large part of economy. Services grow and manufacturing declines and it has had to be dealt with. Services have had to become more productive and efficient. Thus a discipline called service science has been created. *"We have no choice but to make services more science- and technology-based if we are to improve the value delivered from the services sector. This is true of not just IT services, but especially of other services such as health, education and government,"* Robert Morris, vice president for services research at IBM Research.

In September 2004, while starting up the IBM® Research Service Research department, Jim Spohrer was complaining to Henry Chesbrough, a professor of business and innovation at the University of California at Berkeley, about having trouble finding the job candidates who would have the right mix of knowledge, including computer science, engineering, management, and social science. In this conversation, the idea, that there ought to be a new scientific discipline called service science has its roots.

2.1   Service Science in Definitions

The service science is the incipient study of service systems, which are dynamic, cocreating configurations of resources, and they combine organization and human understanding with business and technological understanding. By resources we mean people, technologies, organizations, and shared information (Maglio and Spohrer 2008).

It is an interdisciplinary study, focusing not only on one aspect of service, but on service as a system of interacting parts that include people, technology, and business. It explains many types of service systems and how service systems interact and evolve to cocreate value (Maglio and Spohrer 2008). Service science involves methods and theories from a number of existing disciplines including computer science, cognitive science, economics, organizational behavior, human resources management, marketing, operations research, industrial engineering, psychology, information systems, design, and more (Auer et al. 2011; Gregus and Kryvinska 2015).

The main objective of the service science is to advance ability to design, improve, and scale service systems and to create service innovations (Stoshikj et al. 2016).

According to Maglio and Spohrer (2008) there are four categories of resources, those are transferred and shared within and among service systems in the service science concept. These categories encompass resources with rights, resources as property, physical entities, and socially constructed entities (Kryvinska and Gregus 2014).

2.2 Service System Analysis

Service systems are dynamic configurations of resources, both operant and operand, that can create value with other service systems through shared information (Spohrer et al. 2007), all connected internally and externally to other service systems by value propositions. Service systems interact to cocreate value. Many things, such as people, foundations, corporations, government agencies, cities, nations, families, can be considered as service systems or dynamic configuration of resources. Service systems are *"value-creation networks composed of people, technology, and organizations"* (Maglio et al. 2006, p. 81). We can see relationships and actions among service provider, service client and service target on Fig. 2.

The service system is an open system, which is able to improve the state of other system through applying or sharing its resources and able to improve its own state by acquiring external resources. Atomic service system is a service system that uses no other service systems as resources, such as an individual person (Maglio et al. 2009). Also we can distinguish a service system with one resource and a service system with many resources. A composite service system is formed by combining atomic service systems or other resources. Service systems are regarded as the basic unit of analysis in service science.

Service interactions are interactions of value cocreation that are happening between service systems, but not all service system interactions qualify as service

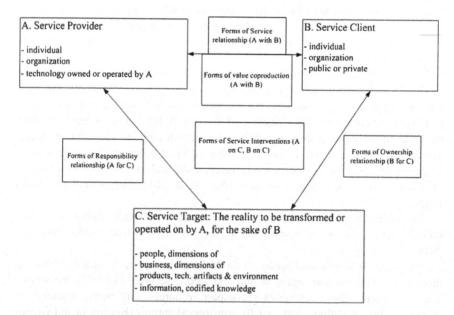

Fig. 2 Relationships and actions among service provider, service client and service target in terms of service systems (*Source* Maglio et al. 2006)

interactions (Maglio et al. 2009). For a service interaction to be a service interaction it must meet three criteria: proposal must be made by one party to another, parties must come to an agreement, and value must be realized by both. Non-service interactions include casual interactions between people and between organizations, informal conversations, inquiries, and they can be welcome or not welcome interactions.

Maglio et al. (2009, p. 400) developed ISPAR (Interact-Serve-Propose-Agree-Realize) framework of service systems interaction episodes, which are *"series of activities jointly undertaken by two service systems."* ISPAR model covers the space of possible interactions between systems, and the total number of such different interactions is ten as shown in Fig. 3.

Different outcomes include: value cocreation is realized, the proposal is not communicated, the proposal is not agreed to, value is not realized and not disputed, value is not realized and disputed but it resolved in OK resolution for interested parties, value is not realized and disputed and it resolved in not OK resolution for interested parties, interaction is not a service interaction but it is welcome, not welcome non-service interaction is not criminal, not welcome non-service interaction is criminal and justice is realized, not welcome non-service interaction is criminal and justice is not realized.

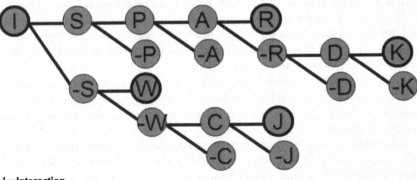

I = Interaction

S = Service interaction

-S = Not a service interaction

P = Proposal communicated

-P = Proposal not communicated

A = Agreement

-A = Agreement not reached

R = Realized value co-creation

-R = Not realized value co-creation
(as judged by one or both service systems, or another interested service system stakeholder)

D = Dispute

- D = Not disputed

K = OK resolution for all interested

-K = Not OK resolution for interested

W = Welcome non-service interaction

-W = Not welcome non-service interaction

C = Criminal (illegal) interaction

-C = Not criminal interaction

J = Justice realized

-J = No justice realized

Fig. 3 ISPAR model (*Source* Maglio et al. 2009)

ISPAR model as proposed by Maglio et al. (2009), enables seeing the world as population of different types of service systems interacting, such as people, government agencies, businesses, and so on. Important mechanisms for improving service systems and learning are disputes and how effectively they are resolved. According to Maglio et al. (2009), this view of the world as people, businesses, and governments as interacting service systems can lead to enhancements in service productivity, regulatory compliance, quality, and sustainable innovations, although service–system abstraction is under development and there are still many abstraction needed for service science (Engelhardt-Nowitzki et al. 2011).

Each service system integrates in three main activities that form a service interaction:

- proposing a value-cocreation interaction to another service system, called proposal;
- agreeing to a proposal, called agreement;
- realizing the proposal, called realization.

There are two particular types of proposals which can be either agreed-to or rejected. First, to cocreate a new instance of service system, second, to cocreate a new type of service system. We also distinguish between formal service systems, which have a set of legal rights and responsibilities, and informal service systems, which may not have them. Formal service systems also depend more on monetary economic and informal service systems hinge more on traditional social systems.

Measurement of work and formal representation in service systems is not an easy task for the services economy. Many businesses are thinking of hiring service scientists who will study and handle service systems, solve problems, and utilize opportunities in creating service innovations.

In the paper Service Systems, Service Scientists, SSME, and Innovation Maglio et al. (2006) illustrated complexity of formally modeling service systems using four examples as service systems that are, education, IT service delivery centers, call centers, and patents.

Education: There is no doubt that education belongs to fundamental concepts in any society. According to Maglio et al. (2006), service scientists can help in handling problems of creating service innovations and enhancing the educational service system by:

- identifying the stakeholders and inform them of the service system's boundaries and of problems and opportunities for the stakeholders to see
- creating a formal model of service system that includes all interactions of stakeholders, organizations, and technologies that intervene in those interactions, and owners and not owners of the perceived problems and opportunities
- estimating the detailed evolution of the system and activities of the stakeholders by which service scientists might be able to envisage new service system that could be implemented to solve problems. In some cases what is needed is financial investment that is new stakeholders, sometimes existing stakeholders need to multitask on new activities. This could help service scientists in solving

problems that are known by connecting new service systems to the problematical sides of the primary service system.

IT service delivery centers: Because there exist complicated relationships between businesses, organizations, and technologies, informal work in IT operations is prevalent in many cases. According to the study of Maglio et al. (2006), activities of informal work represent much time of system administrator. Informal work activities encompass negotiating items and schedules of work, looking for information and expertise, and providing them and usage and sharing tools and practices, they are performed outside formal IT service processes, which make them an inefficient addition. In their study, Maglio et al. (2006) identified couple of opportunities to make IT service delivery more effective, for example, they developed a platform to transform informal activities into activities that are supported (Kryvinska et al. 2014b).

Call centers: The following are the possible service provider views of call centers on how to economize:

- if it is possible, stop the incoming call
- minimize time of the call if it has to be answered
- provide service with the lowest labor cost, if the issue cannot be resolved over the phone

The call center system consists of different stakeholders and each has different objectives:

- customer looking for service provider who is dependable and provides high-quality service that is cost-effective
- the service provider's goal is to reduce cost, increase revenue, maximize profit, and reach on its service-level agreements (SLA) at the same time
- call takers have many aspects that are satisfaction of customers, simple use of tools, success of first call resolution, and controlling volumes of call
- individual account managers take responsibility for particular accounts and targets for the customer satisfaction
- schedulers provide forecast demand that is based on SLA agreements and statistics
- the quality management team controls the call's quality, and constantly improves effectiveness of calls by focusing on the top and bottom 25%

Studying and analyzing all stakeholders, their boundaries and measurements indicate that benefits for the whole system can be in focusing on transformation of the system with appropriate processes, technology, and tools that are working in accordance among all stakeholders. And transformation is done by the combination of process, organization, technology, and tools changes (Maglio et al. 2006; Kryvinska et al. 2015).

Patents: A patent system as a service system also consists of different stakeholders with various goals:

- inventors seeking for simplifying filing patents
- owners of the invention's rights want to keep the cost and cost of conflict resolution on minimum level, simplify the use of the system, and sustain in property of the invention
- consumers that are using the invention as indirect beneficiaries of a system which support innovation in cost-effective manner by accessibility of consumables that are better and cheaper
- nations, that are under jurisdiction of the patenting authority are concerned with a larger gross domestic product and prospering economy
- patent authorities take responsibility for costs, realization, and system's fairness

Analyzing patent as service system will enable improvement in quality and prior-art search, and stimulate economic vitality. Producing and capturing value from innovations and net effect on economy and stakeholders are real measures of success.

2.3 Service Science Establishment

We know that there are two perspectives for the consideration of services (Vargo and Lusch 2008).

One, called goods-dominant logic (G-D), has its roots in work of Smith in 1776. G-D logic views goods as the primary focus of economic exchange and services as intangible units of output. In G-D logic, the economic exchange is centered on products which are embedded with value during the manufacturing process and customer does not participate in this process. Products include tangible (goods) and intangible (services) units of output. G-D logic acknowledges value formed by firm and consumed by customers.

Business-to-business (B2B) marketing represents a sub-discipline, and was created more because the G-D logic mainstream marketing was unable "*to provide a suitable foundation for understanding inter-enterprise exchange phenomena not because of any real and essential difference compared to enterprise-to-individual exchange*" (Vargo and Lusch 2008, p. 255). It refers to business which is performed between companies, rather than between company and individual, called business-to-consumer (B2C), or between company and government, called business-to-government (B2G). In the context of communication, it is a type of communication where employees from different companies communicate with each other.

The other perspective for consideration of services, called service-dominant logic (S-D), consider service as the application of knowledge and skills for the benefit of another party, it is a process of applying resources for the benefit of another, based on the idea that service is the basis of all exchange.

Services are no longer viewed as intangible units of outputs. S-D logic considers service itself, rather than in relation to goods. In S-D logic, value is cocreated with customers; it is not formed by firms themselves. Service-dominant logic is considered as a philosophical foundation of service science, while its basic theoretical construct could be the service system (Maglio and Spohrer 2008). However, traditional G-D logic paradigm remains strong in this foundation of service science, whose influence is considerable in language used to describe and examine phenomenon associated with economic exchange, encompassing that related to service science and service systems (Kryvinska et al. 2013b).

In S-D logic, service is not considered as a substitute for goods. In the shift from goods to services or from goods-dominant logic to service-dominant logic, there is a need for understanding service as a transcending concept to goods. This transcendence constitutes relationship where goods-dominant logic is nested within service-dominant logic, and considers theoretical and conceptual components of G-D logic as relevant, but not as deep and general as those of S-D logic.

For the better developing and formalizing the concept of S-D logic and related phenomenon, a comparison of G-D logic concept and S-D logic concept have been made. In this comparison, five key constructs used in the study of exchange among service systems are compared in G-D logic and S-D logic concepts. S-D logic concepts are described below in Table 1.

Service

Regarding the term 'service,' there have been misinterpretations of S-D logic and some have even expressed concerns about using this term. It stems from the fact that in G-D logic concept the term '*services*' (plural) is used to refer to intangible units of output, whilst S-D logic is using the term '*service*' (singular) which refers to a process of doing something for another party.

S-D logic focuses on service as a process which includes the service beneficiary in the process of serving in which the customer participates. The firm's activity is not just about making goods and services, but the firm is now assisting customers in their own process of value creation.

Table 1 Contrasting G-D logic and S-D Logic concepts (*Source* Vargo, Lusch, and Akaka 2010)

Core construct	G-D Logic concepts	S-D Logic concepts
Service	Goods and services	Serving and experiencing
	Transaction	Relationship and collaboration
Value	Value-added	Value cocreation
	Value-in-exchange	Value-in-context
	Price	Value proposing
System	Supply chain	Value-creation network
	Asymmetric information	Symmetric information flows
Interaction	Promotion/propaganda	Open source communication
	Maximizing behavior	Learning via exchange
Resources	Operand resources	Operant resources
	Resource acquisition	Resourcing

Value

According to Maglio et al. (2009, p. 403), definition of value in service science reads as follows: *"improvement in a system, as judged by the system or the system's ability to fit an environment."* Value in S-D logic concept is no longer consider as something produced and sold and the firm can only propose value. Value is rather something which is cocreated with customers.

System

"A system is a configuration of resources including at least one operant resource, in which the properties and behavior of the configuration is more than the properties and behavior of the individual resources."

In S-D logic concept, we are talking about value-creation networks, which represent a process of applying, integrating, and transforming resources in which multiple actors participate (Vargo et al. 2010). In this value-creation process, all systems involved in the value-creation process are considered as service providers and also service beneficiaries which establishes a symmetric framework. This is opposite of asymmetrical framework in G-D logic, where firms, producers, and value creators were distinguished from customers, consumers, and value destroyers (Vargo et al. 2010). In S-D logic, we are also talking about symmetric flow of information and communication internally and externally and symmetric treatment which means that all parties involved in the process are treated as equals.

From S-D logic view, value creation is happening at various levels of aggregation, within and also among service systems (Vargo and Lusch 2008). Networks are not only linear, vertical or horizontal, but there is an infinite number of ways arranged, and traditional concept of linear supply chain, as it was in G-D logic, is no longer adequate.

Interaction

In S-D logic, relationships and models of exchange are dynamic, interactive, nondeterministic, and nonequilibrium which is opposite to G-D logic concept of exchange.

Collaborative communication indicates interactions not only between firms and customers, but also among employees, shareholders, society, and others who may be involved in service exchange. All the parties involved in collaborative communications are as well considers as partners in value creation (Urikova et al. 2012a).

Learning via exchange process is provided by dynamic interaction and collaborative communication. According to Lusch et al. (2007), in S-D logic concept, actors exchange with other actors to improve their existing conditions, mostly by improving the conditions of others. The process of improving the wellbeing of any service systems requires feedback and learning.

Resources

As we move from a product focus to a service focus, there is also a shift from firm resources thought as operand in G-D logic to operant in S-D logic. Operand resources present tangible resources, resources that need to be acted upon. Operant resources have been identified as intangible, invisible, infinite, and dynamic resources, resources which are able to act upon other operand, and operant, resources, such as knowledge and skills (Vargo et al. 2010). Operant resources are not produced or distributed per se, but they can evolve, transform, multiply.

Lusch et al. (2008) defined resourcing as an activity in which value creation only occurs when a potential resource, which is usually operant, is applied and contributes to a specific bonus. Resourcing involves resource creation, resource integration, and resistance removal.

Vargo et al. (2010) examined the importance of proper use of vocabulary in G-D and S-D logic concept, language used to discuss S-D logic and service science and its clear definitions, the importance of distinguished S-D logic concept and G-D logic concepts. They described the clarification of S-D logic as foundation for service science which brought attention to the G-D logic and its influence. They presented several key constructs associated with S-D logic, their comparison with G-D logic (see Table 1), and they stressed the importance of transparent definitions for the misinterpretations of foundational premises of S-D logic to be revaluated.

According to Lusch et al. (2008), in S-D logic customers are seen as operant resources (unlike the operand resources in G-D logic), and as the cocreator of value with the firm. This cocreation of value implies evolving a dialog between parties included. The dialog aims at development of understanding the point of view of every participant included in cocreation of value. They referred to the dialog not as the one-to-one dialog but rather as many-to-many dialog which is especially possible because of the World Wide Internet, through which stakeholders can engage in dialog and the firm does not have to actively participate (Lusch et al. 2008).

2.4 Cocreation of Value

Value cocreation is one of the key components of service systems, sometimes discussed from the perspective of a production orientation.

In general, two broad conceptualizations of value have been recognized over the years: "*value-in-exchange*" and "*value-in-use*" (Vargo et al. 2008). Although the traditional research primarily focused on value-in-exchange; recently, the attention has refocused on value-in-use, to some extent indirectly through service-marketing and B2B research (Vargo and Akaka 2009).

As I mentioned above, in S-D logic value is cocreated with customers not produced by the firms, which was also stimulated by the increasing emphasis on value-in-use conceptualization.

Value-in-use is also considered as one of the key components of service systems, as it was developed by Prahalad and Ramaswamy in 2000 (and also by Normann and Ramirez in 1993) and adopted and elaborated in service-dominant logic (Vargo et al. 2010).

Vargo and Lusch also appointed the term service ecosystems that are resource-integration networks, loosely coupled systems of service systems. It comes out of the need for more extended venue for value creation in the process where customer participates in value creation than it is in the firm or firm–customer interaction. This leads to a network-within-network concept of relationships which converge on value creation through a web of resource integration (Vargo and Akaka 2009). This implies that every part of value creation is unique to an individual service system and can be evaluated from the perspective of the individual service system only.

As the center point of value creation has been redirected from value-in-exchange to value-in-use, phenomenological and experiential conceptualization of value emphasized, and this has been recognized as value-in-context in service-dominant logic (Vargo et al. 2008). Value-in-context stresses the importance of key variables in the value creation and value determination that are time dimensions, place dimension, and network relationships.

In his article, Gronroos (2011) analyzed implications for value creation and marketing by adopting service logic in business relationships, and how processes marketing and value creation are intertwined with interaction as a clarifying factor. Adopting service logic in business enables creation of value for both customer and supplier. Emphasizing value-in-use (in his article the terms value creation and value-creating process are only used for the creation of value-in-use by customer; the terms value generation and value-generating process are used for more comprehensive process consisting of developing, manufacturing, designing, delivering, firm's front-office and back-office activities, and it also includes customer creation of value-in-use), business aimed at mutual value creation with mediating factor service in the process. His analysis suggests that marketing and value creation are intertwined. Suppliers participating in their customer's value creation are given opportunities to extend their marketing and sales activities into the customer's zone by incorporating activities during interactions of a firm with customers which enables new marketing strategies. A supplier who is directly and actively involved in customer's value creation through value-cocreation activities with them provide interactive marketing. Firms that adopted goods-dominant logic do not have opportunities of interactive marketing (Grönroos 2011).

Cocreation of value emerges from the interactions of many parts. To cocreate value, a provider and a customer must interact directly or indirectly. The customer and the provider have to be able to grant each other access to some set of resources which can be divided into four parts depending on whether they are physical or not physical, and whether they do or do not have rights. Maglio and Spohrer (2013, p. 667) explored value-proposition design as one type of business model innovation using four basic principles of service science. "*A value-proposition can be viewed as a request from one service system entity to others to run a procedure or an algorithm. Business model innovation can be understood as value-proposition design.*" As business model innovation can aim at cost advantage or differentiation, value-proposition design can aim for adaptive advantages without taking proper account of restraints (Maglio and Spohrer 2013). Value-proposition design can provide a systematic search for adaptive advantages using technology to create new offerings, improve an existing offering, or reconfigure ecosystems. In their study

Maglio and Spohrer (2013) described four basic principles of service science, which can bridge various disciplines, such as marketing, engineering, design, operations and management, economics, computing, policy, and social sciences to help describe, understand, and increase cocreation of value through new business model innovation.

3 Service Management

In enterprises, which for our consideration could be educational organizations, businesses or government entities, the roles of service providers and service clients are adapting to provide services to clients and they manage their own services. Because an enterprise can be a provider and a user of services, and the fact that many internal services are managed as businesses, they sometimes deploy into external service providers, there is only a tenuous line of division between management and business (Katzan 2008a, b).

Service management is a set of specialized organizational capabilities for providing value to customers in the form of service. The specialized organizational capabilities include the processes, activities, functions and roles, which are used by service providers to enable them to deliver services to their customers. These capabilities also include the ability to organize and manage knowledge and understand how to facilitate outcomes that create value.

Businesses nowadays have benefited from the application of information and communication technology (ICT). In many organizations, the rise of ICT has enabled them to be more effective and efficient in the application of services, and to respond more quickly to changing market conditions, that leads to revenue growth. The aim of ICT is to create and support information systems that integrate with processes and people to provide Government and Business Services (GBS) (Galup et al. 2007).

According to Katzan (2008a, b), there are three forces operating in the service processes domain. First, information systems refer to the use of ICT enablement that provides revenue growth, efficiency, and effectiveness for traditional, enhanced services, and for conventional business processes. Second, providing IT services to external organizations is in consulting services domain. And third, it is IT Services Management, which refers to the use of ICT to manage information systems and services.

Service provisioning is a process which determines who pays for the service and how the organization of that support is managed. Service lifecycle is a cyclic process in which internal processes of effective service management are moving. Service lifecycle includes:

- service strategy,
- service design,
- service transition,

- service operation,
- and continual service improvement

The service strategy is considered to be the most important element (Katzan 2008a, b). Because conditions are changing and successful service operations are not sustainable over long periods, service strategy is necessary. Service strategy is a long-term plan that is based on customers' needs and it enables the organization to adapt to conditions that are changing. A service document, where service strategy is recorded, should indicate whether certain service strategy is intended for a client or the provider, whether management of services is done internally or outsourced, key collaborators, as well as important service management functions should be included, too.

The service design embraces processes, service architecture, policies, necessary documentation, and it also includes capacity, availability, and security management as well as key responsibilities in the organization.

The service transition is considered as a bridge between service design stage and service operation stage. In this stage services are implemented into production environment. Service transition stage involves also implementation of required changes to existing services if they are needed, building framework, and observance of formal policy for implementation and integration of changes, establishing a supplementary training.

The service operation stage is responsible for managing and delivering services that were established in service design stage. During this phase monitoring of the event is of paramount importance and business value is delivered to the enterprise (Katzan 2008a, b).

Continual service improvement is related to sustaining the value. Important output of this stage, called service reporting, gives the feedback into the previous four stages, and presents the service lifecycle. This stage includes seven steps as it is defined in IT Infrastructure Library (we are going to describe IT Infrastructure Library in another section):

- Step 1: Identifying the strategy for improvement, thus identifying what will be measured
- Step 2: Identifying what can be measured
- Step 3: Gathering and measuring the data
- Step 4: Processing the data
- Step 5: Analyzing the data
- Step 6: Presenting and using the information
- Step 7: Implementing corrective actions

Katzan (2008a, b) named two aspects of service management. One aspect concerns components, which are entities of organization for instantiating services, and it tells about the ability to pass information and tasks between components without obvious direction, in short, choreography of components. Another aspect regards monitoring the components and their attributes, for which a computer database is usually used.

3.1   IT Service Management

IT service management is a set of tasks that deal with monitoring and controlling IT services (Hochstein et al. 2005). It is process-focused, it aligns enterprise IT services with business, and it refers to the implementation and management of quality IT services. According to Katzan (2008a, b, p. 4), IT service management involves *"keeping track of things,"* and he called these *'things'* service elements. Service elements, for example, could be hardware, software, configurations, and so on, those are evident, or service elements such as categorization of services, contractors, outsourced projects, business partners. These service elements are less evident and they mostly concern enterprise operations which are able to offer a challenge.

IT service is a service that is provided to one or more customers by an IT service provider, and it is based on the use of information technology.

It is important to note that the view of IT service management is different from the service client and service provider perspective. There is a mutual denominator between these perspectives that is the set of common issues related to a service lifecycle as they involve strategic planning, business partners and relationships, sourcing, governance, etc. (Kryvinska et al. 2009).

3.2   Information Technology Infrastructure Library (ITIL)

ITIL is a framework developed in the 1980s by the UK's Office of Government Commerce, The Central Computer, and Telecommunications Agency (CCTA), proposing Best Practice in Information and Communication Technology (ICT) Service Management (Potgieter et al. 2004). According to Potgieter et al. (2004), using ITIL framework improves customer satisfaction. In their study they monitored if there exists a direct correlation between using ITIL and customer satisfaction. The methodology of their study was in using SERVQUAL instrument (Zeithaml et al. 1990), which is a widely used instrument by academics and business, to design customer satisfaction surveys. Using the SERVQUAL scale, which has five generic dimensions (tangibles, reliability, responsiveness, assurance, and empathy), they compared customer expectations and their perception of actual performance. They do not focus due to the deployment of ITIL framework. The findings of their study implicate that increased using of ITIL framework results in improvements of customer satisfaction and operational performance.

Many organizations have adopted ITIL framework mainly because it offers a systematic approach to provide and manage information technology services (Cervone 2008). ITIL framework provides many benefits for organizations, such as reducing costs, improving productivity and customer satisfaction, and also can help to provide effective ways to define metrics and measure their outcomes. ITIL's focus is on the service lifecycle that is associated with a project. In digital libraries, ITIL focus is not only on technical issues, as in other best practices and guidelines but it also includes how functions and services within an IT organization align with and add value to the larger organization. Moreover, ITIL focus is not primarily on operational issues. Many stakeholders are part of the team within the ITIL framework, and part of the service implementation function.

According to Cervone (2008), it is important to maintain close cooperation with customers and a little bit of understanding the processes in ITIL by customers for better serving of IT services to the purposes of the organization.

As for the understanding of the ITIL framework, it is not an easy task. Previous methodology of ITIL framework was described in a set of nine books and it was reduced to five books in version 3 which involve: Service Strategy, Service Design, Service Transition, Service Operation, and Continual Service Improvement. This version of ITIL has its added benefit in providing material which is useful for people outside of ITIL instead on focusing solely on technical staff in information technology organizations. Version 3 of ITIL also makes documentations of standardized definitions of processes and IT services whose using can help in reducing the costs and providing end users with results and costs (Cervone 2008).

Information Technology Infrastructure Library is a collection of best practices for Information Technology Service Management (ITSM). ITSM constitutes a manual to the IT service's processes that exist in the organization (Suhairi and Gaol 2013). ITMS focus is on reducing differences between IT language and business unit managers that are using IT services. Thus the alignment between IT and business might be implemented from the beginning of the lifecycle of the information technology.

3.3 Information Technology Service Management (ITSM)

According to Galup et al. (2007) ITSM is "a subset of the Service Science discipline that focuses on IT operations delivery and support. It is a set of processes that detail best practices based on ITIL standards to enable and optimize IT services in order to satisfy business requirements and manage the IT infrastructure both tactically and strategically." In other words, "ITSM provides a framework to align IT operations-related activities and the interactions of IT technical personnel with business customers and users processes" (Galup et al. 2009). It is important to manage IT as it fundamental for organizations to support their businesses, and it is also important to establish and engage best practices processes in order to optimize IT services. Part of ITSM approach is also a common vocabulary, approach for ensuring stability in the environment of information technologies, and a set of principles for management. This is particularly needed in situations such as when the provider of the service is outside the country and operation of the service is complicated due to diverse regulations of government and cultures of the country.

It is a distinction between IT management and ITSM. Whereas IT management is technology-oriented, ITSM approach is process-oriented, and so IT service providers now have to be more careful about the quality of services they provide and the relationships they have with customers. Because of the ITSM's process-focused, it shares common themes with the process improvement movement, such as Total Quality Management, Six Sigma, Business Process Management, and Capability Maturity Model Integration. In Fig. 4 we can see the evolution of ITSM best practice standards that start with the Information Technology Infrastructure Library, and continue with British Standards 15000 and ISO (International Organization for Standards)/IEC 20000 (International Electrotechnical Commision). Other standards, such as COBIT, eTOM, CMMI, etc., that influenced the formation of ISO/IEC are listed at the bottom of Fig. 4.

ITSM and ITIL are often invoked together. The focus of ITSM as subsection of ITIL is on service delivery and service support.

The British standard 15000 was developed by the British Standard Institute in the United Kingdom and ratified in 2000, and it was the world's first standard for ITSM (Galup et al. 2009). BS 150000 represents best practice guidance inherited within Information Technology Infrastructure Library framework, and it also supports other IT service management frameworks. BS 15000 describes a framework through which processes can be established and evaluated. It is based on the ITIL framework and specifies management processes which are mainly operations-oriented.

International Standards Organization/International Electrotechnical Commision 20000, the world's first standard for IT service management, is the successor of BS 15000. ISO/IEC 20000 was first published in December 2005 and revised in 2011 and it is divided into five parts: ISO/IEC 20000-1, ISO/IEC 20000-2, ISO/IEC 20000-3, ISO/IEC 20000-4, and ISO/IEC 20000-5. The 2011 version of ISO/IEC 20000-1 is a formal standard and specifies requirements about design, transition, delivery, and improvement of services to deliver quality services that provide value for service provider and also the customer. It consists of following sections:

- Scope
- Normative references
- Terms and definitions
- Service management system general requirements
- Design and transition of new or changed services
- Service delivery processes

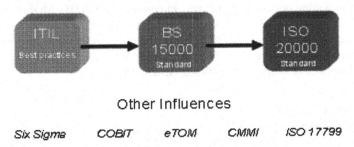

Fig. 4 Evolution of ITSM (*Source* Adapted from Galup et al. 2009)

- Relationship processes
- Resolution processes
- Control processes (Galup et al. 2009)

ISO/IEC 20000-2 describes best practices for service management based on requirements of ISO/IEC 20000-1. ISO/IEC 20000-3 represents guidance on scope definition and applicability of ISO/IEC 20000-1. ISO/IEC 20000-4 represents process reference model. And ISO/IEC 20000-5 constitutes exemplar implementation plan for ISO/IEC 20000-1 (Cots and Fa 2014).

According to Galup et al. (2009) main benefits for businesses that implemented the ITSM are:

- consistence of outsourced customers handling across data centers,
- quality of delivered service is improved,
- functional visibility across data centers is improved,
- financial aspects of IT operations management are improved.

There are some other frameworks using the ITIL as their foundation. PRM-IT that is Process Reference Model for IT from IBM, ITSM Reference Model from Hewlett Packard, and MOF, Microsoft Operating Framework.

The Process Reference Model for IT *"is a powerful management tool for investigating and identifying areas for IT improvement. PRM-IT is an integrated collection of the processes involved in using IT to assist businesses in carrying out many or all of their fundamental purposes"* (Jacob et al. 2008, p. 9) It is an integrated collection of 41 processes across eight categories that are:

- IT governance and management system
- IT customer relationships
- IT direction
- Solution development
- Solution deployment
- IT operational services
- IT resilience
- IT administration (Jacob et al. 2008)

There categories are shown in Fig. 5.

Microsoft Operations Framework (MOF) helps organizations in implementing ITIL by providing operational guidance. In comparison to ITIL, MOF focuses less on governance and more on IT operations, it gives more prescriptive and specific recommendations about changes in improving processes and supporting the changed processes with products from Microsoft. According to Galup et al. (2007), MOF comprises of several foundational elements that are:

- The Process Model
- The Team Model
- The Risk Management Model

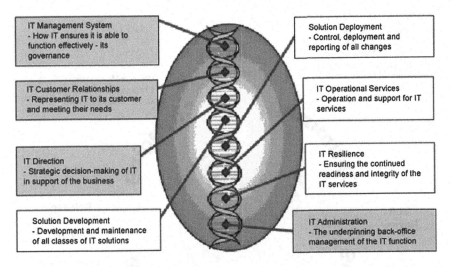

Fig. 5 Process categories of PRM-IT (*Source* http://www.ibm.com/developerworks/rational/library/mar07/hanford/)

MOF Process Model is organized around four quadrants, Changing, Operating, Supporting, Optimizing, and several Service Management Functions, as Fig. 6 shows. MOF Team Model role is to simplify the appearance of team roles and support the MOF Process Model by providing guidelines to organize people into teams or clusters and it describes the key activities for each role cluster.

The MOF Risk Management Model role is to help organizations in managing risk whilst running the businesses.

MOF version 4.0 was updated in April 2008; it encompasses the whole IT lifecycle in terms of three phases and a foundation layer:

- Plan Phase—ensures that there is alignment among businesses, IT objectives, financial management, policy compliance, and reliability
- Deliver Phase—regards envisioning, planning, building, stabilizing, and deployment of requested service
- Operate Phase—handles efficient operation, monitoring, control, and support of deployed services in line with service-level agreement (SLA) goals
- Manage Layer—helps IT professionals in managing governance, risk, and compliance

According to Galup et al. (2009), there are several initiatives to transition ITSM into university pedagogy:

- Service Science, Management, and Engineering (SSME)
- Information Technology Service Management Forum (itSMF)
- Association of Information Systems (AIS)

Service Level Management
Capacity Management
Availability Management
Security Management
Infrastructure Engineering
Financial Management
Workforce Management
Service Continuity Mgmt.

Change
Initiation
Review

Change Management
Configuration Management
Release Management

SLA
Review

Release
Readiness
Review

Service Desk
Incident Management
Problem Management

Operations
Review

Service Monitoring & Control
System Administration
Network Administration
Directory Services Administration
Security Administration
Storage Management
Job Scheduling

Fig. 6 MOF process model quadrants (*Source* http://consultingblogs.emc.com/markwilson/archive/2005/02/10/973.aspx)

3.4 Service Science, Management, and Engineering

SSME is a term that was introduced by IBM originally to describe the service science. SSME is the "application of scientific, management, and engineering disciplines to tasks that one organization (service provider) beneficially performs for and with another (service client). SSME aims to understand how an organization can invest effectively to create service innovations and to realize more predictable outcomes" (Spohrer et al. 2007, p. 71). It is an IBM initiative that emphasizes a program for undergraduates and graduates which focuses on support and development of IT organization's internal operations and government and business services (GBS). Nowadays, more than 450 universities over the world offer some sort of service science program.

Global service economy is growing which has led to a huge increase in people's daily interactions with highly specialized service systems such as education, healthcare, financial, retail, transportation, legal, entertainment, legal, government, retail, communications, professional, and other interactions. People can be customers and also providers in these interactions, thus they can play many roles in many service systems which brings us to the fact, that people are individual service systems themselves (Spohrer and Kwan 2009). Hence it is highly important to understand service systems. The discipline whose aim is to understand and innovate service systems is called Service Science, Management, Engineering, and Design (SSMED).

Service systems, their creation, improvement, understanding, and innovations is an area of interest for service science professionals. Because of innovations of information and communication technologies, and higher level of creation and sharing of specialized knowledge assets, service systems are evolving in costs reduction.

The world nowadays creates the impression of accelerating complexity of economics, technology, society, politics, and environment. People live in this world and constantly interact with each other, business, and societal service systems. Daily service interactions include healthcare, education, retail, transportation, government, business, financial, professional, utilities, energy service, communication service, entertainment service, online self-service websites, and others, which represent a vast and growing investment of time, money, attention, and effort. Customers, providers, government entities, and competitors of innovations are seen as service systems interacting mutually. Business professionals and academics are adopting a new view of people, organizations, and institutions as service systems that are embedded in a world of comprehensive, interacting populations of service systems. Spohrer and Kwan (2008) call this view the service systems worldview. *"The service systems worldview can be used to interpret the world that we live in as a world of (1) interacting service systems, (2) connected by value propositions (to cocreate value), (3) with governance mechanisms (to resolve disputes) among the many stakeholder service systems, (4) that collectively form many dynamic, interlocking service networks"* (Spohrer and Kwan 2008). According to Spohrer and Kwan (2009), in the service systems worldview, people, as individuals are all service systems, all customers, and all providers. As an example, when we are visiting a hairdresser, we play the role of customer entering a provider's service system. But when we call a repairman into our house, he plays the role of service provider entering our service system. Both situations represent people as service systems who are adapting roles in the service system of someone else in order to cocreate value.

Service Science, Management, Engineering, and Design represent an *"interdisciplinary approach to the understanding of service systems and the value propositions and governance mechanisms that connect them into service networks"* (Spohrer and Kwan 2008). Both, the formal service systems study as well as informal service systems study are included:

- the formal system's study comprises: the study of economic markets, formal, written contracts among service systems, and legal system for enforcement of contracts

- as examples of formal service systems we consider legal entities such as people, businesses, government agencies, nations, cities, hospitals, universities, and many others which have rights and responsibilities, can own a property, and are able to make contracts with other legal entities

- the informal system's study includes: the study of relationships among service systems, social systems, cultural norms, beliefs, and political systems to maintain those relationships

  - as examples of informal service systems we consider families, open source communities, and others social or societal systems governed by unwritten cultural and behavioral norms

Service science endeavors to create and understand the service, both formal and informal nature of service, as regards to entities, interactions, and outcomes.

According to Spohrer and Kwan (2009), there are three foundational concepts that underlie the service systems worldview:

- service systems—knowledge-value thinking entities (people, organizations, machines) that are sophisticated enough to get involved in rationally designed service interactions leading to win–win outcomes of value cocreation; entities are able to construct models of possible worlds (past, present and future) that include a model of others as well as themselves; entities can be seen as populations of stakeholders who interact in service worlds
- value propositions—shared capabilities and needs among entities, which model interactions among entities; value propositions are applied to outline the win–win outcomes of value cocreation
- governance mechanisms—shared information among entities, which model interactions among entities; governance mechanisms are applied to outline the collective win, contested decisions, which refers, for example to government authorities and legal processes, risk taking, and learning to enhance performance

And also other concepts are important to understand the service systems nature, which are value, stakeholder perspective, measures, and resources.

SSMED aim to answer to the four fundamental questions:

- Science—Questions of evolution, interaction of service systems, and what service systems are.
- Management—Discusses the questions of investments due to improvements in service systems and service value networks.
- Engineering—Discusses the questions of improvements in scaling of service systems by the invention of new technologies or restitution of already existing ones.
- Design—Discusses the issues of best improvements in experience of people in service systems

3.5   T-Shaped People

As the complex service systems have been more affecting people's everyday lives, and their importance and complexity has been raising, wide range of knowledge was needed to understand service systems (Urikova et al. 2012b). There was a need for a service science specialist with deep knowledge of service systems and expertise from many existing disciplines. In their article, Spohrer and Kwan (2009) reviewed disciplinary areas that support directly the rational design of complex service systems, and are organized as follows:

- Evolution: Learning from history of interactions—this includes economic and legal, social and political, knowledge and linguistic
- Measures: Four basic roles from stakeholder perspective—customer and quality, provider and productivity, authority and compliance, and competitor and innovation
- Resources: Four logical categories—people (physical and can contract), technology (physical and cannot contract), information (not physical and cannot contract), organization (not physical and can contract)
- Strategy: Learning from possible future worlds—management and strategy, and finance and investment

Students attending disciplinary areas indicated above might add to their studies "*deep disciplinary knowledge interactional expertise in SSMED-related disciplines*" (Spohrer and Kwan 2008).

According to Spohrer and Kwan (2009), T-shaped professionals are created by interactional expertise in the SSMED-related disciplines. Interactional expertise means that those who have adopted this expertise are able to communicate effectively with academic discipline's specialists, who are able to understand problems and proposed solutions, but they are not able to solve the problems. T-shaped people reflect the depth of expertise in at least one area but a horizontal breadth of knowledge in a broad set of related areas, which allows them to solve problems with colleagues across disciplines (see Fig. 7).

Spohrer and Kwan (2009) also indicated that T-shaped professionals can better learn and adapt to the changing needs of business.

Hansen and Nohria (2004) in their article described how managers can promote collaboration. They indicated that the T-shaped role of managers tends to bring satisfying results in prioritizing and delegating to subordinates. Managers who adopted the T-shaped role have primary responsibility in delivering results for their own business unit (that is the vertical part of the T), and as the horizontal part of the T, manager's responsibility is to seek help and aid others (Hansen and Nohria 2004).

Bullen et al. (2009) in their article examined the workforce trends in IT provider companies. Their results indicate that more than technical capabilities, provider firms also look for client-facing capabilities, knowledge of business domain, and project management. Their implications for IS curriculum and hiring suggest that

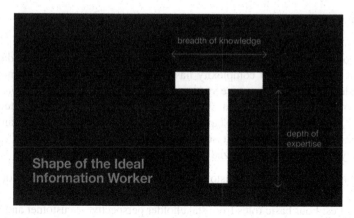

Fig. 7 T-shaped people (*Source* http://www-03.ibm.com/ibm/history/ibm100/us/en/icons/servicescience/)

students will need to be trained in technical and also nontechnical skills. People who adopted T-shaped role have broad general skills and deep technical skills, and according to the data in the study of Bullen et al. (2009) highly valued people would also have broad technical skills and deep business skills (Bullen et al. 2009; Stoshikj et al. 2014).

Water nowadays plays a central role in many sectors. As a consequence of population growth and our climate, water supply is increasingly limited. Thus the change is increasingly important in sectors where water plays a key role. There is a need for change in terms that essential services, such as water, food, energy, are managed and delivered in a more effective and integrated way. McIntosh and Taylor (2013) in their article developed a concept of the T-shaped water professional. It provides a framework for the design of curricula for educational programs in order to raise the capacity of water professionals who would stimulate and control processes of innovation and change which, in twenty-first century, constitutes an increasingly key topic for water professionals (Mcintosh and Taylor 2013). T-shaped water professionals, in order to effectively lead teams, need to have an in-depth knowledge of a particular discipline and broader, general knowledge to recognize opportunities for idea generating, integration, and collaboration.

4 Outsourcing

"Outsourcing is the transfer of the ownership of a business process to a supplier, which includes management and day-to-day execution of that function" (Katzan 2008a, b, p. 9). Business processes such as information technology, customer support, accounting, call center operations, and human resources are mainly outsourced, but core business competencies are usually not outsourced. Also a company that focuses on information technology can provide consulting as well as outsourcing as business services. The difference is that with consulting the company tells the customer how to do things, and with outsourcing the company does it for the customer. The objective of outsourcing can be reducing costs, benefiting from special capabilities of provider firm, or focusing firm's business on more profitable activities. Usually, outsourcing is associated with offshoring. It means the relocation of a business process from one country to another, when the other country can provide business activities in less expensive manner (Katzan 2008a, b). When a company establishes business agreement in the transfer of the whole business function to another company in another country, this company is both offshoring and outsourcing.

There have been studies that have been dealing with knowledge sharing through outsourcing partnership and its effect on the success of outsourcing. Knowledge sharing was defined as *"activities of transferring or disseminating knowledge from one person, group, or organization to another"* (Lee 2001, p. 324). Between service provider and service receiver knowledge sharing arises, which is one of the most eminent motives for establishing the partnership based on mutual trust. Knowledge sharing between different organizations, however, is not easily transferred when such organizations have different cultures, goals, and structures. In that case, for successful outsourcing, both the service provider and receiver should set common goals and vision for that partnership, and this was termed partnership quality (Lee 2001). Ability to learn and acquire requisite knowledge from other organizations is another important factor for successful outsourcing partnership. An organization should be able to exploit the external knowledge, recognize the value of new information, assimilate it, and apply it for an organization capability. According to Lee (2001) and his study, knowledge sharing is highly associated with the level of achievement of outsourcing benefits. Also the service receiver should have the ability to absorb, integrate, and leverage the needed knowledge for the higher effect on such benefits, and his ability to do so is also important for effective knowledge sharing. Moreover, his study indicates that the partnership quality has a significant role in knowledge sharing and outsourcing success as a mediator between them. His study also showed that for successful outsourcing explicit knowledge sharing is more effective than the implicit knowledge sharing. Implicit knowledge sharing is also a significant predictor in successful outsourcing but explicit knowledge sharing was found to be easier to understand and share with other organizations.

Grover et al. (1996, p. 93) say that the success of outsourcing can be evaluated in terms of three benefits, which *"need to be weighed against the increase in transactional costs, decrease in flexibility, and conflicting objectives of the outsourcer vis-a-vis the firm."* These benefits are: strategic benefits, economic benefits, and technological benefits. Strategic benefits mean that the firm is able to focus on its core business, where through outsourcing arrangements routine IT activities can be left outsourced and the firm can focus on the strategic use of IT. Economic activities mean that the firm is able to make use of expertise and economies of scale in human and technological resources of the service provider and is also able to make unequivocal contractual arrangements for better management of the cost structure. And third, technological benefits mean that the firm is able to respond quickly to changes in IT, adapt to these changes, and avoid the technological obsolescence.

In the study they explored firms that outsource IT functions, if they are successful and which variables might influence their success. Their study showed a positive relationship between IT outsourcing and the level of achievement of benefits. A long-term interactive relationship that is based on communication, trust, satisfaction, and cooperation has also the significant effect on outsourcing success. The study further implies that the establishment of elements of partnership and service quality are important factors for successful outsourcing. However, the study also discusses difficulties in maintaining partnerships and that elements such as trust, communication, satisfaction, and cooperation might be difficult to build and sustain. Increasing service quality can improve firm's chances for success, especially in transaction that are asset-specific, such as end-user support or systems planning management (Grover et al. 1996).

Implementing internal or external outsourcing within an organization can also lead to concerns over management control and operational flexibility and a syndrome called "*tail wagging the dog*" resulting in bringing major services, e.g. IT outsourcing, back into the parent organization as proposed by Katzan (2008a, b).

4.1 Opensourcing

Opensourcing is a global sourcing strategy. Open source software development model is similar to outsourcing and offshoring, as it also offers many advantages such as reducing salary costs, reducing cycle time, cross-site modularization of development work, accessing the larger pool of skilled developers, innovation and sharing best practice, and closer proximity to customers (Agerfalk and Fitzgerald 2008). The open-sourcing phenomenon has been characterized as "the *use of the open source software development model as a global sourcing strategy for an organization's software development process*" (Agerfalk and Fitzgerald 2008, p. 386). The open source software development model enables firms to subcontract activities related to development to another party, which is similar to outsourcing.

Research on open source has focused on the supply side of the relationship, on detection of the development process and projects and their characteristics, and not on customer side as the offshore outsourcing tends to be (Agerfalk and Fitzgerald 2008).

4.2 Psychological Contract Theory

A psychological contract theory (PCT) has been used for the better view of "*mutual relationships between managers of offshore outsourcing customer organizations and members of their global OSS community*" (Agerfalk and Fitzgerald 2008, p. 386). In the outsourcing point of view, three implications of the psychological contract are mostly relevant: First, it is important in obligations in a social context because of its mutuality and reciprocity that are critical to the OSS development model and its success. Second, psychological contracts are different from legal contracts, because they embrace written and also unwritten terms. Developers contributing to OSS development projects are expected to be familiar with both written and unwritten rules and norms. The third factor is related to motivation of developers to contribute to OSS development projects. The PCT's focus is on individual's expectations, it promotes individual level of analysis because whether contribution of the developer is eminent or not depends mainly on the level of individual.

For the outsourcing to be successful, customers must also contribute. According to Koh et al. (2004) there are four particular commitments:

- accurately describe and explain the requirements of the services covered by outsourcing,
- pay on time to suppliers, no unnecessary withheld payments,
- attending project meetings and discussions, and active control of the project progress,
- to ensure that senior management promotes strong leadership, support, and commitment to the outsourcing project by project ownership.

For the successful outsourcing, the supplier must also take responsibility for these five obligations (Koh et al. 2004):

- structures of authority must be clear, so that all parties involved know what their roles and responsibilities are,
- solving problems or completing the job with minimal customer involvement,
- ensuring that high-quality staff is working on the project and prevent staff turnover during the project,
- building and maintaining effective interorganizational teams where relationships between all parties involved in the project are good working,
- active transfer of knowledge in educating customers because their role in OSS is significant as they can contribute to testing, documentation, etc.

In their study, using interviews, they identified customer and community obligations in the context of outsourcing. These obligations are summarized in Table 2.

Then they further explored these obligations by means of survey between community and customer representatives with outsourcing experience, where respondents were asked to consider an opensourcing project that they have participated in, and on scale estimate to what extent these obligations were met and to what extent the project was considered as successful. The results of their study indicate that opensourcing success and fulfillment of certain community and customer obligations are significantly associated. Also, these obligations are "*partly symmetrical and complementary*" and so there is a tension between community and

Table 2 Summary of refined customer and OSS community in opensourcing (*Source* Agerfalk and Fitzgerald 2008, p. 397)

Customer obligations	Community obligations
Achieving consensus on development roadmap (vision)	Clear and democratic authority structure and process transparency
Project ownership	Responsible and innovative attitude
Marketing project to increase visibility	Creating a sustainable ecosystem
Transparency and close project monitoring	
Creating a sustainable ecosystem	

customer obligations that need to be managed jointly, but the realization needs to be done differently by the community and the customer for the open-sourcing to be successful (Agerfalk and Fitzgerald 2008).

The contribution of this study is also in adopting the perspective of both community and customer, while previous studies have mostly focused on single perspective of the customer or the supplier.

5   Business Process Management (BMP)

The idea of process thinking came out in the late eighties. "Process thinking should enhance the service to clients by extending beyond ad hoc, local decision-making that pays little attention to the effectiveness across the process" (Reijers 2003, p. 1) The presence of business processes in organizing and managing work nowadays is related to specialization and its development across different periods of time. The higher degree of specialism was in raise during the Industrial Revolution. Over the nineteenth and twentieth century the dominant organization of work was in creating functional departments within the company for better differentiating responsibilities among managers.

Nowadays, the emphasis is on the process, particularly the practical interest is in business processes. Managing business processes, such as an insurance company, work in a bank, call centers, and many others, is a difficult task, and also scientific interest has focused on the area of business processes. Business Process Management is a term referring to the field of study between Management and Computing Science which involves business processes. According to Reijers (2003, p. 9), we can consider Business Process Management "as the field of designing and controlling business processes." This is constructed using the distinction between two fundamental aspects; build time aspect, which focuses on the creation of a business process, and run time aspect, which focuses on execution of a business process.

Business process has been defined as "a collection of activities that takes one or more kinds of input and creates an output that is of value to the customer" (Hammer and Champy's 1993, p. 53). The output of a business process is called a product, it is either goods or service. A business process which delivers service is also often called as a workflow. The main reason to consider business processes, and all related parts is to support a decision of some form. There are three criteria that can be used to differentiate between decision-making levels within an organization:

- frequency of decision-making
- the range of the decision to be taken
- discuss the issue whether it is dynamic or static state of the process that is more relevant

The first dimension of the business process management definition stated above, the design of business processes is traditionally viewed as a strategic issue. Examples of strategic decisions that fall within the scope of BMP are decisions on finances, logistics, quality, decisions of a restructuring of the business processes, and other. Strategic decisions that are not relevant from a BMP view are for example, decisions whether products should be continued or abolished from a product lifecycle, decisions of which markets should be abandoned and which should be conquered, questions of preferred corporate image, or decisions of funding the organization.

The control of business processes, that is the second dimension of the BMP definition stated above, refer to the decisions taken in real-time, and tactical and operational levels of decision-making. Examples of the activities that fall within this dimension of the BMP are planning of production, assignment of resources, budgeting, and handling the exception.

According to Reijers (2003), elementary parts of the Business Process Management were defined as design and control of business processes. There are similarities as well as differences between these two dimensions of the BPM, but as the technological developments raised, the difference between design and control, which should be acute, is vanishing. However, the term business process management in business practices and sciences is frequently used; there is no accurate agreement on its meaning. There are rather themes jointly gathered under the term business process management respecting business processes, such as analysis, modeling, design, control, and implementation of business processes (Reijers 2003).

In his study, Van der Aalst (2013, p. 1) is referring to Business Process Management as *"the discipline that combines knowledge from information technology and knowledge from management sciences and applies this to operational business processes,"* and BMP systems as *"generic software systems that are driven by explicit process design to enact and manage operational business processes."* BMP is aimed at improving business processes which can lead to increased productivity, and saving costs. This, when possible, BMP is doing without using the newest technologies for example, by analyzing and modeling business processes with the use of simulation.

Workflow Management

Workflow management (WFM) can be considered as related to BMP, but while WFM main focus is on the automation of business processes, BMP focuses on a wider range, that is from automation and analysis of the process to operations management and the organization of work. There are many BMP systems available, and conferences that are BMP-related, so the relevance of the BMP discipline by practitioners and academics is acknowledged.

Van der Aalst (2013) in his article provides twenty BMP use cases that show "*how, where, and when*" BMP techniques can be applied. The use cases refer to the practical application of BMP tools and techniques. These cases can also be tied together creating composite use cases that suits to practical BMP scenarios. His survey also describes six BMP key concerns that emphasize significant research area within the BMP discipline. The key concerns have not been frequently encountered in practice, so far, but they require fundamental research.

Nowadays, there are many BMP systems, tools and technologies available for the practitioners' using to model, enhance, and enact business processes. Despite the development of the BMP discipline, there are also paucities especially in BMP language, as van der Aalst (2013) pointed out, where many papers present a new modeling, often unclear, language which may lead to difficulties in using, comparison, and presentation of the results. His survey also revealed neglects in some use cases, thus the active classification of publications and tools that are using use cases should be introduced. Given these and some other weaknesses and the significance of BMP, van der Aalst (2013) also highlighted the urgency of these weaknesses to be take care of (Van der Aalst 2013).

6 Discussion

The service science discipline includes a wide range of studies, articles, books, and other related material. As it is an interdisciplinary study, and involves methods and theories from many existing disciplines, it can provide and adopt multiple approaches to determine various issues in service sector.

The need for a discipline called service science is delineated in many studies. For example, Vargo and Lusch (2008) described the shift from goods to service(s), from manufacturing to service economy, and suggested perception of firms redirecting the production and marketing strategy from manufacture oriented to those concerned with service(s). They consider this shift to service focus very important for the firm's wellbeing. Chesbrough and Spohrer (2006) also argued the need for service science discipline. They suggested that the growth of service sector and its relevance for firms as we now live in service-based economy requires deep understanding of how to innovate services. Vargo et al. (2010) described the evolution of service science as it stems from the need to understand the intangible and dynamic aspect of exchange. I would summarize the need for the new discipline called service science as follows:

- a shift from goods to service(s)
- majority of service industries in gross domestic products, most workforce employed in the service sector
- the growth of the service sector and arising fundamental need of scientific understanding of modern service
- the rise of information and communication technologies (ICT) as a result of the people's shift from manufacturing to the knowledge-intensive service industries
- the need for generating innovations in service economy
- deep understanding of customer needs
- to answers questions such as, "*why industries and companies vary in their productivity*" using business modeling and business process modeling

In the service science with S-D logic as its philosophical foundation, value is cocreated with customer. Thus deep understanding of customers, their behavior, and perception in service encounters is fundamental for business and many studies support this. Chase and Basu (2001) indicated the importance of perception in service encounters using behavioral science. Firms that want to retain their customers in long-term relationships should focus on the service encounter and how managers can optimize those moments. For example, one of the findings for service-encounter management which emerged from the behavioral-science research is the principle '*finish strong*' indicating that the end of service encounter is far more important than the beginning. Zhang and Chen (2008) also delineated the importance of involving customers in cocreating value as an important strategy for business and for gaining competitive advantages. Adopting service perspective on business enables engaging suppliers with their customer in value creation offering the suppliers opportunities to extend their marketing activities into the customers' sphere, which according to Grönroos (2011) allows new marketing strategies. These provide interactive marketing opportunities for the firm that has adopted the service perspective on business.

Giving the importance of customer in value creation, customer loyalty and customer satisfaction have been the subjects of several studies. Enhanced customer loyalty indicates increased revenue, reduced acquisition cost on customer, increased firm's performance (Reichheld 1993; Rust et al. 2000). Customer satisfaction is also an important aspect of value creation, and enhances firm's competitiveness as well. We confront '*customer satisfaction*' everyday: when we are in a retail shop and the saleswoman is rude, we are not satisfied with the offered service and we are not coming back; when the food in a restaurant is not tasty, or when we are not satisfied with the haircut at the hairdresser, we also might not come back. Given these and many other existing examples, we would underline the importance of customer satisfaction in interaction of firms with their customer, thus organizations should be given attention to enhanced satisfaction of their customers knowing real customers' demands.

The emergence of service science discipline has also given opportunities for innovations in service economy. Creating service innovations is also one of the main objectives of the service science (Maglio and Spohrer 2008). SSME prime aim is on understanding how organizations can invest effectively to create service innovations and to realize more predictable outcomes. Understanding and innovating service systems is also the aim of another discipline called SSMED. As Maglio et al. (2006) described, real measures of success in interacting service systems include producing and capturing value from innovations as well as net effects on economy and stakeholders (Kryvinska et al. 2013a). According to Maglio and Spohrer (2013), service innovations are key priorities for nations, businesses, and citizens in the way our world works. While cocreating and delivering value, competitive advantage can be achieved by business model, by means of business model innovation (Chesbrough 2010). As a business model is a result of strategy (Casadesus-Masanell and Ricart 2010, p. 212), such strategic interaction between competitors lead to competition that is based on business model modifications or innovations. According to Boons and Lüdeke-Freund (2013), business models innovation is a significant aspect in creating competitive advantage and aspect for renewing organizations. However, given today's growth of population, and smarter machines, business model innovation will require systematic research of reconfiguration in the resources, and will hinge on value propositions that better use billions of new interconnected people around the world, and the access to the information possessed (Maglio and Spohrer 2013). Nowadays, also social network service providers, such as LinkedIn, Facebook, or Twitter use business models depending on access to shared information. We can see in our everyday life how the technology is changing and moving forward, and as we are adapting to these changes, organizations and business also have to adapt to these changes in our competitive environment. Business model innovations help us to make innovations more systematic and more sustainable to encounter entire business and societal challenges. In a manner of innovations, managers are essential in applying principles of service science for innovativeness of entities the way it remains equitable, sustainable, and resilient.

Given the rise in ICT, specialization of businesses and professions, and global regulations as aspects of an emerging discipline of the service science, there is a need for properly educated professionals with a wide range of knowledge. Many articles discuss T-shaped professionals, and how they can better understand complex service systems. Spohrer and Kwan (2009) discussed the need for T-shaped professional with a deep knowledge of service systems and expertise from many existing disciplines to understand service systems. Their study also indicated that T-shaped professionals can better learn and adapt to the changing needs of business. Hansen and Nohria (2004) also stressed the need for managers to adopt T-shaped role that would help them promote collaboration, and tends to bring satisfying results in prioritizing and delegating to subordinates. Bullen et al. (2009) examining workforce trends in IT provider companies concluded that those companies are seeking for professionals who adopted T-shape role not only having broad general skills and deep technical skills, but also for those having broad technical skills and deep business skills.

With the rise of service sector in our world, T-shaped professionals are becoming relevant in various spheres of business. McIntosh and Taylor (2013), seeing the need for change in terms of essential services, such as water, food, and energy to be managed in more effective and integrated way, developed a concept of T-shaped water professional. These professionals would also have to develop an in-depth knowledge of a particular discipline and broader, general knowledge to recognize opportunities for idea generating, integration, and collaboration.

The nature of service science itself as an interdisciplinary study that involves methods and theories from a number of existing disciplines, such as computer science, cognitive science, organizational behavior, economics, human resource management, operational research, marketing, psychology, industrial engineering, information systems, design and others refers to the need for T-shaped professionals who would have the ability to understand multiple fields, and deep understanding in one particular field. Business in different areas requires in-depth knowledge of that particular area but also generates knowledge in, for example communication skills for better competitive advantages, geographical and demographical skills if for example you are finding new areas for providing your service, or leading skills for better collaboration with your subordinates. Given this aspect of service science, our view suggests that T-shaped professionals and managers should be in focus of various kinds of businesses, not only those related to essential services or IT.

The first step in developing T-shaped professionals should be in schools, especially business schools. Davis and Berdrow (2008) described a challenge for academia to develop integrated curricula. SSME, an IBM initiative, emphasizing programs for undergraduates and graduates is now offering some sort of service science programs in more than 450 universities all over the world. However, there is still a gap between the skills that business schools are providing and the skills that companies need (Davis and Berdrow 2008; Bennis and O'Toole 2005). Considering the gap between provided skills and needed skills, academia and business need to engage in partnerships to overcome these gaps and form programs which both students and also employers demand. This brings suggestions for the educational programs to be redefined to better meet the needs of today's businesses and better define a knowledge-based service management approach, and for academic institutions to more interact with business and organizations.

The rise of ICT specialization and the importance of service management as a set of specialized organizational capabilities for providing value to customers in the form of service, also indicate the need for new and better tools or frameworks to apply principles of service science. ITSM as a set of processes that detail best practices based on ITIL standards enables and optimizes IT services in order to satisfy business requirements and manage the IT infrastructure (Galup et al. 2007). Many organizations have adopted ITIL framework offering a systematic approach to provide and manage information technology services. As Potgieter et al. (2004) suggested, using ITIL framework improves customer satisfaction. ITIL also provides other benefits for an organization such as reducing costs and improving productivity (Cervone 2008). PRM-IT from IBM is an example of management tool that investigates and identifies areas for IT improvement. MOF helps organizations in implementing ITIL by providing operational guidance.

Reviewing these examples it is obvious that for our service-oriented world in which ICT are on the rise, it is essential for the community of service science to work on new tools and educational programs which will improve the ability of service science professionals and others involved to make value-proposition design, more systematic search over time, and enable better implementations of ongoing changes in this service-oriented environment.

However, examining available literature indicates differences in language use. There is a need for an alignment between IT and business. For example, ITSM also aim on reducing differences between IT language and business unit managers that are using IT services. As Reijers (2003) indicates that the meaning of the term business process management which is used in business practices and sciences is also not accurate agreement. Van der Aalst (2013) pointed out new, often unclear language in BMP, too. There is, therefore, a necessity to overcome these differences for better modeling, enhancement, and enactment of business processes.

Service science depends on S-D logic and in S-D logic value is cocreated with customers. Given this nature of service science where the customer is involved in value cocreation with the provider, and businesses cooperate with customers to cocreate value, questions of understanding the processes in the firm by the customer arise. Cervone (2008) indicates that a little bit of understanding the ITIL processes by customers is important IT services to better serve the purposes of the organization. I am not sure whether it is important in every business, but given the limited space in this work. I would let the questions of importance of understanding the processes in a firm by customers for future research.

7 Conclusion

The service sector in global economies grows, and in most developed countries more than 70% of economic activities take place in the service sector. Nowadays, modern businesses rely on information, communication, automation, technology, and globalization, which require of them to operate in a complex web of customers, suppliers, and all involved in the process of value cocreation for mutual benefit (Fauska et al. 2014). As service science involves methods and theories from a range of disciplines, it is an emerging study of such complex web of customers, suppliers, and other stakeholders.

Living in nowadays service-based economy, businesses need to be more efficient and effective in the application of services, and respond quickly to the changing market conditions to be successful in today's competitive environment. It is in best interest for businesses to adjust everyday operations in order to do so.

This chapter discussed the different aspects of service management and business in relation to the service science. The main aim of the work was to perform recherché, examination, and systematization on the different aspects of service management and business in relation to the service science within an available scientific literature. A partial aim of the work was to provide an overview for the need of the service science discipline to emerge. Another partial aim was to analyze the importance of service innovations creation for businesses. A further aim was to analyze the need for properly educated professionals and tools to apply the principles of service science. We managed to fulfil these objectives. Examining available literature we also analyzed the differences in used language, especially differences between IT language and managers in business that are using IT services and we emphasized the necessity to overcome these differences. In the concluding section we discussed the results of the research, analyzed and compared them with works of various authors, and contemplated further development and research.

The contribution of this work is in providing the analysis of different aspect of service management and business in relation to the service science using available scientific literature with our own analytical, proposal, and recommendation capabilities.

Given the nature of service science as the discipline that involves methods and theories from a number of existing disciplines, there are many opportunities for future research. It could be possible for further research to describe the importance of understanding processes in businesses by customers, deeper analysis of tools and technologies that enable business to be successful in today's competitive environment or better elaborate the need for T-shaped professionals in various kinds of businesses, and related educational programs to better meet the needs of business.

References

Ageralk PJ, Fitzgerald B (2008) Outsourcing to an unknown workforce: exploring opensourcing as a global sourcing strategy. J Manag Inf Syst Q [online] 32(2):385–409

Auer L, Belov E, Kryvinska N, Strauss C (2011) Exploratory case study research on SOA investment decision processes in Austria. In: Mouratidis H, Rolland C (eds) 23rd International conference on advanced information systems engineering (CAiSE-2011), 20–24 June 2011. LNCS, vol 6741. Springer, London, UK, pp 329–336

Bennis WG, O'Toole J (2005) How business schools lost their way. Harv Bus Rev [online] 83(5): 96–104

Boons F, Lüdeke-Freund F (2013) Business models for sustainable innovation: state-of-the-art and steps towards a research agenda. J Clean Prod (Special Issue 'Sustainable Innovation and Business Models') 45: 9–19

Bullen CV, Abraham T, Gallagher K, Simon JC, Zwieg P (2009) IT workforce trends: implications for curriculum and hiring. J Commun Assoc Inf Syst 24(9):129–140

Casadesus-Masanell R, Ricart JE (2010) From strategy to business model and onto tactics. Long Range Plan 43(2–3):195–215

Cervone F (2008) ITIL: a framework for managing digital library services. J OCLC Syst Serv 24 (2):87–90

Chase RB, Dasu S (2001) Want to perfect your company's service? Use behavioral science. Harv Bus Rev 79(6):78–84

Chesbrough H (2010) Business model innovation: opportunities and barriers. Long Range Plan 43 (2–3):354–363

Chesbrough H, Spohrer J (2006) A research manifesto for service science. Mag Commun ACM—Serv Sci 49(7): 35–40

Cots S, Fa MC (2014) Exploring the service management standard ISO 20000. J Total Qual Manag Bus Excellence 413–438

Davis MM, Berdrow I (2008) Service science: catalyst for change in business school curricula. IBM Syst J 47(1):29–39

Dickinson E Dictionary.reference.com. [online]. [s.l.]: IAC [s.a.]. Available online at: http://dictionary.reference.com/browse/service

Engelhardt-Nowitzki C, Kryvinska N, Strauss C (2011) Strategic demands on information services in uncertain businesses: a layer-based framework from a value network perspective. In: The first international workshop on frontiers in service transformations and innovations (FSTI-2011), in conjunction with EIDWT 2011, Tirana, Albania, pp 131–136, 7–9 Sept 2011

Fauska P, Kryvinska N, Strauss C (2014) Agile Management of complex good & service bundles for B2B e-commerce by global narrow-specialized companies. Springer, Glob J Flexible Syst Manag (Special Issue on Flex Complexity Management and Engineering by Innovative Services) 15(1):5–23

Free dictionary. [online]. [s.l.]: Farlex [s.a.]. Available online at: http://www.thefreedictionary.com/Service

Galup S, Quan JJ, Dattero R, Conger S (2007) Information technology service management: an emerging area for academic research and pedagogical development. In: Proceedings of the 2007 ACM SIGMIS CPR conference on computer personnel research: the global information technology workforce, pp 46–52

Galup SD, Dattero R, Quan JJ, Conger S (2009) An overview of IT service management. Mag Commun ACM—Secur Browser 52(5): 124–127

Gregus M, Kryvinska N (2015) Service orientation of enterprises—aspects, dimensions, technologies. Comenius University in Bratislava

Grönroos CH (2011) A service perspective on business relationships: the value creation, interaction and marketing interface. J Indus Mark Manag 40(2):240–247

Grover V, Cheon MJ, Teng JTC (1996) The effect of service quality and partnership on the outsourcing of information systems functions. J Manag Inform Syst 12(4):89–116

Hammer M, Champy J (1993) Reengineering the corporation: a manifesto for business revolution. Harper Business, New York

Hansen MT, Nohria N (2004) How to build collaborative advantage. MIT Sloan Manag Rev 46 (1):22–32

Hill TP (1997) On goods and services. Rev Income Wealth 23(4):315–338

Hochstein A, Zarnekow R, Brenner W (2005) ITIL as common practice reference model for it service management: formal assessment and implications for practice. In: Proceedings of the 2005 IEEE international conference on e-technology, e-commerce and e-service (EEE'05) on e-technology, e-commerce and e-service, pp 704–710

Jacob B, Khungar R, Otalora C, Pittard J, Raghunathan TP, Stephenson, D (2008) IT asset management processes using tivoli asset management for IT. IBM Redbooks publication, p 220

Kaczor S, Kryvinska N (2013) It is all about services—fundamentals, drivers, and business models. Soc Serv Sci, J Serv Sci Res 5(2):125–154 (Springer)

Katzan H (2008a) Foundations of service science concepts and facilities. J Serv Sc—Third Quart 1 (1): 1–22

Katzan H (2008b) Foundations of service science management and business. J Serv Sci—Fourth Quart 1(2): 1–16

Koh C, Ang S, Straub DW (2004) IT Outsourcing success: a psychological contract perspective. Inform Syst Res 15(4):356–373

Kryvinska N, Gregus M (2014) SOA and its business value in requirements, features, practices and methodologies. Comenius University in Bratislava

Kryvinska N, Strauss C, Auer L, Zinterhof P (2009) Information technology investment decision-making under uncertainty. In: Fourth IIASA/GAMM workshop on coping with uncertainty (CwU'2009), managing safety of heterogeneous systems, 14–16 Dec, IIASA, Laxenburg, Austria

Kryvinska N, Barokova A, Auer L, Ivanochko I, Strauss C (2013a) Business value assessment of services re-use on SOA using appropriate methodologies, metrics and models. Inderscience Publishers, Int J Serv, Econ Manag (IJSEM) (Special Issue on Service-centric Models, Platforms and Technologies) 5(4):301–327

Kryvinska N, Olexova R, Dohmen P, Strauss C (2013b) The S-D logic phenomenon-conceptualization and systematization by reviewing the literature of a decade (2004–2013). J Serv Sci Res 5(1):35–94 (Springer)

Kryvinska N, Kaczor S, Strauss C, Gregus M (2014a) Servitization—its raise through Information and communication technologies. In: 5th international conference on exploring services science (IESS 1.4), 5–7 February 2014. Lecture Notes in Business Information Processing (LNBIP 169), Springer, Geneva, Switzerland, pp 72–81

Kryvinska N, Kaczor S, Strauss C, Gregus M (2014b) Servitization strategies and product-service-systems. In: The IEEE fourth international workshop on the future of software engineering FOR and IN Cloud (FoSEC 2014), June 27–July 2, 2014, at Hilton Anchorage, Alaska, USA, within IEEE 10th World Congress on Services (SERVICES 2014), pp 254–260

Kryvinska N, Kaczor S, Strauss C, Gregus M (2015) Servitization—transition from manufacturer to service provider. In: Gummesson E, Mele C, Polese F (eds) Service dominant logic, network and systems theory and service science: integrating three perspectives for a new service agenda, naples forum on service 2015, 9–12 June. Naples, Italy

Lee Jae-Nam (2001) The impact of knowledge sharing, organizational capability and partnership quality on IS outsourcing success. J Inform Manag 38(5):323–335

Lusch RF, Vargo SL, O'Brien M (2007) Competing through service: insights from service-dominant logic. J Retail 83(1):5–18

Lusch RF, Vargo SL, Wessels G (2008) Toward a conceptual foundation for service science: contributions from service-dominant logic. IBM Syst J 47(1):5–13

Maglio PP, Spohrer J (2008) Fundamentals of service science. J Acad Mark Sci 36(1):18–20

Maglio PP, Spohrer J (2013) A service science perspective on business model innovation. J Indus Mark Manag 42(5):665–670

Maglio PP, Srinivasan S, Kreulen JT, Spohrer J (2006) Service systems, service scientists, SSME, and innovation. Mag Commun ACM—Serv Sci 49(7): 81–85

Maglio PP, Vargo SL, Caswell N, Spohrer J (2009) The service system is the basic abstraction of service science. IseB 7(4):395–406

Mcintosh BS, Taylor A (2013) Developing T-shaped water professionals: building capacity in collaboration, learning, and leadership to drive innovation. J Contemp Water Res Edu 150 (1):6–17

Normann R, Ramírez R (1993) From value chain to value constellation: designing interactive strategy. Harv Bus Rev 71(4):65–77

Potgieter BC, Botha JH, Lew C (2004) Evidence that use of the ITIL framework is effective. In: Proceedings of the annual conference—national advisory committee on computing qualifications, pp 161–168

Prahalad CK, Ramaswamy V (2000) Co-opting customer competence. Harv Bus Rev 78(1):79–87

Rechheld FF (1993) Loyalty-based management. Harv Bus Rev 71(2):64–73

Reijers HA (2003) Design and control of workflow processes: business process management for the service industry. Springer, Berlin, Heidelberg

Rust R, Zeithaml V, Lemon K (2000) Driving customer equity. Free Press, New York, NY

Spohrer J, Kwan SK (2008) Service science, management, engineering, and design (SSMED): outline & references. In: Spath D, Ganz W (eds) Die Zukunft der Dienstleistungs-wirtschaft, Trends und Chancen heute erkennen (The Future of Services—Trends and Perspectives), Carl Hanser Verlag, Germany, München Wien

Spohrer J, Kwan SK (2009) Service science, management, engineering, and design (SSMED): an emerging discipline–outline & references. Int J Inform Syst Serv Sect (IJISSS) 1(3):1–31

Spohrer J, Maglio PP, Bailey J, Gruhl D (2007) Steps toward a science of service systems. J Comput 40(1):71–77

Stoshikj M, Kryvinska N, Strauss C (2014) Efficient managing of complex programs with project management services. Glob J Flexible Syst Manag (Special Issue on Flexible Complexity Management and Engineering by Innovative Services) 15(1):25–38 (Springer)

Stoshikj M, Kryvinska N, Strauss C (2016) Service systems and service innovation: two pillars of service science. Elsevier J Procedia Comp Sci (Special Issue on The 7th International Conference on Ambient Systems, Networks and Technologies (ANT-2016)) 83:212–220

Suhairi K, Gaol FL (2013) The measurement of optimization performance of managed service division with ITIL framework using statistical process control. J Netw 8(3):518–537

Urikova O, Ivanochko I, Kryvinska N, Strauss C, Zinterhof P (2012a) Exploration of factors affecting the advancement of collaborative e-business in the enterprises—research efforts examination. In: First international workshop on inter-clouds and collective intelligence (iCCI-2012), in conjunction with AINA-2012, Fukuoka, Japan, March 26–29, 2012, pp 1227–1232

Urikova O, Ivanochko I, Kryvinska N, Zinterhof P, Strauss C (2012b) Managing complex business services in heterogeneous eBusiness ecosystems—aspect-based research assessment. Elsevier J Procedia Comput Sci (Special Issue on The 3rd International Conference on Ambient Systems, Networks and Technologies (ANT-2012)) 10:128–135

Van Der Aalst WMP (2013) Business process management: a comprehensive survey. ISRN Soft Eng 2013(2013):37

Vargo SL, Akaka MA (2009) Service-dominant logic as a foundation for service science: clarifications. J Serv Sci 1(1):32–41

Vargo SL, Lusch RF (2008a) From goods to service(s): divergences and convergences of logics. Ind Mark Manage 37(3):254–259

Vargo SL, Lusch RF (2008b) Service-dominant logic: continuing the evolution. J Acad Mark Sci 36(1):1–10

Vargo SL, Maglio PP, Akaka MA (2008) On value and value co-creation: a service systems and service logic perspective. Eur Manag J 26(3):145–152

Vargo SL, Lusch RF, Akaka MA (2010) Advancing service science with service-dominant logic clarifications and conceptual development. In: Handbook of service science, service science: research and innovations in the service economy, pp 133–156

Zhang X, Chen R (2008) Examining the mechanism of the value co-creation with customers. Int J Prod Econ 116(2):242–250

Ziethaml V, Parasuraman A, Berry LL (1990) Delivering quality service: balancing customer perceptions and expectations. Free Press, New York

Chapter 7
Improving Information Accuracy with SEO for Online Marketing Services

Jakub Žilinčan

Abstract Search engine optimization techniques, often shortened to SEO, should lead to first positions in organic search results. Some optimization techniques do not change over time, and still form the basis of SEO. However, as the Internet and web design evolves dynamically, optimization techniques arise and die. In the first section of this chapter, we will look at the most important factors and techniques that can help to improve position in search results. However, none of the factors can guarantee it because search engines have sophisticated algorithms, which measure the quality of web pages and derive their position in search results from it. In the next section we will introduce and examine the object of optimization, which is a website http://bratislava-slovakia.eu. This website was created for the sole purpose —to implement and test all main SEO techniques. The main objective of this chapter is to verify whether search engine optimization increases traffic and, if so, to what extent.

Keywords SEO · Optimization · Internet traffic

1 Consumer Decision Journey

Marketing tries to reach consumers at the moments that most influence their decisions. For years, touch points have been understood through the metaphor of a "funnel"—consumers start with a number of potential brands in mind (the wide end of the funnel), marketing is then directed at them as they methodically reduce that number and move through the funnel, and at the end they emerge with the one brand they chose to purchase (Fig. 1) (Gregus and Kryvinska 2015; Urikova et al. 2012).

In 2009, McKinsey & Company released the publication that the purchase funnel that days is rather circular, than linear (Fig. 2—The classic journey) (Court

J. Žilinčan (✉)
Faculty of Management, Comenius University, Bratislava, Slovakia
e-mail: jzilincan@gmail.com

© Springer Science+Business Media Singapore 2018   217
N. Kryvinska and M. Gregus (eds.), *Agile Information Business*,
Flexible Systems Management, DOI 10.1007/978-981-10-3358-2_7

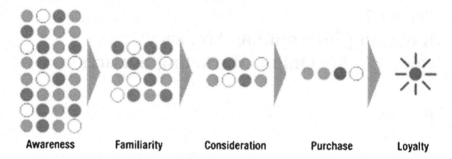

Fig. 1 Linear decision funnel (Court et al. 2009)

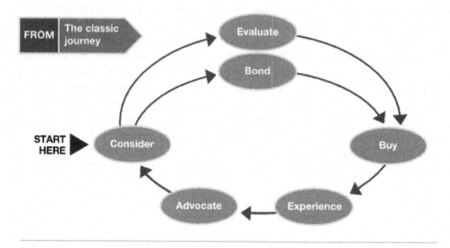

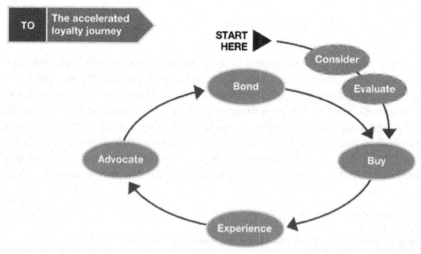

Fig. 2 The new consumer decision journey (Court et al. 2015)

et al. 2009). In step 1, the consumers consider an initial set of brands, based on brand perception and exposure to recent touch points. Next they add or subtract brands as they evaluate what they want. Ultimately, consumers select a brand at the moment of purchase. After purchasing a product or a service, the consumers build on experience to inform the next decision journey (Kaczor and Kryvinska 2013; Stoshikj et al. 2016).

In 2015, same company introduced a model of "new consumer decision journey" taking into consideration current trend of mobile, social media and other technologies, which give users power to compare prices, find best deals and interact with the brand online. Research has been conducted among 100 digital-business leaders worldwide and the outcome proved, that "brands today can not only react to customers as they make purchasing decisions but also *actively shape those decision journeys*." (Court et al. 2015).

> Companies today can use journeys to deliver value to both the customer and the brand. Companies that do this well can radically compress the consideration and evaluation phases —and in some cases even eliminate them—during the purchase process and catapult a consumer right to the loyalty phase of the relationship (Fig. 2 – The accelerated loyalty journey). The journey itself is becoming the defining source of competitive advantage. (Court et al. 2015)

The survey also uncovered that top performers understood the entire customer journey much better than their peers (20% vs. 6%) and had better processes for capturing insights about customers and feeding them back into their marketing programs to improve performance (30% vs. 11%). Company's ability to deliver that value relies on four distinct but interconnected capabilities

- *Automation* streamlines journey steps.
- *Proactive personalization* uses information about a customer—either based on past interactions or collected from external sources—to instantaneously customize the experience.
- *Contextual interaction* uses knowledge about where a customer is in a journey to deliver them to the next set of interactions.
- *Journey innovation* extends the interaction to new sources of value, such as new services, for both the customer and the brand. The best companies design journeys that enable open-ended testing to allow for constant prototyping of new services or features.

Activating customer journeys to capture value requires journeys to be treated like products that need to be actively managed, measured and nurtured. How good companies are able to do that will dictate how successful they are in making customer journeys a competitive advantage.

2 See-Think-Do-Care Framework

STDC (see, think, do, care) is a business framework evolved from the traditional AIDA (attention, interest, desire, action) model and is entirely focused on describing online decision journeys of consumers. It describes a list of events that may occur when a consumer engages with an advertisement in a simpler, customer-centric way. STDC framework was developed by Avinash Kaushik, a web analytical expert focusing on advanced measurement.

The foundational elements of the framework are the consideration stages and the audience in each stage as described in Table 1. From the online strategy point of view all stages should be addressed by different touch points (Table 2) and have a dedicated content ready to serve users in different stages of purchase cycle (Kaushik 2009).

Targeting strategy in the *See* stage will be broad, focused on demographic or/and psychographic of/and geographic signals. The ad purpose will be primarily branding, so the goal for the campaign should be set respectively to measure the target audience reach, frequency, brand awareness or ad recall.

In the *Think* stage, ad creative will be a little narrower and the targeting strategy should focus on specific types of sites, specific content and customers with specific

Table 1 See-think-do-care framework (Kaushik 2009)

Consideration stage	Audience definition	Example
SEE	Largest possible way how to define the target audience	All people who wear clothes
THINK	Subset of the see audience delineated by even the slightest amount of intent	All people who wear clothes who think they might need some
DO	Subset of the think audience ready to perform an action	All people who wear clothes who think they might need some, and are currently looking to buy them
CARE	Returning customers who have purchased more than twice	

Table 2 Online channels and their association to separate stages of purchase funnel

		Stages of purchase funnel			
		Loyalty (CARE)	Purchase (DO)	Consideration (THINK)	Awareness (SEE)
Online channels	Video	✓		✓	✓
	Display ads	✓		✓	✓
	Paid search	✓	✓	✓	
	Organic search		✓	✓	✓
	Social media	✓		✓	✓
	Email marketing	✓	✓	✓	
	Direct traffic	✓	✓	✓	
	Company blog			✓	✓

interests. The ad purpose should be to present the value of the brand but also to drive initial direct engagement with the brand. The measurable goals should be for example: number of email addresses signed up for newsletter, click-thru rate, page depth, number of video views, app downloads and other micro-conversions.

Audience in the *Do* stage should be targeted by as much intent signals as possible, i.e. retargeting driven by prior history, full of intelligence from another customer like-type behaviour, etc. The main purpose of targeting people in this stage is to drive revenue. Measurable goals include conversion rate, ROI, avg. order value, checkout abandonment rate, number of orders or the length of purchase cycle in days/hours/minutes and last but not least profit itself (Kryvinska et al. 2014a).

As "monetizing" returning visitors is cheaper than gaining new ones, marketers should not forget about the loyal customers and develop a strong *care* strategy through customized mobile apps, special websites, unique search/display/social strategies. Also the goal should be adjusted to measure life-time value or retention (Kryvinska et al. 2014b).

3 Digital Touch Points

Measuring the full consumer journey and attributing value to each channel involved is a big challenge. People nowadays usually own more than one device (e.g. personal computer, computer in work, mobile, tablet) and each of them can be part of the decision journey. For instance, people looking to book a vacation can start their research on mobile device, then look for some additional information few days after on personal computer, watch video on tablet same evening and finally book the hotel on another computer (Stoshikj et al. 2014).

In the real world we know that this customer is one person. In the digital world, persons are usually represented by cookies, which usually cannot be transmitted from device to device (unless the customer is signed in or offers any other signal about his "uniqueness"). And not only device is taken into consideration when evaluating the full journey, but also a big variety of online channels. Following the previous example, customer comes into contact with several channels. This fact brings us to an exponential growth of all the touch points, which marketers need to analyse to truly understand the full consumer decision journey. Each of the channels is entering the purchase funnel in a different stage as illustrated in Table 2.

3.1 Last Versus Assisting Interaction

Marketing channels (such as email, display ads, paid search ads, social and direct visits to a website) influence the consumer at different stages of their decision journey (Think with Google 2014):

- Assisting channels build awareness, consideration and intent earlier in the customer journey.
- Last interaction channels act as the last point of contact prior to a purchase.

Understanding the proximity of a concrete channel to the final purchase is vital for marketers. Trying to push a hard-selling message via assisting channels (more on the left in Fig. 3) is contra-indicatory and does not target the right audience. On contrary, soft call-to-actions in the last interaction channel (located more on the right in Fig. 3) may miss the opportunity to push the consumer to the final decision of purchase. The modern online customer journey is complex and it is important to focus on the key moments that can help persuading people to buy a product or service (Kryvinska et al. 2015).

Theory described previously in Table 2—Online channels and their association to separate stages of purchase funnel is supported by the research conducted by Google in 2014 analysing millions of consumer journeys in a shopping industry, which led to an online purchase. As visualized in Fig. 3, channels to the left tend to play an early and assisting role in the typical sale, while channels to the right are more likely to be the last interaction before a purchase.

Legend (not in particular order)—More to the left: assisting role; more to the right: last interaction.

4   Search as a Digital Touch Point

People use search engines to find product-related information, compare prices and find the most suitable retailer. According to Consumer Barometer, search engine is chosen as the primary online source of information in all countries worldwide (mostly in Asia). In Slovakia, 59% of people used search engines for their last purchase. This makes Slovakia one of the most search engine-oriented countries in Europe. United Kingdom ranks lower, where 48% of people used search engines, and in Germany "only" 40% of people used search engines while making their last purchase (Ward 2013).

From the point of advertiser, search traffic can be divided into two main categories:

- paid search—traffic coming from the AdWords
- organic search—traffic coming from the non-paid Google search

Each of this category can contain a brand-relater keyword (e.g. "nike shoes") or non-brand generic keyword (e.g. "running shoes"). This categorization is also important in terms of association to the funnel stages.

While generic keywords signalize that user is only gaining information about the topic of interest (awareness/consideration stage), brand-related keywords are usually connected with research or purchase intent (consideration/purchase/loyalty stage).

The number of organic searches is usually dependant on the awareness itself. In other words, users do not search for something, they do not know. Thus the

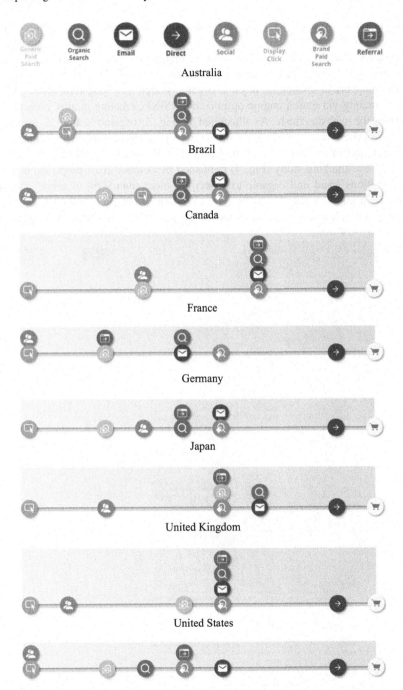

Fig. 3 How online channels for large businesses in the shopping industry influence the purchase decision (Think with Google 2014)

marketers must engage with the customers via other digital touch points before focusing on organic search in order to bring immediate traffic to their websites. As soon as the customers are familiar with the brand, they can perform brand-related searches and finish the action on the most relevant retailer's website.

Building brand awareness through organic search is a long-term strategy controlled mainly via search engine-optimization (SEO), creating quality content, and keeping the website fresh. As illustrated in Fig. 3, organic search as a channel appears in the lower-to-mid part of the funnel signalizing its ability to influence the consideration in the last stages before purchase (Search Engine Land 2012).

They eye tracking study (Fig. 4) published in October 2014 proposes, that first five positions (paid and organic together) get more than 90% of users' attention while scanning the search results page. With the right paid and organic search strategy, Google allows one advertiser to occupy two positions in a search result

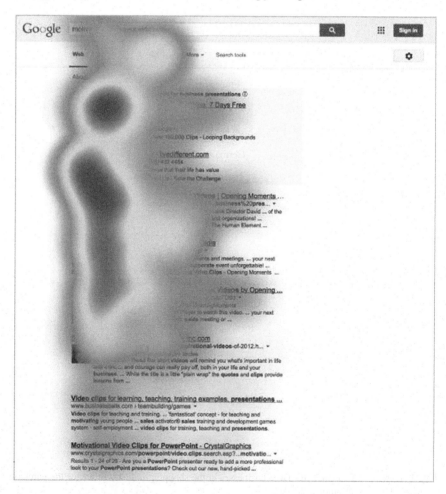

Fig. 4 Eye tracking study in Google search results page (Google Webmaster Central 2009)

page—one in a paid slot, one in an organic slot[1]—making it possible to "own" almost all of the above-the-fold[2] content.

This split could, however, lead to a phenomenon called "Cannibalization". This occurs when a website ranking in the first organic positions adds a paid search campaign and immediately starts to show above the organic result. Some users, which would have clicked on the organic search results (non-paid), are now rather clicking on the ad (paid search result). In other words, advertisers are now paying for visitors, whose acquisition was "free" before. A study conducted by Google does not deny the fact of cannibalization, but it also reveals that launching a paid campaign leads to an additional increment of $\sim 79\%$ clicks on desktop and 88% on mobile. Due to this fact it is recommended for brands to advertise on their own brand keywords despite being present in the organic search (Google Webmaster Central 2009; Schema 2013; Sullivan 2010).

5   Search Engine Optimization

According to Google (2010), SEO is a series of modifications and techniques, which make it easier for search engines to crawl, index and understand the content of a website.

Generally, SEO is divided into two groups

- On-page—modifying the structure of a website
- Off-page—techniques independent of website's structure

Right combination of both can bring significant increase in traffic thanks to higher position in SERP.

Before optimization itself it is crucial to know the customer, market and our capabilities. It is impossible to make a search engine optimization for every word on a page, thus it is important to select 5–10 keywords, which represent the content most accurately. It is important to keep in mind, that optimization is always performed according to a specific query, which is likely to be searched by a user.

5.1   On-Page SEO

On-page SEO includes the elements that are in direct control of a publisher. In following demonstrations, we will concentrate on optimization for Google, as it owns 90% of search engines market worldwide (Statcounter 2013). Following lines

---

[1]Depending on the quality of website and a search query it is possible to "own" more than one slot by one website in organic search.
[2]Content visible on screen without scrolling.

will describe fundamental techniques, which are recommended to prepare a perfectly optimized website.

Content

A process of writing a text for the purposes of advertising or marketing is called copywriting. While creating a helpful, information-rich website, copywriters should write pages that clearly and accurately describe a specific topic. It is important to think about the words users would type to find pages and include those words on a site (Google 2012). The aim is to create a unique, content-rich website, which is likely to be referenced, and subsequently would have gone viral.

To find out, what content goes viral and why, a research has been done on University of Pennsylvania. Elements, which cause that some articles are shared more often than others, are (Berger and Milkman 2011; Ward 2013)

- Length—"word count was more closely correlated with sharing than any other variable examined. [...] While long posts appear more likely to be shared through email and links, a separate study on blog comments found that users are less likely to comment on long posts."
- Certain emotions—"content that inspires low-energy emotions like sadness is less likely to be shared, where content that inspires high-energy emotions like awe, anger, and anxiety is far more likely to be shared."
- Surprise—"content that is surprising, interesting, and practically useful receives more shares than the obvious, boring, and useless content."
- Known authors—"the fame of the author was just slightly more important than content. [...] While content is innately influential, it usually only carries the authority of its creator or publisher".
- Humour—"content that is truly and broadly viral is almost always funny". A study proved, that "despite 62% of ads being aired by Fortune 500 companies, 60% of viral ads were being generated by the smaller companies "thanks to funny content" (Porter and Golan 2006).

According to Google, creating compelling and useful content will also influence a website ranking more than any of the other factors. "Users know good content when they see it and will likely want to direct other users to it. This could be through blog posts, social media services, email, forums, or other means. Organic or word-of-mouth buzz is what helps build site's reputation with both users and Google, and it rarely comes without quality content" (Google 2010).

SEO copywriting is a method used to compose text that helps a page to rank higher in the search results, while still producing readable and human-friendly content. The content-creators should bear in mind following questions (Search Engine Land 2012):

- Are pages well written and have substantial quality content?
- What are the keywords people may use to find the content?
- Do visitors spend time reading or "bounce" away quickly?
- Are pages fresh and about "hot" topics?

Based on this knowledge, we can derive the best practices to bear in mind while creating a quality content (Google 2010):

- Relevant content to a website topic should be rich on keyword phrases.
- Easy-to-read text should be formatted in paragraphs. Use bolding to emphasize the keywords.
- Human-readability—Content should be prepared for users, not for search engines.
- Conclusions at the beginning of a text will put keywords higher to a top of article.
- Use lists instead of paragraphs whenever possible—they are easy to read for users and a clear source of keywords for search engines.
- Use internal linking with descriptive keywords in anchors.
- Use headings to separate content.
- Images should always contain an "alt" attribute to describe the visualization in human readable text.

On the other hand, you should avoid (Google 2010)

- Dumping large amounts of text on varying topics onto a page without paragraph, subheading, or layout separation.
- Copying existing content that will bring little extra value to users.
- Duplicating content across a website.
- Keyword stuffing—loading a text with unnatural number of keywords.
- Hiding text from users but displaying to the search engines.
- Misspellings and grammatical mistakes.
- Putting text as a part of an image—visitors cannot copy it and search engines cannot read it.

Duplicate content is something that might harm the credit of a website more than any other factor mentioned here. Duplicate content is a problem because when there is more than one piece of identical content on the Internet, it is difficult for search engines to decide which version is more relevant to a given search query. There are several factors, which can cause duplicate content (Google 2012):

- Dynamic URLs—usually append parameters to URL, which are for example just sorting content for users, but URLs are considered as unique by search engines. On URL is expected to offer unique content.
- Example: /products?order=price versus /products?order=name.
- *Solution*: Canonicalization—preventing search engines indexing every dynamic URL. To direct search engines to an original URL, use *rel* = "*canonical*" tag or 301 Redirect Header (Moved Permanently).
- Domain version—usually it is possible to get to a website by typing "www" in front of a domain name but also by omitting this. Search engine perceives this as two different pages.
- Example: example.com versus www.example.com.

- _Solution_: Setting preferred domain (with or without "www") in Google Webmaster Tools and using 301 Redirect Header (Moved Permanently) to redirect to domain with or without "www".
- Trailing slash—URL accessible by using (or not using) the "/" symbol at the end of an URL can be considered as duplicate content.
- Example: example.com/page/ versus example.com/page.
- _Solution_: Canonicalization—using 301 Redirect Header (Moved Permanently) without "/" at the end of the URL.

Google itself does not advise to block access to duplicate content by using robots.txt or "noindex, nofollow" tag.

Titles

A title tag tells both users and search engines what the topic of a particular page is. [...] If a document appears in a search results page, the contents of the title tag will usually appear in the first line of the results. [...] Words in the title are bolded if they appear in the user's search query. This can help users recognize if the page is likely to be relevant to their search (Google 2010)

In the survey among the leaders in SEO industry, 35 of 37 participants said, that keyword usage in the title tag was the most important place to use keywords to achieve high rankings. A study showed, that among keywords placements, keywords in title tag are probably one of the most influential elements to rank in the first positions in search results (94.4% influential value) (Seomoz 2013) (Fig. 5).

Best practices while creating a good title tag include

- Relevancy—title tag must be descriptive in relation to the content on the page.
- 70 characters—this is the maximum amount of characters that will display in the search results. Phrases should be short and simple.
- First positions—keywords should be placed close to the front of the title tag, separated by pipe symbol "|".
- Brand name should be mentioned in the title. If the brand is strong and aware, it should be placed in the beginning of the title tag replacing the main descriptive keyword.
- Readability must be considered. The website is created for users, thus even titles should be written in human natural language.

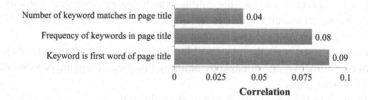

Fig. 5 Page level keyword usage—correlated data

On the other hand, you should avoid (Seomoz 2013)

- Keyword stuffing—loading a title with unnatural number of keywords.
- Duplication—title tag should be unique for every page on a website.
- Using long titles, which consist of full sentences of even paragraphs.

To give an idea about a well-formatted title tag, see the example below. A brand name has been used in front of the title tag to immediately associate the website with the official manufacturer. The word "and" has been replaced by "&" for better readability and a pipe symbol has been used a separator between brand name and descriptive title (Fig. 6).

Domain name

> Domain names are the human readable Internet addresses of websites. Root domains, which are identified by their domain names, have extensions such as .com, .org, .net, etc. Subdomains are a lower level component a root domain and precede the domain name. (Seomoz 2013)

Selecting a suitable domain name is vital, because it cannot be changed over time easily. While thinking of a good, domain name, these are the best practices (Seomoz 2013):

- Keyword-rich domains are usually ranked higher because the domain name is one of the key ranking factors.
- Length should be less than 15 characters in terms of memorability, ease of sharing and lower chance of typos.
- Relevancy to the content of page is also an important factor.

Practices, which negatively influence the rankings, and you should avoid, are (Seomoz 2013)

- More than three hyphens within a domain are considered to be spam. Domain name longer than three words should not be used.
- Low-quality TLDs (.biz, .info, .name, …) are considered to be less credible.
- Redirecting several domains to one site is not effective anymore. Google devalues links from sites once they expire or change ownership.

In the example below we used the .com domain as it is the most common TLD and thus trustworthy for users and search engines. We also suggested a short

Search query:	*iPhone 5 features and tech specs*
Bad title:	iPhone - features and tech specifications of Apple's iPhone 5
Good title:	Apple | iPhone 5 - Features & Tech Specs

Fig. 6 Well-formatted page title

Search query:	*iPhone 5 features and tech specs*
Bad domain name:	iphone-review.info
Good domain name:	iphone-features.com

Fig. 7 Well-formated domain name

phrase, which is easy to remember and has a high probability of exact domain match when being searched (Fig. 7).

URL structure

A URL is human readable text that identifies the file structure on the given website. It is separated by "/" from the domain name and follows right after it. In search engines, "URL to a document is displayed as part of a search result, below the document's title and snippet. Like the title and snippet, words in the URL on the search result appear in bold if they appear in the user's query" (Google 2010, 2012).

As URL is an important part of SEO optimization, follow these best practices to ensure, that users and search engines understand the file structure of your website (Google 2010, 2012):

- User-friendly URL is easy to read even for the search engines.
- Static URLs with a clear directory structure are easier to navigate and better understood by users and search engine. Allow a part of URL to be removed without causing the 404—Not found error.
  <u>Example</u>: example.com/dir/sub/page.html
- Relevancy—Use relevant descriptive keywords within URL.
- Use hyphen symbol "-" as the words separator.
  <u>Example</u>: example.com/words-separated-by-hyphen
- Use lower case letters only. Users expect them and are better to remember.

While defining the URL structure, avoid (Google 2010, 2012):

- Dynamic URLs, which are not clear and hard to read.
  <u>Example</u>: example.com/index.php?dir=1572&sub=5
- Using punctuation and accents. Do not use "_" as a words separator.
- Long URLs with unnecessary parameters and session IDs.
- Generic names of files.
  <u>Example</u>: /page1.html
- Keywords stuffing.
  <u>Example</u>: /baseball-cards-baseball-cards-baseballcards.htm
- Deep nesting of subdirectories.
  <u>Example</u>: example.com/dir/dir/dir/dir/dir/page.html

In the example below we suggest user-friendly URL, which is easy to read and gives a clear explanation where the user will land. As Google advises, we used

Search query:	*iPhone 5 features and tech specs*
Bad URL:	example.com/index.php?cat=224&sub=71&id=ip5
Good URL:	example.com/iphone-5/features-tech-specs

Fig. 8 User-friendly URL

hyphen "-" as the words separator. Moreover, we skipped the word "and" as it gives no additional value to our keyword-rich URL (Fig. 8).

Headings

Similar to books, even a web page should be divided into chapters using the heading tags. It is possible to use six levels of headings, ordered by priority from 1 (most important) to 6 (least important). Headings present page structure to users. The h1 heading tag is the most important in terms of SEO as it represents the name of a main chapter. It can be the same as the page title. Best practices suggest (Google 2010):

- Descriptive short phrases in headings should contain keywords.
- One h1 tag per page. This is not an obligatory rule, as Google allows even more h1 tags, but it is worth considering whether to use one or more tags.
- Different styles of headings allow users to quickly scan the page and reveal the main sections.
- Hierarchy of headings should be adhered. Start with h1 tag as the most general topic name and continue to the lower levels of hierarchy, as the text gets more specific.

On contrary, avoid these practices (Google 2010):

- Long phrases or even whole paragraphs in the tag.
- Keyword stuffing—loading a heading with unnatural number of keywords.
- Not using headings at all is bad not only for users, but also for SEO. However, sites without headings can still get to the first positions.

In an example below we have used exactly the same phrase as we are expecting from user to search. Heading is keyword-rich and gives a clear explanation of the content occurring on a page (Fig. 9).

Search query:	*iPhone 5 features and tech specs*
Bad h1:	Apple smartphone overview
Good h1:	iPhone 5 features an tech specs

Fig. 9 Well-formatted heading

Internal linking

"Internal links are links that go from one page on a domain to a different page on the same domain. They are commonly used in main navigation" and thus build a main structure of a website (Seomoz 2013). A search engine considers the number of links, which lead to a page and how they link to it and derives the importance of a page (Whalley 2012).

Best practices

- Tight architecture—a visitor should be able to get to any page within two clicks.
- Linking from reputable pages, i.e. from a homepage to a product page, gives a search engine signal, that the linked page is important.
- Descriptive anchors should briefly describe the content of a page where they follow.
- Title parameters within a link should be used to describe what a user finds on the linked page.

Avoid

- General anchor texts like "click here".
- More than 150 links from one page—this is a spam indicator. Search spiders might stop crawling a website and thus could not discover eventually important content.
- Hiding links in JavaScript or Flash.
- Pointing links to the pages, which are blocked by Meta Robots or Robots.txt (Fig. 10).

Meta tags

"A page's description meta tag gives Google and other search engines a summary of what the page is about. Whereas a page's title may be a few words or a phrase, a page's description meta tag might be a sentence or two or a short paragraph. [...] Words in the snippet are bolded when they appear in the user's query. This gives the user clues about whether the content on the page matches with what he or she is looking for" (Google 2010). This meta tag might be used as a descriptive snippet of a page in search results, if a search engine does not decide to use another relevant section of a page. Even though since September 2009 Google does not use description meta tag as ranking factor, it is still one of the decision factors for visitors (Google Webmaster Central 2009).

Best practices (Seomoz 2013)

- Descriptive meta tag must be relevant to the content of the page.

| **Bad anchor text:** | For more information about iPhone 5 features click here. |
| **Good anchor text:** | Read more about iPhone 5 features and tech specs. |

Fig. 10 Well-formatted anchor text

- 150–160 characters is the maximum amount of characters that will display in the search results. Phrases should be short and simple.

Avoid (Seomoz 2013)

- Using single keywords. Use phrases and full sentences instead.
- Duplication—meta tag should be unique for every page on a website.
- Quotes in description cause cutting of the description. It is best to remove the non-alpha and non-numerical characters.
- General descriptions, like "This is a web page" (Fig. 11).

Page speed

Page speed reflects how quickly a website responds to user's requests. In 2010, Google included a page speed signal to a search-ranking algorithm. The faster page loads, the higher search rank it might get. Even though this is probably not the most important ranking factor, between two equally relevant websites the one, which is loading faster, could be prioritized (Google Webmaster Central 2010). Tips and best practices on how to decrease page load time (Search Engine Land 2012):

- gzip compression—encodes source code using fewer bits than the original representation.
- Reduce the number of fetches to minimum, so that the server does not have to wait for execution of each of them.
- Enable caching of a website with defined expiration.
- Optimize code, remove unused parts and use as few declarations as possible.
- Split static sources like images and CSS over 2–4 servers.
- Optimize images to have the lowest file size.

6 Structured Data

Structured data are basic html tags that "webmasters can use to mark-up their pages in ways recognized by major search providers. Search engines including Bing, Google, Yahoo! and Yandex rely on this mark-up to improve the display of search results, making it easier for people to find the right web pages". In other words, webmasters can help search engines to understand content better by marking up

Search query:	*iPhone 5 features*
Bad:	This is a page about iPhone featuers.
Good:	All-new design. The thinnest, fastest and lightest iPhone ever with 4-inch Retina display and ultrafast Wi-Fi. Starts at $499!

Fig. 11 Well-formatted meta tags

specific information. Schemas are managed and accepted by neutral schema.org website. The most common types of schemas, recognized and shown in Google search results, are (Schema 2013):

- Breadcrumbs—categories leading to a specific page
- Reviews—number of reviews, average review, reviewers...
- People—name, address, contacts, family information...
- Products—price, availability, quantity...
- Business—address, contact, geo location...
- Recipes—time, summary, ingredients...
- Events—location, duration, attendees...
- Music—song name, author, length...
- Video—thumbnails, length, description...

Structured data are not only good because they directly explain the content to a search engine, but they also

- Draw user's attention to relevant result.
- Provide instant information related to the query.
- Increase click-through rates and lessen the amount of bounces (Fig. 12).

Sitemap

Sitemap is a structured list of pages, which could be found on a website. Creating and submitting a Sitemap helps Google to understand the structure and discover all pages faster. In addition, Sitemaps can also provide Google with metadata about specific types of content on a website, including video, images, mobile, and news.

Sitemaps should be particularly used, if a website has pages that are not easily discoverable by Google bot during the crawl process—for example, pages featuring rich AJAX or images. They are also very useful for new websites, which do not get so much attention from Google bot in early days.

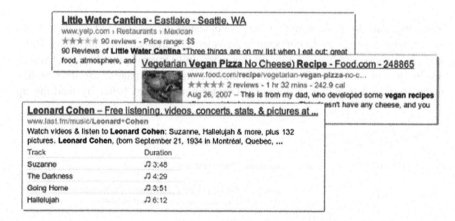

Fig. 12 Example of various rich snippets within Google search results (Google 2012)

6.1 Off-Page SEO

Off-page SEO includes elements influenced by readers, visitors and other publishers. These elements are not in direct control of a publisher but can positively influence the search rankings and boost traffic to a website.

Social networks

Social networks are the phenomenon of today's world. They represent a mass of people who are willing to read and share the information for free. This word-of-mouth promotion is probably one of the most valuable marketing techniques.

In 2010, both Bing and Google confirmed that links shared through Twitter and Facebook have a direct impact on rankings (Sulivan 2010). However, 4 years later, Google announced that Facebook and Twitter signals are not a part of search engine algorithm anymore (Slegg 2014). Google+ remains the only social network, which is being considered while ranking the websites in search. Activity on social networks is, however, not important only due to the search rankings, but also to build relationships with users.

Best practices

- Post relevant content often, but do not overdo it. There is a tight balance between engaging news and spam.
- Use short URLs when posting a link to "save" space for readable text.
- Engage "fans" by asking questions and actively joining discussions.
- Use links to your website wherever possible—in posts, descriptions, ….

Avoid:

- Posting forbidden content. You should be aware of the terms and conditions of particular social network you are using.
- Misusing of personal information.
- Deleting reactions of users, which express dissatisfaction with your services.

Blogs

In blogs, unlike on the official company websites, authors can publish subjective opinions, react on the current trends, or present study results and get the direct response from the readers. Blog is not suitable for everyone, but if you decide to run one, you should be aware of some best practices:

- Post relevant content often. Publish news, findings or inside stories, which are shocking, humorous and not obvious.
- Engage readers by opening a discussion.
- Use links to your official website wherever possible.

Avoid

- Selling your products directly in the blog posts. Those posts should be more or less neutral.

- Deleting reactions of users, which express dissatisfaction with your services in comments or guest boards.
- Posting secret information, which might harm your business.

Creating and maintaining a blog is an important part of off-page optimization. Blogs are usually full of content that is relevant to an official company website, thus creates a great internal linking source. Moreover, it indirectly helps to present company's skills and expertise.

There are several tools that offer blog creations in just a few steps. Some are totally free and hosted on third-party servers (i.e. blogger.com), some are open sources able to host on own servers (i.e. WordPress), and there are also paid solutions as customized blogs developed for individual customer.

Forums and discussion boards

Forum is an online discussion site where people can hold conversations in the form of posted messages. On one side there are people looking for the information, on the other side people willing to provide the answer.

In terms of building relationship with (potential) customers it is essential to appear in these debates. It will not just boost the awareness of brand we represent in discussion, but might also help to create a strong basis of backlinks.

Best practices

- React to questions related to your field and provide comprehensive answers.
- Use references in reactions and link to sources.
- Fill in your signature and full profile and put links to your company website.

Avoid

- Posting forbidden content. You should be aware of terms and conditions.
- Ignoring the reactions, which are cumulated about your brand.
- Spamming by posting only links.
- Duplicating content.

Audiovisual media sharing

It is not just a text content that can bring traffic to a website. Rich media, as videos or images, can be good promotion, too. It is not just they are more likely to be shared and virally distributed, than text, but they also can bring traffic from image search results as they appear in SERP.

Best practices

- Info graphics are a good way to share interesting information about company.
- Videos should be funny, interesting or reveal something hidden.
- Use links in descriptions.
- Images should include name and authorship information.
- Name of the files should be descriptive like "*iphone-front-view.jpg*".
- Rich formatting (schema.org) can be used to effectively describe media content to search engines.

Avoid

- Posting forbidden content. You should be aware of the terms and conditions.
- Copyright infringement.

Using low-quality material like videos from mobile phones or disproportionally rescaled images.

Link-building

"External links are hyperlinks that point at any domain other than the domain the link exists on. Top SEOs believe that external links are the most important source of ranking power. External links pass Link Juice (ranking power) from source page to target page differently than internal links because the search engines consider them as third-party votes" (Seomoz 2013), thus are more influential.

In 1997, Google founders created an algorithmic method to determine importance and popularity of links called PageRank, which is based on several key principles

- Links on the web can be interpreted as votes that are casted to target by source
- All votes are, initially, considered equal
- Over the course of executing the algorithm on a link graph, pages which receive more votes become more important
- More important pages cast more important votes

Nowadays, majority of search engines use many metrics to determine the value of external links. Some of these metrics include:

- Trustworthiness of linking domain.
- Popularity of linking page.
- Relevancy of content between source and target page.
- Anchor text used in the link.
- Amount of links to the same page on source page.
- Amount of domains that link to target page.
- Amount of variations that are used as anchor text in links.

There are several possibilities how to get high-quality links. It is important to continuously bear in mind, that relevant links from similar and high authority websites are much more valuable than numerous links from low-quality sources. List below presents the best practice techniques widely used by webmasters to gain links (Vaidhya 2008)

- Link exchange and partnerships—exchanging links with content-related websites can help increasing link popularity, which is a major factor of Google's PageRank algorithm.
- Directory submissions—some experts believe that this method is not important anymore. However, it still depends on the relevancy. Choosing the topmost quality directories like DMOZ or Yahoo Directory and selecting a proper category helps search engines to categorise website better.

- Social bookmarking—as content of bookmarking websites is updated frequently, search engines like these types of sites and visit them often. Posting a link to a social bookmarking websites, like Digg, Delicious or StumbleUpon, might increase traffic if the tags and descriptions are used properly.
- Developing gadgets and widgets—if we put a link directing to our website within a gadget we have developed and offered to public, we can build a wide linking network thanks to developers who will place this gadget to their website.

Tool, that can help analysing the link popularity, is called MozRank. MozRank "reflects the importance of any given web page on the Internet. Pages earn MozRank by the number and quality of other pages that link to them. The higher the quality of the incoming links, the higher the MozRank" (Seomoz 2013). At the same time, MozTrust analyses global link trust. Even though it is not a search-ranking factor, it helps analysing the strength and trustworthiness of a link.

Best practices while link-building include

- Getting links from authority websites, ideally with PageRank higher than 3 and domain age more than 3 years.
- Descriptive anchor texts should be used instead of general phrases like "*click here*".
- Getting links from one relevant source is much more influential than getting a link from ten irrelevant sources.

Avoid

- Linking to a website with malicious content—use rel = "nofollow" to prevent search engines passing a Link Juice to that site.
- Linking to more than 150 pages from one page (internal + external links).
- Buying links—All major search engines, especially Google, give punishments for paid linking and might even ban a website.

Trustworthiness

It is vital to act as a trustworthy website on the Internet. It means creating quality content, update website frequently, link to and get links from relevant sources and last, but not least, serve for visitors and not for search engines. There are several more factors, which influence the trustworthiness perceived by search engines:

- Domain age—even though the age of a domain might not be the most important ranking factor, it gives signals to search engines that a website works for a long time and might be more relevant to a topic than the younger ones.
- Domain authority—this algorithm, developed by SEOmoz, gives predictions how a website will perform in search engine rankings. It might help webmasters to compare the performance against the competition. While Domain authority measures the authority of a domain, Page authority measures the authority of a single page (Seomoz 2013). While this is not a direct search-ranking factor, domain authority algorithm can be used to analyse the current performance and uncover possibilities for future improvements.

Personal settings

In order to display the most relevant search results, search engines take into consideration even personal factors, which customize the search results for every one of us. Some of the factors are language, location, web search history or frequency of visits to specific websites. If Google recognizes a website, which is visited often by a specific person, next time it will rank it higher in the search results for him (Horling and Kulick 2009).

Webmasters cannot do much about the personalized search results. However, there is still a possibility to target users based on geographic location in Google Webmaster Tools. Language targeting is obvious from the content of a website.

7   Objective of the Experiment

The main objective of this work is to test the impact of Search Engine Optimization on website's traffic. If there is a direct implication on traffic increase, we will:

- Analyse keywords, which have the highest traffic potential
- Analyse competition, to find niche market
- Compare traffic sources (direct, referral, search) to find out, which brings the most valuable visitors

7.1   Hypotheses

We will test, if following hypotheses are true:

H1: An organic search brings majority of traffic after implementation of search engine optimization techniques.
H2: Bratislava travel guide websites are in low saturated market, where it is possible to rank on the first search results page in Google (rank <10).

8   Methodology and Methods of Research

8.1   Characteristics of an Object

This study focuses on website http://bratislava-slovakia.eu. This website has been created to test SEO techniques and their influence.

Website consists of well-structured content about Bratislava and provides practical information mainly for tourist in English language. Based on keyword research, website has been categorised in following structure:

- About Bratislava—basic information about city and country, i.e. locality, weather, money and currency, or city parts.
- Travelling—describes how to get to/from Bratislava to other cities, i.e. Vienna, Budapest, or Prague.
- Places—introduces the most important places for tourists in Bratislava, i.e. airport, train station, bus station or sightseeing spots.
- Others—other categories which might be interesting for visitors, i.e. summer and winter activities, shopping, or planned tours.

Website has been launched in March 2012. Since then it has been continuously filled by unique content. In January 2014 it went through complete redesign and prepared for mobile devices. In October 2014 another complete redesign occurred bringing more engaging features and medial content.

8.2 Workflow

Keyword research
The very first part of creating a SEO-optimized website should be the keyword research. We have analysed the market, competition and potential of each keyword to drive traffic to our website.

First of all, we needed to find out whether this topic is searched and has some potential to bring visitors. We used Google Trends tool to analyse "Bratislava" keyword. This tool not only provides general interest data about the topic over time, but also showed regional interest and related terms with rising potential.

This research has shown that the keyword is mostly searched in Slovakia, Czech Republic, Austria and Hungary. Even though it could look like that these markets are not relevant due to language, we assume that majority of searches occur from tourists already based in this countries and searching for further travel opportunities. However, to get more related English keywords, we were focusing on United Kingdom and United States.

We decided to use a keyword-rich domain name, where the main key phrase is placed as the first word of whole name (http://bratislava-slovakia.eu). We have also used general and trustworthy TLD .eu, instead of .info or .net domain name. The best solution would be to use the .com domain, however, this one has already been taken. On the other hand, whole domain name now gives clear signal either for Google, or for visitors, that Bratislava is in Slovakia located in Europe.

Charts below represent the search volume for keyword "Bratislava". As we can see there is a slight decline in the volume of searches what might predict diminished interest in travelling to Bratislava (Figs. 13 and 14).

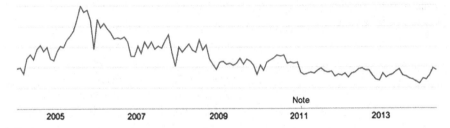

Fig. 13 Keyword "Bratislava" search volume in United Kingdom

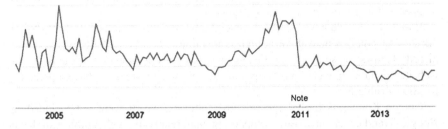

Fig. 14 Keyword "Bratislava" search volume in United States

Google Trends tool also proposed terms, which were searched right after the initial search of term "Bratislava". This gave us better look at how visitors narrow their searches to get the results they look for.

Terms are represented in Tables 3 and 4. Based on these data we can assume, that people from United Kingdom are willing to travel to Bratislava—either to stay here or to get to Vienna. Their searches included terms connected with transportation and getting to Bratislava. On the other hand, people from United States rather explore where Bratislava is, how does it look like and what to do there.

These data explore how searchers behave. However, there are still other websites, which represent a strong competition for us for particular keywords. In order to find keywords, which are worth focusing on, we used Google Keyword tool. This tool shows the estimates of monthly searches and competition level for each keyword.

From the previous findings, we merged both tables into one representing the keywords with highest search volumes. We skipped keywords not directly related

Table 3 Related terms to keyword "Bratislava" in United Kingdom

United Kingdom		
Position	Top related term	Rising related term
1	Bratislava airport	Bratislava to Budapest
2	Bratislava flights	Bratislava to Vienna
3	Bratislava Vienna	Bratislava weather
4	Vienna	Ryanair Bratislava
5	Flights to Bratislava	Vienna airport

Table 4 Related terms to keyword "Bratislava" in United States

United States		
Position	Top related term	Rising related term
1	Slovakia Bratislava	Airport Bratislava
2	Slovakia	Bratislava castle
3	Hotel Bratislava	Budapest to Bratislava
4	Map Bratislava	Map of Bratislava
5	Vienna to Bratislava	Time Bratislava

to Bratislava (i.e. Vienna, Slovakia) and merged terms, which were very similar (i.e. Bratislava Vienna and Vienna to Bratislava). For each keyword we analysed competition and number of monthly searches.

Based on this data we skipped general phrases like "Bratislava flights" and "Bratislava hotel" where there is high competition. A new website, which is not directly focused on selling flight tickets or offering accommodation (exactly as our website), cannot compete with big portals. In this stage it does not have a potential for SEO (Table 5).

Google Keywords tool suggested other phrases, which were not included in Google Trends, yet have low competition and relatively high number of local searches. Keywords are rather long-tailed than too general. The final set of keywords we will focus on in our website presents the list below.

- Bratislava—Where is Bratislava, Bratislava weather, Bratislava currency, Bratislava nightlife, What to do in Bratislava
- Bratislava Vienna—Bratislava to Vienna, Vienna to Bratislava, Bratislava to Wien, Wien to Bratislava, Bratislava to Vienna by train, Bratislava to Vienna by boat, Bratislava to Vienna by bus
- Bratislava Budapest—Bratislava to Budapest, Budapest to Bratislava, Bratislava to Budapest by train, Bratislava to Budapest by bus

Table 5 Analyses of keywords

Term	Competition		Local monthly searches	
	UK	US	UK	US
Bratislava	Low	Low	90,500	40,500
Bratislava flights	High	High	5400	390
Bratislava airport	Low	Low	4400	590
Bratislava weather	Low	Low	2900	590
Bratislava airport	Low	Low	4400	590
Slovakia Bratislava	Low	Low	1600	2400
Bratislava hotel	High	High	4400	1900
Bratislava map	Low	Low	720	480
Bratislava castle	Low	Low	320	590
Bratislava time	Low	Low	480	590
Bratislava to Prague	Low	Low	590	390
Bratislava to Vienna	Low	Low	5400	1600

- Bratislava Prague—Bratislava to Prague, Prague to Bratislava, Bratislava to Prague by train, Bratislava to Prague by bus
- Places—Bratislava airport, Bratislava train station, Bratislava castle, Bratislava old town

Content creation

As we found out the main keywords, we started preparing our own unique content. Based on research described in the first chapter, quality content is the fundamental part of search engine optimization. During the copywriting, we adhered to the following principles:

- Write for people—texts are comprehensive and easy to read. They provide full and detailed information.
- Keywords—content is keyword-rich. We used variations of keywords and repetition of phrases across whole texts to explain search engines, what the page is about. However, we avoided unnatural keyword stuffing.
- Headings—text is separated with headings, which provide clear navigational structure.
- Linking—we have created an automated system which recognizes specific keywords and creates links to specific content which guarantees the internal links uniformity. Where applicable, we used references to external sources.
- Media—we have published our own professional photos of places in Bratislava. Those are attached to relevant articles. Also one interactive map has been created to place all the important spots in Bratislava to one map.
- Engagement—we created a discussion place for visitors, where they can ask questions. We reply as soon as possible with relevant answers, which are automatically sent also by email.

Even though this is the most important part of search engine optimization, we have implemented even more techniques to ensure first positions in search results. These techniques will be demonstrated on the example of article Vienna to Bratislava by train.

On-page SEO

Following paragraphs describe techniques, which have been used to positively influence search rankings.

Titles, as one of the strongest search ranking factors, were designed to contain phrases that have the highest possibility to exactly match user's query. In this case they would be bolded and would attract users in SERP.

Example of title tag: Vienna to Bratislava by train—Train from Bratislava to Vienna.

URL addresses of our pages contain only full-meaning keywords. If it is needed, we use hyphens to separate phrases; we use hyphens instead of any other character or even merging words, however, we try to use as few hyphens as possible. Keyword-rich URL is a good signal for search engine, that a page is about specific topic, and (if not replaced by Rich Snippets Breadcrumbs) bolded if matches user's query.

Example of URL: http://bratislava-slovakia.eu/travel/vienna-bratislava/train.

We used also meta tags, even though meta description and meta keywords tags are not used as search ranking factor anymore. However, meta description could still be shown in the search result's snippets. Thus it provides a great place where to put key phrases. Those are then bolded, if match user's query and signalize that the website is about the topic he or she is looking for.

Example of meta description tag: There is a direct connection between Bratislava and Vienna. It takes approximately 1 h to get from Bratislava central station to Vienna train station. Bratislava's central station is called Bratislava—Hlavna stanica.

Example of meta keywords: Vienna central train station, Wien Sudbahnhof, Vienna Sudbahnhof, Wien Hauptbahnhof, Vienna central station, train from Vienna, train to Vienna.

We avoided duplicate content by using canonicalization. This means directing search engines to one and only content per one URL. In case that URL changed over time we used 301 Moved Permanently Header to redirect users and search engines to primary page.

Example of duplicate content: The primary URL for the page is /travel/vienna-bratislava/vienna. However, following links also direct to the same content and thus could be recognized as duplicate content, if canonicalization would not have been used:

- /index.php?id=14
- /travel-to-bratislava/vienna-to-bratislava/vienna-train
- /travel/vienna-bratislava/vienna-train?comment=225&level=1

Numerous headings were also used to separate content and provide clear navigational structure. H1, as the most important heading tag, has been placed on top of the HTML code and contains main key phrase. H2 tags were also placed in the article to contain the names of sections to help search engine understand content better.

Example of headings:

- h1: Vienna to Bratislava by train
- h2: Tickets and prices, Timetable, Transport from the station
- h3: Gallery, Map, Discussion

Pictures on the page were used to illustrate the topic and make a website more user-friendly. In terms of SEO, images might also have an influence on boosting traffic. Some pictures appear directly in the search results and the others might be found in Image search. Every image's file name has been changed to contain keywords. Keywords were also used in picture's EXIF information and image titles. Watermark with URL has been printed to the image to prevent copyright abuse, however, this does not have any effect on SEO.

We took advantage of structured data to pass as much additional information as possible to search engines. This is our big competitive advantage compared to other websites, which still do not use Rich snippets or other schema.org structured data.

We use following rich snippets to ensure that our website will be visible in SERP and will "take" as much space as possible:

- Breadcrumbs—to show the path to the article instead of URL
- Reviews—to show stars rating
- Author—to show author's credentials
- Publisher—to associate a website with Google+ profile

In terms of page speed, we try to load as much content from static sources as possible. We enabled gzip compression and minified source codes.

For Google, we have created a sitemap, which includes all the links to articles published on a website. This will help Google to discover even the newest articles relatively fast. Other than links sitemap, we have created also a sitemap of images. Both sitemaps have been successfully uploaded to Google Webmaster Tools.

Off-page SEO

Things that we cannot directly influence, as they depend on third parties, are called off-page optimization. Following paragraphs describe techniques that have been used in terms of off-page SEO.

First and one of the most important parts was the activity on social networks. We analysed the most used and most influential social media websites and created profiles there. As mentioned in the first chapter, Google uses links from Google+ as ranking factor. We filled every possible field to describe our website with strong keywords. Wherever possible, we used links to our specific pages, not just homepage. Afterwards, we started publishing engaging content and building community. To simplify sharing, we enabled "social buttons", which publish website link on a specific social network:

- "Like" button which posts content to Facebook
- "Tweet" button which interacts with Twitter
- "+1" button which is used by Google+

To customise the look of the shared content, we used

- OpenGraph tags to design Facebook links
- Meta itemprop tags to design Google+ links

Using these tags lets social networks display specific title, description, link and even an image in the "news feed".

Afterwards we started linking to our content from external websites. Link-building is the most essential part of whole off-page SEO. We analysed potential websites, which could link to our website. The evaluation criteria were:

- Content relevancy
- Domain age and authority
- Popularity and trustworthiness
- Ability to post links
- PageRank

Table 6 Sites selected for link-building (October 2014)

Website	Domain authority	PageRank	Alexa rank	Google position[a]
TripAdvisor.com—travel forum	95	7	205	3
LonelyPlanet.com—travel forum	95	8	1673	2
WikiTravel.org—wiki travel page	89	7	3301	1
Wikipedia.org	100	9	6	1
Quora.com	90	7	269	–

[a]Organic position on Google search results page for keyword "travel Bratislava"

Finally, we have selected four main websites (presented in a Table 6), which met the criteria. It is possible to post user-generated content to these websites hence we were able to publish links to our website.

As these websites provide information for tourists, we started answering questions published in the threads. We published long and quality posts, which fully answered the question. If available, we attached even links directing to our website with descriptive anchor texts to provide "read more" opportunity.

Even though all of these websites automatically append rel = "nofollow" tag to any posted link, which prevents search engines from passing Link Juice, we have seen a significant increase in traffic, mainly in traffic from referrals.

- In terms of media sharing, we needed to publish as many quality unique pictures as possible, as they could be also found in Google Image search. And not only have that—in some cases they even provided a space to write meaningful descriptions full of links. Following list describes websites, which have been used and how they have been used:
- Google+ Photos—this image service recently replaced Google Picasa. Google might sometimes push image search results to organic text results.
- Flickr—Image-sharing social network provides space for professional picture presentations. As it provides space to post html-formatted descriptions, it is a great link-building place (although links are no-followed).
- Pinterest—relatively new image-sharing social network allows users "like" and "repin" images, what helps sharing pictures across the web. For every image, a source link can be used which directs to our website. Some links are even followed and pass link juice. Pinterest is considered as the most valuable image-sharing network in terms of link-building for us.
- Google maps—sightseeing places presented on our website have been put to custom Google map. To every spot, full html formatting can be used. This provides opportunity to easily get links from Google domain.

Every image has been watermarked by website name. Even though this does not have any effect on link building, as this watermark is not a link, it is a great way of "branding".

8.3 Methods of Data Collection and Sources

To analyse the traffic and influence of specific factors, we used several online services. Data are collected automatically either by putting tracking code to the website, or by service-provider's estimations.

Website data

Data about real traffic were collected by high-quality service called Google Analytics. Tiny snippet of code is able to track visitor's behaviour, describes traffic sources and analyses content popularity. As Google itself provides these analytics, it is considered to be highly reputable (Kryvinska et al. 2013; Kryvinska and Gregus 2014).

Another way of collecting specific data and benchmarking with competition is the Alexa service. It collects data from external sources and provides quality estimations about global rank, national rank, or even some information about traffic. Big advantage is that Alexa provides free information about the competition and enables easy benchmarking.

Social media data

Each social network offers its own data about audience, which is engaged with website. Facebook Insights provide complete statistics about "fans", about their demographics and behaviour. These data can be used to better focus our content to the specific audience.

We also used Google Analytics and Flickr Insights to track data about pictures. Other indicators, like number of "likes" on Facebook or "pins" on Pinterest might also offer relevant information about images' popularity. These data can be also found in Google Analytics.

Other data

To track website's performance, we used Open Site Explorer. From information offered we could detect domain authority, page authority and linking profile.

There are several free website services, which offer PageRank check, as Google itself does not provide official information about this number. PageRank reflects strength of linking profile and is a good indicator of how popular the website is.

To obtain general information about social medias, search engines, or specific technical parameters, we used Global Stats Stat Counter. This service provides valuable benchmarking information, separated by country and ordered by time.

To analyse real visitors' behaviour we used Inspectlet. This service generates eye tracking, click and scroll heatmaps, which are very important in case of UI/UX analysis. According to these visualizations we can optimize content design and provide more relevant information in a short period of time.

9 Evaluation Methods and Interpretation of Results

After fully launching the website in May 2012 we started to see almost immediate increase of traffic.

Acceleration during first 3 months was caused mainly by increasing number of visitors from referral websites. At that time, referrals were the most important source of traffic bringing ∼50% of all visitors.

However, August 2012 was the last month when we could have seen equal numbers between referral and organic search traffic. In September, organic traffic started to gather its importance and a month after, visitors from organic search accounted for ∼70% of all traffic. Thus we can assume, that it took us 5 months to "persuade" Google about the importance and quality of our website. In this time, our website started to occur higher and higher in search results, occasionally even reaching the top 1 position (Fig. 15).

Number of visitors was growing at satisfactory rate of ∼30% month over month. This only confirms that keeping website fresh with new content is a clear signal to Google to rank your website higher.

In April 2013, 13 months after full launch, for the first time we have hit 10,000 visitors per month. At that moment, referral traffic accounted only for 5% of our traffic sources. Three out of four visitors would come from organic search. But started to observe another important source of traffic in our statistics—the direct traffic.

Surprising 18% of people already knew our website and were able to write the address directly to browser, without performing any search or click from another website. Vast majority of these people already visited our website some time ago, thus we assume that they bookmarked our articles for later reading. This fact only proves that a well-organized and easy-to-read text is important not only for Google, but mainly for a user.

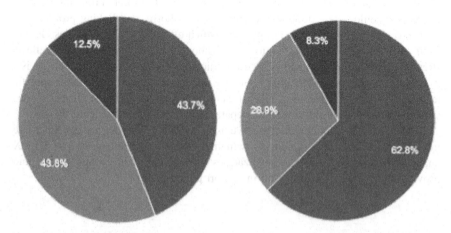

Fig. 15 Percentage of visitors from various traffic sources (Aug'12 vs. Sep'12). Legend: *Blue* organic search traffic, *Green* referral traffic, *Orange* other traffic sources (Color figure online)

Years 2013–2015 were unexpectedly successful. During these 36 months we have served 640,000 unique visitors who have 2 min reading of our articles in average. In total, 1.5 million pages have been displayed to our visitors.

The monthly growth of traffic, however, slowed down and reached 0% YoY in December 2015. As the content of website was not being updated and no new articles have been published we can assume that we have hit the plateau. To maintain the growth of traffic in following years we must either publish and promote new discoverable content or increase positions in organic search by very focused search engine optimization (Fig. 16).

Since launch, search engines brought ~80% of all visitors to our website. Right mix of on-page and off-page optimization techniques described in previous chapter was essential while building our search strategy. However, there is one more important step in whole process of SEO—planning.

Selecting the right keywords, which are worth optimizing for, is the key of optimization. It is necessary to prepare a plan which is ambitious, yet realistic and based on data, not on wishes.

We have focused on long-tail keywords (i.e. "Vienna to Bratislava train") rather than highly competitive ones (i.e. "Bratislava"). As we assumed in the beginning of this chapter, probability of getting to the first positions in search results was high. Following figure compares the performance of main keywords, which we have set as core for search engine optimization.

As we can see in the following chart, keywords on average positions between 1 and 5 get significant number of clicks (CTR mainly between 25 and 45%). Exactly matched website title with search phrase could be a possible reason why is that so. However, there are three phrases, which do not gather high CTR despite relatively high position (Fig. 17):

- "Where is Bratislava"

  – Users probably prefer Wikipedia, which ranks on the first positions.

Fig. 16 Evolution of traffic by months

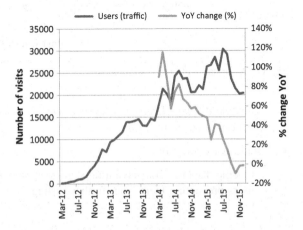

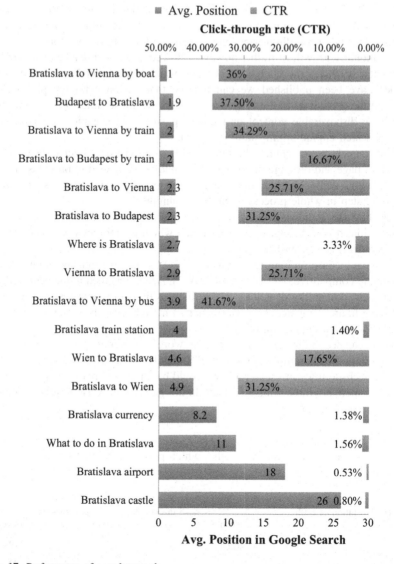

Fig. 17 Performance of core keywords

- Google displays Bratislava on map and gives a direct answer to users preventing them from further surfing.
- "Bratislava train station"
  - Google displays Bratislava train station on map and gives a direct answer to users preventing them from further surfing.

- Inappropriately chosen title ("Central train station") does not exactly match with searched query.

- "Bratislava currency"

  - Page description displayed in search results gives direct answer to users what probably prevents them from further surfing.

To test the saturation of the market, we have selected all keywords with more than 100 search impressions. This would reduce very long-tailed and niche keywords searched only couple of times during last three months.

From total 201 keywords, which led to our website since January to March 2013, up to 104 of keywords had average position in Google better than 10. In other words, 51.7% of keywords, which were searched and led to our website, were placed in the first search result page.

This ratio, however, changed dramatically nowadays. Since August to October 2014 we displayed on 280 keywords with more than 100 impressions in Google search. 95% of these keywords ranked in a first Google search page and 45% ranked even in the first position.

From these results we can assume that Bratislava travel guide websites are operating in low saturated market with weak competition. In this market it is easy to own near half of the top positions of selected keywords. Our hypotheses are thus confirmed.

10 Conclusion

Search engine optimization proved to be an important part of driving traffic to a website. Hypotheses defined by this article have been tested by experimental approach of creating a website http://bratislava-slovakia.eu and implementation of the described SEO techniques. Since launch in May 2012, website served more than 650,000 visitors and proved both hypotheses to be true:

- H1: An organic search brings majority of traffic after implementation of search engine optimization techniques—confirmed, as organic traffic accounted for 80% of all website traffic.
- H2: Bratislava travel guide websites are in low saturated market, where there is possible to rank on the first search results page in Google (rank <10)—confirmed, as in 95% of searches our website was displayed in the rank <10.

We have implemented all relevant SEO techniques including providing unique and quality content written according to copywriting guidelines, off-page promotion via link-building and on-page optimization of source code.

Further research needs to be done to evaluate the importance of each technique in the whole process of search engine optimization.

References

Berger J, Milkman KL (2011) What makes online content viral? J Mark Res 2–14. ISSN 0022-2437

Court D, Elzinga D, Mulder S et al (2015) The new consumer decision journey. McKinsey&Company.   http://www.mckinsey.com/Insights/Marketing_Sales/The_new_consumer_decision_journey. Accessed Jan 2016

Court D, Elzinga D, Mulder S, Vetvik OJ (2009) The consumer decision journey. McKinsey&Company.   http://www.mckinsey.com/insights/marketing_sales/the_consumer_decision_journey. Accessed Nov 2016

Google (2010) Google search engine optimization starter guide. Google.com. http://static.googleusercontent.com/external_content/untrusted_dlcp/www.google.com/sk//webmasters/docs/search-engine-optimization-starter-guide.pdf. Accessed Jan 2016

Google Webmaster Central (2009) Google does not use the keywords meta tag in web ranking. http://googlewebmastercentral.blogspot.sk/2009/09/google-does-not-use-keywords-meta-tag.html. Accessed Jan 2016

Google Webmaster Central (2010) Using site speed in web search ranking. http://googlewebmastercentral.blogspot.sk/2010/04/using-site-speed-in-web-search-ranking.html. Accessed Jan 2016

Google Webmaster Tools (2012) Steps to a Google-friendly site. http://support.google.com/webmasters/bin/answer.py?hl=en&answer=40349&topic=2370419&ctx=topic. Accessed Jan 2016

Gregus M, Kryvinska N (2015) Service orientation of enterprises—aspects, dimensions, technologies. Comenius University in Bratislava

Horling B, Kulick M (2009) Personalizes search for everyone. http://googleblog.blogspot.sk/2009/12/personalized-search-for-everyone.html. Accessed Feb 2016

Kaczor S, Kryvinska N (2013) It is all about services—fundamentals, drivers, and business models. J Serv Sci Res (The Society of Service Science, Springer) 5(2):125–154

Kaushik A (2009) Web analytics 2.0. Wiley, New Jersey. ISBN 9780470596449

Kryvinska N, Barokova A, Auer L, Ivanochko I, Strauss C (2013) Business value assessment of services re-use on SOA using appropriate methodologies, metrics and models. Int J Serv Econ Manag (IJSEM) (Special Issue on Service-centric Models, Platforms and Technologies, Inderscience Publishers) 5(4):301–327

Kryvinska N, Gregus M (2014) SOA and its business value in requirements, features, practices and methodologies. Comenius University in Bratislava

Kryvinska N, Kaczor S, Strauss C, Gregus M (2014a) Servitization—its raise through information and communication technologies. In: 5th international conference on exploring services science (IESS 1.4), Geneva, Switzerland. Lecture Notes in Business Information Processing (LNBIP 169). Springer, pp 72–81, 5–7 Feb 2014

Kryvinska N, Kaczor S, Strauss C, Gregus M (2014b) Servitization strategies and product-service-systems. In: The IEEE fourth international workshop on the future of software engineering FOR and IN cloud (FoSEC 2014), 27 June–2 July 2014, at Hilton Anchorage, Alaska, USA, within IEEE 10th world congress on services (SERVICES 2014), pp 254–260

Kryvinska N, Kaczor S, Strauss C, Gregus M (2015) Servitization—transition from manufacturer to service provider. In: Gummesson E, Mele C, Polese F (eds) Service dominant logic, network and systems theory and service science: integrating three perspectives for a new service agenda, Naples Forum on service, Naples, Italy, 9–12 June 2015

Porter L, Golan GJ (2006) From subservient chicken to brawny men. J Interact Advert 6(2) 26–33. ISSN 1525-2019

Schema (2013) What is schema.org. http://schema.org/. Accessed Jan 2016

Search Engine Land (2012) The periodic table of SEO ranking factors. http://searchengineland.com/seotable. Accessed Jan 2016

Seomoz (2013) 2013 search ranking factors. http://www.seomoz.org/article/search-ranking-factors#metrics. Accessed Jan 2016

Slegg J (2014) Facebook, Twitter social signals not part of Google search ranking algorithm. http://searchenginewatch.com/article/2325343/Matt-Cutts-Facebook-Twitter-Social-Signals-Not-Part-of-Google-Search-Ranking-Algorithms. Accessed Jan 2016

Statcounter (2013) Top 5 search engines worldwide. http://gs.statcounter.com/#search_engine-ww-monthly-201202-201302. Accessed Mar 2016

Stoshikj M, Kryvinska N, Strauss C (2014) Efficient managing of complex programs with project management services. Global J Flex Syst Manag (Special Issue on Flexible Complexity Management and Engineering by Innovative Services, Springer) 15(1):25–38

Stoshikj M, Kryvinska N, Strauss C (2016) Service systems and service innovation: two pillars of service science. J Procedia Comput Sci (Special Issue on The 7th International Conference on Ambient Systems, Networks and Technologies (ANT-2016), Elsevier) 83:212–220

Sullivan D (2010) What social signals do Google & Bing really count? http://searchengineland.com/what-social-signals-do-google-bing-really-count-55389. Accessed Feb 2016

Think with Google (2014) The customer journey to online purchase. https://www.thinkwithgoogle.com/tools/customer-journey-to-online-purchase.html. Accessed Feb 2016

Urikova O, Ivanochko I, Kryvinska N, Zinterhof P, Strauss C (2012) Managing complex business services in heterogeneous eBusiness ecosystems—aspect-based research assessment. J Procedia Comput Sci (Special Issue on The 3rd International Conference on Ambient Systems, Networks and Technologies (ANT-2012), Elsevier) 10:128–135

Vaidhya (2008) 21 Off-Page SEO strategies to build your online reputation. http://www.seomoz.org/ugc/21offpage-seo-strategies-to-build-your-online-reputation. Accessed Feb 2016

Ward C (2013) Why content goes viral: the theory and proof. http://www.seomoz.org/blog/why-content-goes-viral-the-scientific-theory-and-proof. Accessed Jan 2016

Whalley, B (2012) How to use internal linking to improve your website's SEO. http://blog.hubspot.com/blog/tabid/6307/bid/31388/How-to-Use-Internal-Linking-to-Improve-Your-Website-s-SEO.aspx. Accessed Jan 2016

Chapter 8
Sharing Knowledge and Information Through Corporate e-Learning

Martina Halás Vančová and Zuzana Kovačičová

Abstract Corporate e-learning is a way how a company can spread desired information among all employees without any time or space limitations. It is considered as a simple and low-cost method of educating employees. Companies are constantly growing and with an increasing number of employees it is easier but also more convenient to implement e-learning for the purposes of education. The chapter describes implementation of e-learning from the perspective of a company providing e-learning systems but also from the view of a company actively using e-learning. Both views are supported by a questionnaire survey realized among employees using e-learning at work. Combination of three points of view enables us to achieve a complex picture about the current state of e-learning, its advantages as well as disadvantages, and last but not least, to give us the insight into importance of implementation of e-learning in companies.

Keywords Corporate education · e-Learning systems · Learning management system · Implementation of e-learning

1 Introduction

It is undeniable that education enables a company to increase potential of its employees. Since human resources are considered as the most important company's asset, it is necessary to build a strategic educational program, which will be efficient and reliable for company's future needs, even under the influence of external environment. A strategy of corporate education must contain selection of means of education, in order to support the most beneficial way of transferring and distributing knowledge or skills.

M.H. Vančová (✉) · Z. Kovačičová
Faculty of Management, Comenius University, Bratislava, Slovakia
e-mail: martina.halas@fm.uniba.sk

Z. Kovačičová
e-mail: zuzana.kovacicova@fm.uniba.sk

© Springer Science+Business Media Singapore 2018
N. Kryvinska and M. Gregus (eds.), *Agile Information Business*,
Flexible Systems Management, DOI 10.1007/978-981-10-3358-2_8

Thus in recent years, e-learning has become the common way of education in many companies. It offers a flexible, low-cost and sophisticated form for development of employees. Many companies consider e-learning as a method of future learning. Companies need people for their efficient operating. Moreover, they are searching for highly educated people to become their employees in order to achieve added value for its processes, products and services. However, people need continuous education during their presence in a company. In addition to this, companies need to educate more people at once with up-to-date information. Thus, e-learning provides cheap and rather effective ways for achieving this goal.

The chapter is focused on corporate e-learning and its current state in Slovakia as well as abroad. It summarizes development of e-learning in recent years and its most significant advantages as well as disadvantages with the emphasis on cost cutting and methods of evaluating efficiency of e-learning. Furthermore, we present research findings and discussion in the area of implementation of corporate e-learning, based on the information obtained from one of the biggest e-learning providers in the world and a private banking institution based in Slovakia. Additionally, findings are supported by the survey focused on opinions of general public about e-learning education.

2 e-Learning in Slovakia and Abroad

e-Learning offers a wide scale of studying opportunities for companies and people. Implementation of e-learning in Slovak and foreign companies has an increasing tendency. Moreover, e-learning systems have been developing for many years and they bring new interactive and modern ways of studying. Generally, education, including education of employees, has always been very important and its meaning is growing in today's knowledge companies.

Human resources management covers various functions such as staff planning, work analysis, allocation of employees and many others. One of its functions is also education and development of employees. It is a continuous and permanent process focused on developing of skills, knowledge and motivation of employees with the aim to increase their productivity and competences. As a result, a company can reach higher quality of workforce and decreasing difference between its own requirements and employees' actual competencies. In recent years, companies have been applying e-learning methods of education. They are accessible 24 h a day from any location with the use of electronic media such as computers, tablets and smartphones with the Internet and intranet (Kachaňáková et al. 2007; Balco et al. 2014).

Education has always been the way of the improvement for the whole population. In Slovakia, compulsory school education was introduced in the eighteenth century by Maria Theresa of Austria. Recently, a number of reforms have been applied in the country to improve the status and quality of education. In the year 2006 Slovakia has reported that 91% of population has completed secondary education and thus, Slovakia reached the third place in the whole Europe. However, in the same year, tertiary education was reported at one of the lowest levels. Nowadays, Slovakia still belongs to countries with the lowest level of tertiary education in the EU. Slovakia struggles with an insufficient budget for education what is, naturally, reflected in the quality of education in the country. Public expenditures for education in Slovakia are one of the lowest in the European Union (Statistical Office of the Slovak republic 2013).

According to the OECD (2013), probability to be employed on a full-time contract is increasing with the level of education. In average 64% of people with lower than secondary education has a full-time job but on the other hand, 75% of university educated people works full-time.

The modern age can be characterized by continuous dynamic changes that influence our daily life and our approach to decision-making, information but also to education. Companies in the whole world and also in Slovakia are trying to reach the highest profitability resulting in significant cost cutting with more emphasis on innovations and increasing potential of employees, creativity and intelligence. We live in the world of knowledge companies and knowledge management. Therefore, information is the key. As mentioned by Papula (2009), it is undeniable that knowledge management is one of the ways how to increase productivity of a company. It focuses mostly on acquiring new information and knowledge, processing and multiplication of knowledge. For realization of the mentioned processes we need the following subjects: People, Culture, Processes and Technologies.

3 Definition of e-Learning

Companies know that people are their most important part and they must put a lot of effort on their enhancement. Companies apply different tools for improving skills and knowledge of employees and e-learning is one of the most used and useful forms of education.

e-Learning, however, is not the inventory of the modern age. The idea can be only realized today as we can use various media and technology. Beginning of e-learning is connected with the development of the Internet. Nowadays, learning management systems (LMS) allow us to use variety of online e-learning methods such as online conferences, chats, or even virtual classes (Frk 2010; Harasim 2006).

Based on the definition by Cisco (2015), e-learning is the way how to bring information, knowledge and education to the most remote parts of the world. However, educational standards must be improved meaning that schools and libraries must go online first. Furthermore, if a country supports educated and trained population, companies come and invest money into both, people and a region itself. But poor education and literacy will never allow a country to maintain its economic boom.

4 Development of e-Learning

The important factor in applying e-learning is digital literacy as ability to work with computer and IT tools may be a limiting factor. Based on the research by Velšic from the Institute for Public Affairs (2011), in Fig. 1 we can see that the ratio of digital literacy in Slovakia in 2011 was only 76%. Therefore, companies might be affected by lower preferences of employees in selection of e-learning as a preferred form of acquiring knowledge since they might not be able to work with a computer or moreover, they might be technophobic.

Application of e-learning at schools and organizations has an increasing tendency. It is clear that a number of computers and possibilities of the access to the Internet at households has increased in Slovakia and also in the whole world. Figure 2 shows that the Internet connection in households in the Europe but also in Slovakia has been significantly increasing (Eurostat 2012).

The application and use of e-learning tools is increasing. Money spent on e-learning in the whole world has arisen from $35 billion in 2011 to $56 billion in 2013 and are forecasted to be double in 2015. Corporations have stated that e-learning is the second most valuable training method and at least 50% of costs was saved by replacing classroom-based education with e-learning. Additionally, 60% of time for instructing has been cut down. In 2013 46% of university students are taking minimally one online course. More than 41% of Fortune 500 Companies use some form of technology to educate employees during formal learning hours and the trends have been reported as steadily increasing for future years. Another significant fact is that almost 25% of all employees leave their jobs because they did not find enough learning opportunities in the company. In addition to this, companies who offer e-learning can make 26% more revenue per employee. 72% of companies stated that e-learning helps them to keep up-to-date changes in the industry. Companies with strong learning culture are better in the market compared to those who do not (Ferriman 2014). During introduction of e-learning there were expectations that it will cover up to 90% of corporate learning. But employees still prefer classroom education to another minutes or hours spent at the computer. Therefore, combination of e-learning with classroom education seems to be the most attractive and useful. We can also compare approach to corporate education in past years and now (and in future) (Horník 2007) (Table 1).

Fig. 1 Digital literacy in Slovakia, 2011 (Color figure online)

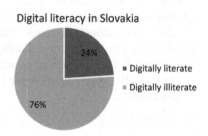

Digital literacy in Slovakia

24%

- Digitally literate
- Digitally illiterate

76%

Fig. 2 Percentage of households with access to the internet (Color figure online)

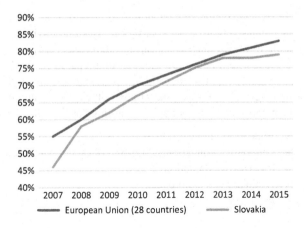

Table 1 Trends in e-learning

	In the past	Nowadays and expected in future
Design of courses	Long-term courses usually exceeding a month	Short-term courses
	Complex topics	Partial topics
	Simple classroom course	Blended e-learning
	Effort to use technical equipment	Courses for everyone with applicable for the least equipped computer
	Lecturer, tutor	Lecturer is not available
Process and motivation	Limited access only for chosen people	Open courses
	Study control, testing used as scoring	Testing used for further development
	Test result as element of motivation	Competition as element of motivation
	Chat used for expressing ideas about course	Co-authorship—possibility to influence course content

Source Processed by the authors based on Horník (2007)

Nowadays, e-learning is very often connected with other forms of education. So-called "blended learning" describes the company's approach to include various forms of education to reach a desired goal. In order to use the most effective way of e-learning, we need to choose and coordinate delivery of education. The blended learning can reach the best results only if it consists of the right forms of education in the right time. For applying the right method of education we need to analyse various criteria such as complexity of education, stability and structure of content of education, time point of view but also a number of attendants. If we want to deliver or teach easier information we can use asynchronous education—so we can apply only e-learning course containing an interactive and interesting content. However, more difficult and complex topics require combination of more education forms—for better understanding and practice, a tutor and real-time cooperation of attendants might be necessary. The dynamic environment very often requires creation of immediate education for employees. In such case, it is more reasonable to use classroom education that can be prepared faster than e-learning course.

As stated by Horník (2007), companies usually apply e-learning for those topics that are needed for a higher number of employees and they are usually standardized. Generally, companies apply e-learning for the following courses:

- Education about products
- Obligatory education based by law (e.g. occupational health and safety)
- Process of adaptation
- Evaluation of employees
- Feedback.

5 Forms of e-Learning

e-Learning can be divided into the online and offline form. Online e-learning can be further divided into synchronous and asynchronous forms. Currently, online e-learning is the most common and it uses the Internet as well as intranet. Synchronous e-learning means real-time communication or participation at education. This form of e-learning is very beneficial because it uses cooperation in real time and supports effectiveness of the educational process. Synchronous e-learning has various forms:

- Audio and video conference—currently, the market offers many choices for real-time conferences, for example, Skype, Google or Facebook.
- IM—instant messaging offers the possibility of real-time chat via software. The most popular IM applications are ICQ, Jabber, MS Messenger, but also corporate tools such as Lotus SameTime.
- Shared applications—software that allows its users to share a document and write or draw on it while communicating with other participants. A very popular example is Whiteboard, or a shared desktop.

An asynchronous form of e-learning does not require attendance of participants at the same time. Offline forms of e-learning do not require the Internet connection and they are usually based on various applications, programs or CD-ROMs (Frk 2010).

Based on the fact whether a lecturer is or is not available during a course, we can divide e-learning into the following:

- Synchronous with a lecturer—this course is very similar to classroom-based courses and its only advantage in comparison to classroom-based course is a reduction of costs and time for travelling.

- Synchronous without a lecturer—a course is set up for particular time and it has a strict schedule. Usually, this type of course is not very popular as it is strict and timed. However, it can be made more attractive by an online discussion and a message board.
- Asynchronous with a lecturer—a course attendant can choose time based on his/her preferences and discussion and communication with a lecturer and other attendants is done in an offline message board or by individual consulting.
- Asynchronous without a lecturer—this type of course is usually intended for self-study, most often containing various interactive elements and animations. Needless to say, this type of course is most often used in corporate e-learning (Horník 2007).

Companies that are searching for the ways of increasing knowledge of its employees are nowadays focusing mostly on technologies. Modern technologies such as intranet, Document Management Systems, Learning Management Systems, Brainstorming software, data warehouses or electronic libraries are highly spread within companies and employees. Web 2.0 describes various ways of information spreading such as follows:

- Blogs provide an opportunity to make own web notes or diaries and share own knowledge or information
- Wikipedia—a web-based encyclopedia containing various hyperlinks and multi-language information
- Social networks—an opportunity for sharing information, searching for contacts, etc.
- Community webpages are oriented to numerous topics and areas, as an example we can mention webpages Procesy.sk, Porada.sk, Entrepreneur.com, or websites focused on sharing information such as Flickr or YouTube
- Web Applications such as Google Apps
- Widgets applied on websites provides possibility of personalization, for instance, iGoogle or MyYahoo
- Mashup applications for combining different information from various sources.

All the mentioned opportunities include one common feature—collective intelligence. Collective intelligence gathers information and knowledge from thousands of people and consequently the information is provided to people. Therefore, the use of mentioned tools has an increasing tendency by individuals, business people and organizations. Web 2.0 provides very easy, direct, low-cost and effective ways of approaching to information and sharing documents with colleagues or business partners (Papula 2009). Web 2.0 provides collaborative learning, which is more effective than individual education. Cooperation and mutual help among attendants of education has a higher quality than knowledge reached by individual learning (Gokhle 1995).

However, it is also necessary to mention negatives of this method of acquiring knowledge. First, websites providing professional information are created by a wide spectrum of people who provide information based on their experience and then information can be insufficient or wrong. Moreover, their identity is usually not verified what decreases the value of information provided. Second, articles and information are usually not managed and some important related topics or subtopics can be unseen or not covered. Third, relying on information from someone else decreases own searching for information and own investigation and research and then consequently, own intelligence, logic, inventions and thinking. As articles and topics are not managed, the process of searching for answers can be purposeless and required information may not be provided in the resources readers are focused on what may cause demotivation and very often it is a waste of time (Papula 2009). Currently, the market offers various systems of managing e-learning. The term Learning Management System describes the system for organizing and managing electronic education. LMS produced by different companies have different features and they are developed at different levels. LMS are not focused on creating content of education but only on its logistics and communication in the education process. For creating of content of e-learning courses there is LCMS—the Learning Content Management System. The LCMS is the tool for creating a subject of a course. The tool allows editing, adding or improving of content of education. LCMS and LMS are, in general, independent systems. For their connection we need SCORM—the Sharable Content Object Reference Model. SCORMS defines the communication between LCMS and LMS. SCORM allows users to use LMS and LCMS from different producers (Pejša 2007).

e-Learning courses can be divided according to their interactivity. Some e-learning courses are used for distribution of final information, so they can be very similar to an ordinary PowerPoint presentation. A different type of e-learning courses is used with the aim to acquire information. This type includes self-testing with multiple choice questions and in general, it aims to increase interactivity of such a course. The last type of e-learning course includes elements of cooperation. It usually offers interaction with content, other students or lectors. It most often contains a space for discussion or virtual classrooms (Horník 2007).

6 Disadvantages of e-Learning

The most significant disadvantages of e-learning include the following:

- Lack of control—it might be very difficult to track an e-learning process of individual employees. Employees with lower motivation may avoid e-learning or fail deadlines as they are managing their own time for education.
- Approach to learning—a design of e-learning courses cannot be fully adjusted to all learning styles. Some employees prefer reading, others listening and images. It may be challenging for a company to set up courses to completely cover all needs of education.
- Computer Competency and Literacy—not all employees are comfortable with using new and modern kinds of education software in spite of their user-friendly

and intuitive interface. These employees may rather choose classroom education.

- Isolation—in many cases, a learning activity requires face-to-face communication supported by a trainer with an opportunity to answer questions and provide a space for discussions. The isolation can cause demotivation of attendees as they do not feel the required support.
- Technology issues—a company must make sure that employees have all the required technical devices. There may occur many issues such as a poor Internet connection, interruption of e-learning by random faults or non-compatibility with e-learning software.

In addition to this, companies usually face the following limits in applying e-learning:

- Age of employees—in some cases age can be limiting in using IT tools
- IT equipment of a company—not every company is sufficiently equipped with computers and IT devices to be able to apply and provide e-learning
- For some courses it may not be possible to transfer them into e-learning
- Too high initial costs and costs for administration and maintenance of e-learning courses (Horník 2007).

7 Advantages of e-Learning

The advantages of e-learning include the following:

- Flexibility—e-learning courses provide a significant level of flexibility and independence to employees. They can choose the time of education and education can be even split into several parts so they can proceed with learning during several days and adjust learning to their workload.
- Lower costs—e-learning courses give an opportunity to reduce company's education costs per head. At the beginning, it is necessary to buy or create e-learning software and courses but the initial investment may be returned quickly. Moreover, there is no need to have a trainer or an education team.
- Mobility—nowadays e-learning courses can be used via smart phones or tablets, so there is an opportunity to learn during travelling or free time.
- A specific design—e-learning courses can be tailored to one's needs. If an employee already knows some part of the topic it is possible to skip the part and focus on new information.

It is necessary to mention also intangible advantages of e-learning such as follows:

- Increasing of employees' job satisfaction as they may feel a higher commitment to an organization

- Improved teamwork and collaboration and decrease of conflicts
- Increase in customer's satisfaction
- Providing standard knowledge—companies can use e-leaning when they need to deliver standard information for all employees at once, e.g. changes in legislation with the possibility to check effectiveness of the study (Horník 2007).

8   Practical Scenario: Implementation of Corporate e-Learning

We aim to provide the picture of using and implementing e-learning courses in corporations by summarization of the three different points of view. Our objective is to sum up suggestions for companies that are deciding about the application of e-learning courses for education and development of its employees. Furthermore, we aim to describe the process of implementation of an e-learning course in a company from the beginning of the process until it is being used and updated during the years of use. Our view is supported by three different perceptions what leads to very coherent results.

8.1   Research Methods

The research was carried out by gaining and analysing data and information from two companies and also by a questionnaire provided to employed people. Thus, in the practical scenario we were focused on three main sources of information:

- Company A—an international company providing tailored e-learning courses, currently no. 2 in the area of e-learning providers
- Company B—a Slovak banking institution that uses e-learning for education of its employees
- Research group of 44 people, employed in different companies in Slovakia, using e-learning at work.

Thus, the procedure of our research is based on three different approaches:

- Consulting with the company A
- Consulting with the company B
- Questionnaires provided to the research sample of 44 employees of companies situated in Slovakia.

First, we have consulted with the company A and we obtained a wide scale of information about their process of designing e-learning courses for various customers. The company provided their point of view on the market focused on education and especially on the e-learning market. The company expressed their vision on advantages and disadvantages of e-learning courses in general as well as benefits of its application in a company. Moreover, the company described specific processes of applying e-learning for one of its customers.

Second, thanks to the consulting with the company B, we have obtained information about the actual use of e-learning for education and development of its employees. The company provided their opinion on this form of education and described their processes of applying e-learning by various departments and their approach to creating of content.

Finally, we requested information through the survey from employed people using e-learning at work, to be able to support the research with their opinions and approach to this form of education, their preferences and their point of view on advantages and disadvantages of e-learning.

To sum it up, we were focused on the whole process of application of e-learning in today's market conditions.

Furthermore, we used the comparison method to be able to evaluate differences and similar features regarding the e-learning area in two different companies—a company actively using e-learning as a form of education and a company developing e-learning solutions for its clients. By the method of analysis, we described obtained results of the research. During the consulting and communication with companies we obtained a huge amount of information that must have been analysed and further interpreted. Synthesis was used to express the results in a clear and structured form and hence we are able to summarize information into lists and tables. Additionally, acquired information was processed by the method of induction to provide suggestions for the application of e-learning. Using deduction, we were able to create and provide statements based on the obtained material.

Questionnaires were used to gain information from employees in order to have an opinion of the general public. We used questionnaires that included only closed questions. The research sample consisted of 44 employees of various companies in Slovakia. The questionnaires were limited by the minimal age of 18 years and full-time employment. There was no limit for males or females. Questions provided either dichotomous answers, single choice or multiple choices of answers. Our respondents consisted of 61% of females and 39% of males. 59% of respondents came from the Trnava region and only one respondent (2%) did not have the Slovak nationality. 70% of respondents reported finished university education.

8.2 Deciding About Implementation of Corporate e-Learning

Companies usually have their own formal program of education. Today's knowledge companies need continuous, up-to-date and high-quality education and moreover, they need to assure that they can cover mandatory trainings, project trainings and still be able to support motivation of their employees. Companies that are searching for the ways of increasing knowledge of their employees are often focusing on new technologies and they are trying to establish a flexible education environment (Balco and Greguš 2014). As an example, web 2.0 allows information spread via social networks, web applications, blogs, Wikipedia, community web-pages, etc. All the mentioned opportunities include one common feature—collective intelligence. Collective intelligence gathers information and knowledge from thousands of people and consequently the information is provided to people. Therefore, the use of mentioned tools has an increasing tendency among individuals, business people and organizations. Web 2.0 provides collaborative learning, which is more effective than individual education. Cooperation and mutual help among attendants of education has higher quality than knowledge reached by individual learning (Papula 2009; Gokhle1995).

Our research shows that only 8 out of 44 people currently using e-learning at work chose e-learning as their preferred form of education, what expresses 18% of all the answers (Fig. 3). Every company should first communicate with its employees if they are even interested in this form of education. However, this is applicable only for small companies. Bigger companies usually apply e-learning from the cost-saving or cost-cutting point of view. Figure 3 also shows that students mostly prefer interactive lectures, and thus interactive content should be understood as one of the most important components of a good e-learning course. We did not notice any significant difference in the preferred form of education between men and women. Moreover, our research shows that people are more likely to choose education that is connected to their real tasks or on-the-job trainings (Fig. 4). This means that if a company is going to implement e-learning it should bear in mind that it must be connected to real tasks as much as possible if this company wants its employees to be keen on this form of education. Based on information acquired by the consulting with the Company B, it is always better to connect e-learning with real working experience or with additional classroom education.

Based on the consulting, we have found out that decision about implementation of e-learning course is connected with two important variables:

Fig. 3 Preferred form of education at work (Color figure online)

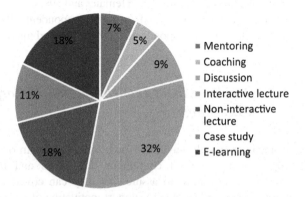

Fig. 4 Connection of
education to real work (Color
figure online)

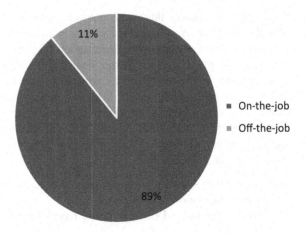

- Time of implementation
- Costs of implementation.

Companies that chose to implement e-learning with the help of an external supplier or provider are negotiating its price and time of delivery. However, companies providing e-learning are very quick and they are able to offer low-cost solutions. Since they are offering e-learning products and services as their core business, it is in their aim to provide solutions that will be effective for their customers.

Every company must decide based on its own preferences, if it is beneficial to implement e-learning courses. The consulted Company A is able to create e-learning courses within few hours and their time is more dependent on a client's IT team, devices and the Internet capability (Balco et al. 2014; Kryvinska 2012). Implementation takes usually one or two days for small- and medium-sized companies or one week for huge international projects. When a company develops corporate details, such as colours, logos and video presentations on their platform, it needs to register members of every single program to be followed. e-Learning contents and formats are developed in cooperation with international management professionals from most renowned business schools in the world. Clearly, it is very important to create e-learnings that are user-friendly. Suppliers seldom develop an individual LMS for every client. The Company A personalizes the interface based on client's needs, desires and feelings. The LMS is already created and it is the same for all clients. The company integrates technologies, options and contents based on clients' wants during the implementation. Price of implementation of e-learning may vary for individual clients. The LMS itself usually has its stable price and it is increased depending on services needed by a client, for example, HR expert advice, time of technicians spent on the project, etc. Other constraints that are taken into consideration are a number of countries linked to the platform as well as a number of learners simultaneously connected to the platform. In general, a project can go up to 200,000 EUR for international clients depending on the size of e-learning. But usually this is the question of contracts. Based on the consulting with the Company A, it is necessary to mention typical conditions that should lead to the decision of e-learning implementation (Fig. 5).

Fundamentally, Fig. 5 shows that companies with a higher number of employees, operating in a more dynamic environment and with a wide range of products and services, will mostly benefit from the implementation of e-learning as it will enable them to cut costs in the sphere of employees' education.

Based on Wild et al. 2002, before the implementation of e-learning a company has to evaluate its organizational readiness. The main aspects that need to be considered are as follows:

- Infrastructure—Does a company have adequate HW and SW infrastructure for the implementation of e-learning?
- Knowledge editor—Does a company have a knowledge editor? Can a company afford it?
- Organizational structure—Is company's structure designed in a way supporting knowledge sharing?
- Employee attitude—Are employees open to new information, education and sharing of knowledge? Are they ready to learn via computers?
- Knowledge needs—What knowledge is required in a company?
- Computer use—What is the level of computer literacy of employees?
- Technology requirements—Does a company fulfil required technological aspects?

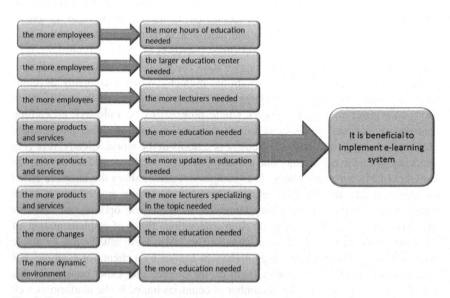

Fig. 5 Typical conditions leading to implementation of e-learning

8.3 Process of Implementation

Based on the information acquired during consulting with two companies included in our research, we have created the list of steps that create the process of e-learning implementation in cooperation with a supplier:

- A company's management decides that they want to implement e-learnings, for example, education about their products.
- The request is processed usually by IT department in cooperation with HR and top management. The company has to evaluate its possibilities and feasibility.
- After the request is internally agreed, the company decides if they are going to implement e-learning with the help of an external supplier. This choice is mostly less demanding on time and money and it is always better to request help of a professional than struggle long time on the project.
- The company reviews portfolios of potential suppliers.
- The company compares solutions and prices.
- The company chooses a narrower circle of potential clients and negotiates prices.
- After successful negotiating, the company chooses its supplier and signs a contract, which may be short-term and focused on one implementation of a smaller number of e-learning courses or long-term and focused on longer cooperation and continuous updating of content of e-learnings in the future.
- The supplier implements a LMS with cooperation of IT department of the company based on technical and IT possibilities.
- The LMS can be further used by the company itself or content and updates might be managed by the supplier.
- The company provides specific content that should be delivered by e-learning courses to its employees.
- Final e-learning is tested and designed based on company's needs and preferences. They can adjust content to be up-to-date, they can adjust a layout, interface, design or add interactive features if it is desired by the customer.
- The testing phase of e-learning follows, bugs are fixed and the final product is being prepared for operation.
- After successful testing, e-learning is introduced into operation and employees are given access to it.
- During the use of e-learning, the company might request additional changes or updates or it might request additional courses to be created or extended.

8.4 Requirements for Successful e-Learnings

In general, no e-learning provided to any company is "typical". Every company has its own requirements and it makes every project unique. Requirements for e-learning depend on profile of learners, learning objectives, type of learning, formats required, etc. Supplier of e-learning must be able to provide flexible solutions. And this might be the hardest part. Solutions and technologies must be adapted to specific needs and wants of a client. Some clients even require implementation of competitor's content into LMS. Similarly, specifics of e-learning are often related to specific markets and countries. It is very often beneficial to implement interactive parts into e-learning and courses should be user-friendly.

Based on our research, only 25% of respondents consider e-learning they are using as absolutely user-friendly while 36% of respondents mostly agree with the statement. 14% of respondents absolutely disagree with their e-learning being user-friendly and probably this is the point where companies should think about e-learning courses used and they should reconsider their approach and redesign courses to achieve more satisfaction of their employees. However, we found a significant difference between opinions of men and women in this question. Mostly women stated that they are not satisfied with e-learning used; especially 80% of respondents, who either disagree or absolutely disagree with their e-learning being user-friendly, are women. Another significant result is that 16% of employees neither agree nor disagree what might mean that they do not know how to evaluate e-learning courses, so in general they are not able to describe if their e-learning is user-friendly or not or they consider some e-learnings user-friendly and some not (Fig. 6).

To have user-friendly e-learning also means to speak the same language as a target audience. Nowadays, it is typical that clients require social features and peer-to-peer communication to be included in LMS. Based on the acquired information we can say that clients very often desire these features and research and development department includes them as top priorities because collaboration is these days very important for every company. Designers of e-learning courses should take into consideration the importance of peer-to-peer as well as peer-to-instructor interactions. This requirement can be fulfilled by creating such activities, which contain participation of creating ideas and content (Johnson et al. 2008).

Fig. 6 Opinions of employees about user-friendliness of e-learning they use (Color figure online)

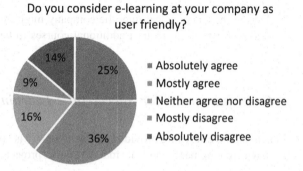

Currently, companies most often require leadership, marketing, finance or soft skills e-learning courses. The Company B uses e-learning only for education about its products. So it means that if they introduce new products they also introduce a new e-learning course as this is the main source of basic information for employees. Nevertheless, these e-learning courses are always supported by on-the-job education or classroom trainings. Thus the Company B takes e-learning as an initial but not complete form of education. For example, if employees want to become financial advisors they must first take e-learning courses about given products (e.g. mortgages) and only after accomplishing of the e-learning they may continue in classroom education, mentoring or real practice at workplace.

Success of implemented e-learning lies in many factors. The user interface is considered as the most important factor in evaluating e-learning courses as it is the place where a learner gets into interaction with the course. The interface must be stable and user-friendly (Shee and Wang 2008). The Company A stated that the most often required features of e-learning to achieve its user-friendly use are as follows:

- Rich media
- Interactivity
- Not too long courses
- Immersive courses
- Specific colour schemes that are attractive for particular learners—specific targeting of colours.

Furthermore, we provide some layout examples of e-learning courses being used by the Company B. Their design has been gradually improved over years based on discussions and brainstorming with their own employees. The company stated that employees recently report high satisfaction with the design of e-learning courses (Fig. 7).

Effectiveness of e-learning can be measured and thus a company can evaluate success of the implementation. The system for measuring was developed by Donald L. Kirkpatrick from Wisconsin University in 1959. The model includes four main stages of evaluating (Strother 2002; Kirkpatrick 1996):

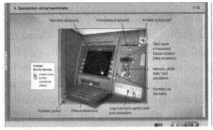

Fig. 7 Examples of e-learning interface in the Company B

- Reaction—what are attendants thinking about the education?
- Education—how much did attendants learn?
- Behaviour—how is their behaviour changed?
- Results—what was the effect of education for the company?

However, Jack Phillips added the fifth stage (Strother 2002):

- Return on investment—are results of the education higher than its price?

Return on investment (ROI) measures efficiency from the accounting point of view. However, when a company decides to introduce an e-learning program, it is necessary to calculate costs and ROI. Additionally, it also indicates company's ability to invest and supports reasonability of the decision. ROI can be easily calculated by the following formula (Horník 2007; Kryvinska et al. 2013):

$$ROI = \frac{\text{Net benefits of e-learning}}{\text{Costs invested for applying e-learning}}. \tag{1}$$

As stated by the Company B in our research, calculation of ROI was one of the most important factors that they considered during the process of e-learning implementation. Moreover, first months and years of using e-learning were connected with deep surveys among employees in order to evaluate success of the decision and possibility to improve the platform.

Additionally, money invested into e-learning does not require only one-time effort. e-learnings must be managed, optimized, continuously improved and re-evaluated on a regular basis. Since the environment within the company is constantly changing, it is necessary to set up rules and standards for regular monitoring of e-learning (Uden et al. 2007). Good practice is applied in the company B, where the team responsible for improving of e-learning effectiveness and content was created in order to gain the most from the initial investment into the platform.

9 Conclusion

It is undeniable that e-learning provides a very wide scale of education opportunities. Furthermore, e-learning is used by companies as a way of modern, cheap and interactive way of providing information and educational materials to its employees. Naturally, the growing popularity and use of e-learning is supported by better quality of education in many countries and rising attendance at universities. Implementation of e-learning goes hand in hand with the level of education in a particular country. Naturally, highly educated employees are the most valuable resource for companies. The dynamic environment requires employees to adapt to changes quickly and moreover, it requires management of companies to provide quick, updated and exact information to its employees. Corporations want employees who are able to perform in the environment full of changes. Online education is the way how to provide up-to-date information for large audiences. Additionally, education provided via e-learning systems can be provided anywhere, anytime and almost for anyone who is digitally literate. In general, e-learning makes around 26% more revenue pre one employee in the company (Ferriman 2014; Kaczor and Kryvinska 2013; Dohmen et al. 2014).

In conclusion, e-learning courses might be very beneficial for companies and employees but we must think also about its negative sides. We cannot say that e-learning is the best and the most appropriate way of learning in today's corporations. However, in many cases implementation of e-learning brings various advantages and if e-learning is properly used it can create an added value for the whole corporate education system. Based on our research we would claim that implementation of e-learning must be premeditated and based on real needs and wants of employees and companies.

References

Balco P, Greguš M (2014) The implementation of innovative services in education by using cloud infrastructure and their economic aspects. Glob J Flex Syst Manage 15(1):69–76

Balco P, Greguš M, Kryvinska N (2014) Education as a Service (EaaS) for Organizations, In: Baines T, Clegg B, Harrison D (eds) The spring servitization conference 2014 (SSC 2014), Aston Business School, Aston University, UK, 12–14 May 2014, pp 174–181. ISBN 978-1-85449-472-6

Cisco (2015) High Tech Policy Guide—Global Policy and Government Affairs (GPGA). http://www.cisco.com/web/about/gov/people/e_learning.html. Accessed April 2016

Dohmen P, Kryvinska N, Strauss C (2014) Viable service business models towards inter-cooperative strategies—conceptual evolutionary considerations. In: Bessis N, Xhafa F (eds) Inter-cooperative collective intelligence: techniques and applications, Studies in computational intelligence, (SCI-495). Springer, Berlin, pp 273–290

Eurostat (2012) Internet use in households and by individuals in 2012. http://ec.europa.eu/eurostat/documents/3433488/5585460/KS-SF-12-050-EN.PDF. Accessed April 2016

Ferriman J (2014) Top 10 ELearning Stats for 2014. http://elearningindustry.com/top-10-e-learning-statistics-for-2014-you-need-to-know. Accessed April 2016

Frk B (2010) e-learning a online vzdelávanie dospelých. http://www.casopispedagogika.sk/rocnik-1/cislo-2/E-learningaonlinevzdelavaniedospelych.pdf. Accessed April 2016

Gokhle A (1995) Collaborative learning enhances critical thinking. J Technol Educ 7(1). ISSN 1045-1064

Harasim L (2006) A history of e-learning: shift happened. The international handbook of virtual learning environments, pp 59–94. ISBN 978-1-4020-3803-7 (Springer)

Horník F (2007) Rozvoj a vzdelávaní pracovníku. Grada Publishing, Praha. ISBN 978-80-24-4578

Johnson RD, Hornik S, Salas E (2008) An empirical examination of factors contributing to the creation of successful e-learning environments. Int J Hum Comput Stud 66(5):356–369 (Elsevier)

Kachaňáková A et al. (2007) Riadenie ľudských zdrojov. SPRINT, Bratislava 2007. ISBN 978-80-89085-87-5

Kaczor S, Kryvinska N (2013) It is all about Services—fundamentals drivers, and business models. Soc Serv Sci J Serv Sci Res, Springer 5(2):125–154

Kirkpatrick D (1996) Great ideas revisited. Training & Development. https://sherri249.wikispaces. com/file/view/Training+%26+Development+Measurement.pdf. Accessed April 2016

Kryvinska N (2012) Building consistent formal specification for the service enterprise agility foundation. Soc Serv Sci J Serv Sci Res, Springer 4(2):235–269

Kryvinska N, Barokova A, Auer L, Ivanochko I, Strauss C (2013) Business value assessment of services re-use on SOA using appropriate methodologies, metrics and models, Inderscience Publishers. Int J Serv Econ Manage (IJSEM) 5(4):301–327 (Special Issue on Service-centric Models, Platforms and Technologies)

OECD (2013) Education at a Glance 2013. http://www.oecd.org/edu/eag2013(eng)–FINAL20June 2013.pdf. Accessed April 2016

Papula J (2009) e-learning 2.0 čo prináša a aké je jeho miesto v znalostnom manažmente podniku. http://www.academia.edu/1485318/E-learning_2.0_co_prinasa_a_ake_je_jeho_miesto_v_ znalostnom_manazmente_podniku. Accessed April 2016

Pejša J (2007) e-learning–trendy, měření efektivity, ROI, případové studie. http://www.e-learn.cz/ soubory/e-learning_trends_roi.pdf. Accessed April 2016

Shee DY, Wang YS (2008) Multi-criteria evaluation of the web-based e-learning system: a methodology based on learner satisfaction and its applications. Comput Educ, Elsevier 50 (3):894–905

Statistical office of the Slovak republic. Slovakia in the EU 2013. http://portal.statistics.sk/files/ Odbory/odb_410/el_publikacie/Slovensko_v_EU_2013.pdf. Accessed April 2016

Strother J (2002) An assessment of the effectiveness of e-learning in corporate training programs. Int Rev Res Open Distance Learn 3(1). ISSN 1492-3831

Uden L, Wangsa IT, Damiani E (2007) The future of e-learning: e-learning ecosystem. Digital EcoSystems and Technologies Conference, 2007. DEST'07. Inaugural IEEE-IES, Cairns, 21–23 Feb 2007, pp 113–117. ISBN 1-4244-0470-3

Velšic M (2011) Institute of public affairs: digital literacy in Slovakia 2011. 9th International Conference on Emerging eLearning Technologies and Applications (ICETA), 2011, pp 223–226. ISBN 978-1-4577-0051-4

Wild RH, Griggs KA, Downing T (2002) A framework for e-learning as a tool for knowledge management. Ind Manage Data Syst, Emerald 102(7): 371–380